D1564880

Estate Planning in Tennessee

Anne M. McKinney
John T. Berteau

Pineapple Press, Inc.
Sarasota, Florida

To a gentleman who, since the age of twelve, has helped me in every
accomplishment, my husband, J. Michael McKinney

Copyright © 1996 by Anne M. McKinney and John Berteau

Inquiries should be addressed to:
    Pineapple Press, Inc.
    P.O. Box 3899
    Sarasota, Florida 34230

LIBRARY OF CONGRESS
CATALOGING IN PUBLICATION DATA

McKinney, Anne M., 1949-
    Estate Planning in Tennessee / Anne M. McKinney and John Berteau.
    -- 1st ed.
            p.   cm.
    Includes index.
    ISBN 1-56164-059-X
    1. Estate planning--Tennessee--Popular works.
    2. Wills--Tennessee--Popular works.
    3. Trusts and trustees--Tennessee--Popular works.
    4. Probate law and practice--Tennessee-Popular works.
I.   McKinney, Anne M., 1949-
II.   Berteau, John, 1941-
III.   Title
        KFT140.Z9M38   1996
        346.76805'2--dc20
        [347.680652]   95-39054
                                                                                CIP

First Edition
10 9 8 7 6 5 4 3 2 1

Design by Millicent Hampton-Shepherd
Composition by Anne M. McKinney

SOME QUESTIONS THIS BOOK ANSWERS:

- Is a will the only way to transfer property at death?

- Why do wills need to be so long?

- Can I write a simple will myself?

- If I need an attorney to make a will, how much will it cost and what questions will I be asked?

- Do I need a will if all my assets are owned jointly with my spouse?

- Should I leave everything to my spouse? In fact, how much do I have to leave to my spouse?

- Should I leave something for the kids?

- I am told life insurance is free from taxes. If this is so, shouldn't I buy a lot of life insurance?

- Speaking of taxes, I am told living trusts save lots of taxes. How can I find out about this and where do I get one?

- What happens if I leave everything I have to my spouse and my spouse remarries? How can I be sure that my children are going to get something?

- What happens if both of us are deceased and our children are still too young to take care of things?

- This is my second marriage. I want to take care of my spouse. We want to provide for each other and we both have our own children. When both of us are gone, each of us would like our assets to go to our respective children. How do I handle this?

- How do I provide for medical decisions if I am incapacitated?

- How do I provide for financial management of my assets if I am incapacitated? Or if my spouse is?

- Will the doctors and hospitals really honor living wills?

- Can I give money away and, with the tax deductions, actually come out ahead?

- When should I start to draw on my pension plan?

CONTENTS

ACKNOWLEDGMENTS

In writing a book such as this, there are many persons who offered comments, suggestions, help and encouragement, but special recognition should be given to my co-author, John Berteau, for his support and patience with me, and for what I now appreciate as the enormous effort required of him to write *Estate Planning in Florida*, after which this book is fashioned. Attorney Gale Allison's help, enthusiasm and thoughtful suggestions, together with her experience as a practicing attorney and technical expertise in the areas of estate planning and taxation, were invaluable in producing the final draft. Thanks, also, to my word processor, Dee Jones, who has typed so many drafts and redrafts, and overcome computer glitches. Attorney Lisa W. Gammeltoft and my legal assistant, Eugene E. Jones, were indispensable in researching and revising several chapters in the book. Thanks to Amanda Oswald and June Cussen for their editorial expertise. Finally, I owe deepest thanks to the thousands of wonderful people who have sat in my office and discussed estate planning. They taught me much over the years and have brought their life experiences, their learning and their insights into this book.

INTRODUCTION

E state planning is making provisions in advance for the management and transfer of assets. It is far more than preparing a will or trust. It is more than considering what the tax collector is going to take. It is even more than finding the least expensive way to transfer property. Cutting costs is important. In fact, it is so important that this is reason enough to do some serious estate planning even if you think your assets are "too small."

Proper estate planning considers the beneficiaries. Will their interests be protected? Will the management of the assets be good? Will beneficiaries be truly benefitted or will their inheritance lead to bad habits, excessive spending, and perhaps, in some instances, even worse results? Will the assets that you worked so hard for be properly used? None of us wants to see the assets for which we have labored squandered away by spendthrifts who give no thought to the future or to the labor that produced what they so easily enjoy.

You are worth more than you think! Fill out a simple financial sheet similar to the one in Appendix A of this book and total the values. The result may surprise you. A pleasant surprise, but one which suggests that good stewardship is required now to protect the assets you have worked to acquire. And your wealth is only a part of your financial picture. You also are an important asset. You provide valuable services for yourself and others who depend on you. A well-conceived estate plan can help you and them to prepare for the time when you are less able or unable to continue these services. Your property and your responsibilities are unique; your estate plan should fit you.

You cannot take it with you, so estate planning necessarily is concerned with the transfer of wealth at death. But it is rarely so limited in scope or time. An effective plan begins during life (the earlier the better), is revised as lives and laws change, and may continue to control certain assets long after your death.

Together, you and I and an assortment of people, both real and imaginary, will explore a practical, money-saving approach to estate planning for you as a Tennessean. We will examine the ways assets can be transferred to the ultimate beneficiaries with

7

the lowest costs, the smallest amount of red tape, and the fewest delays. We will see ways to save federal estate taxes, federal income taxes and Tennessee inheritance and estate taxes (Tennessee does in fact have both an inheritance and an estate tax). We will review common planning tools, including wills, lifetime gifts, Totten trusts, joint property, life insurance, retirement plans, living wills, living trusts, and durable powers of attorney. We also will look at other less familiar ideas.

This book is not a "do-it-yourself" or "how-to-avoid-attorneys" primer. Public opinion to the contrary, such "self-help" books are more likely to change the nature of the attorney's practice and not necessarily the volume, because instead of being given the relatively easy task of structuring the estate properly up front, attorneys are too often called in, after the fact, for cleanup or to provide damage control after someone has attempted to do his estate planning without qualified legal help. This book is also not intended to give specific legal advice. It explains general concepts and gives you basic building blocks used to create most estate plans. This book is not a substitute for good personal legal advice. After all, you would not expect to be able to practice medicine after reading a medical book. It will offer you, however, a number of ideas and approaches to estate planning which will be of great assistance to you as you consider your own estate planning.

This book is intended to answer, in plain English, questions that are commonly asked, to pose questions that should be considered, and generally to make the whole process of planning for the management and preservation of your estate as a resident of Tennessee more understandable, less complex, and sufficiently responsive to meet the changing needs of you and your family.

ESTATE
PLANNING

IN

TENNESSEE

In this chapter, you will learn:

- who is and who is not a Tennessean
- how to become a Tennessean
- whether you need a new will
- how to find a good attorney
- what to do before the first meeting with your attorney
- about legal fees

1

ARE YOU A TENNESSEAN?

An initial step in the estate planning process is to determine which state you belong to. This is easy — unless you have recently moved to Tennessee or you live here only a portion of the year. The technical term for where you usually live is "domicile," although "citizenship" or "residency" are also used on occasion. Let's see why domicile is important in estate planning.

Laws vary among the states. In preparing your estate plan, you need to know which rules to follow. If you are a Tennessean, you are subject to the laws of Tennessee. There are limitations on every state's right to impose its laws (its "jurisdiction") on its citizens, just as there are circumstances that give a state jurisdiction over an individual who is not its citizen. While you are driving through Ohio, you must obey Ohio's traffic laws. It does no good to complain, "I'm a Tennessean and that isn't the law in Tennessee." If you sell your vacation condominium in Florida, the closing will be subject to Florida's laws, including payment of fees and taxes imposed by Florida. This brings us to the real issue in many domicile cases: Which state gets to collect how much in taxes?

The differences in the amount of death and inheritance taxes assessed by various states can be significant. Each state in which you live or own property wants a bite of your estate. They and you have a financial interest in locating your domicile.

Tennessee may not be as well known for its favorable tax climate as for its country music, but both reputations are well deserved. Few states, except perhaps Nevada, are more benevolent in their taxation of estates. Not only are inheritance and death taxes higher in some other states, but many states, especially some in the Northeast, have become increasingly aggressive in asserting that taxes are owed even though the person who died was no longer a resident of the state. This growing trend means there is a need for careful planning in order to reduce exposure to these conflicting claims against your estate. There is even the remote but real possibility that without proper planning, more than one state may determine you are legally domiciled in that state and two or more states will each take a full tax bite!

The Intent to be a Tennessean

You are not a Tennessean solely because you live here. You must intend that Tennessee be your "usual place of residence," and, whenever you are absent from Tennessee, you must intend to return here (the Tennessee definition of "domicile"). Since "intention" exists solely in a person's mind, it is sometimes difficult to know precisely in which state a person usually resides. When you additionally consider that different states have different definitions of "domicile" and different standards for asserting jurisdiction over all or some portion of a person's estate, you can understand the potential for confusion and, occasionally, dual domicile. To avoid the possibility that more than one state might claim jurisdiction over your estate and impose taxes based on such claim, you should clearly establish residence in one state. Visible acts are presumed to indicate your intention. Therefore, if you want to be a Tennessean, it is important that you act like a Tennessean after moving to Tennessee.

What Can You Do to Indicate Your Intention to be a Tennessean?

You can write a Tennessee will. Although there are many more important reasons for writing a will other than to show your intention to be a Tennessean, there are few better ways to show that intention than to execute a will which recites that you are a resident of Tennessee. Register to vote in Tennessee. Vote in person (not by absentee ballot). Pay United States income taxes through the Internal Revenue Service office in Memphis as other Tennessee citizens do. Open bank accounts in Tennessee. Transfer your religious, social, and professional organization memberships here. Join and be active in Tennessee organizations. Spend time in Tennessee. If you travel a substantial portion of the year or live in several places, stop in your Tennessee home between moves from one location to another. Pay the Tennessee Hall income tax if any is due. Get a Tennessee driver's license showing your Tennessee address and put a Tennessee tag on your car. Later we'll talk in more detail about some of the problems of having citizenship in two states, but for the time being, the important thing is to be sure you have done everything you can to make yourself a Tennessean.

Do You Need a New Will?

As you will learn in Chapter 2, you should have a will regardless of the size of your estate. But if you already have a will, how do you know when to have a new one prepared, or when to make an amendment (or *codicil*) to your will? A wise man once advised that whenever something happens that makes you either very happy (such as the birth of a child or a grandchild, a wedding, or the receipt of a large inheritance), or very sad (as with the death of someone you love, a divorce, or the development of a chronic illness in a family member), you should review your will to see if changes are in order. If you move from one state to another, you should ask an attorney in your new state to review your will and to advise you about the need for a new one or for changes in the will you have. It is also a good idea to review your existing will every three to five years. Finally, if your estate should increase to a total figure greater than $600,000, it is time for you to ask an attorney who has experience in estate and gift taxation to do a thorough review of your will and your overall estate plan.

How to Find an Attorney

If you are going to have an attorney help you with your estate plan, your next question may be, "How do I pick a good attorney?" An obvious choice is to talk to the attorney who has been doing other legal work for you. If you do not have one, ask friends or co-workers. The best recommendation is a satisfied client. Ask a bank trust department or a CPA to recommend an attorney who concentrates his or her practice in estate planning. If none of these sources produces the right name, look for a listing in the business section of the telephone book entitled "Lawyer Referral Service." You can also look in the Yellow Pages. Many attorneys who practice in estate planning indicate in their firm listing that they prepare wills and trusts or provide similar services. Don't be misled by large ads. There is often an inverse relationship between the size of the advertisement and the ability of the attorney. You want high-quality, professional legal work at reasonable fees, not extravagant promises and cute pictures.

Areas of Practice

Every attorney who is authorized to practice law in Tennessee may inform the public of his or her areas of practice in the Yellow Pages, on a business card, and through other types of advertising. All Tennessee attorneys are subject to certain rules governing professional conduct, but no specific criteria must be met before naming estate planning as an area of practice. A general practice attorney ordinarily drafts wills and trusts. Many do some estate planning. Attorneys who list wills, trusts, or estate planning as areas of practice probably, but not necessarily, have more interest and more experience in these areas than ones who list only general practice.

Designation or Certification

In many states, attorneys who have substantial experience in estate planning over several years, currently spend a substantial portion of their practice in the area, and have accumulated the required number of hours of continuing legal education may apply to their state governing boards for permission to designate Wills, Estates, and Estate Planning as an area of specialization. Also, in many states attorneys who have met the criteria for certification, have passed a rigorous written exam and peer review, and have a satisfactory professional ethics record can apply for certification in Estate Planning and Probate. However, Tennessee does not yet provide approval or certification of specialty areas in the practice of estate planning, probate, or taxation. That is why, when you see advertisements by Tennessee attorneys, they usually include a statement that "Certification as a specialist in the areas listed is not currently available in Tennessee."

Martindale-Hubbell® Law Directory

There is an excellent resource for locating attorneys and learning about their qualifications which may be available in your local public library (or in your local law school library if you live near a university): the *Martindale-Hubbell® Law Directory*. The *Directory* lists the attorney's date and place of birth, date(s) of admission to the bar, education, law-related memberships, and concentrations of practice. In some cases, the *Directory* even provides a rating of the attorney's legal ability obtained from a solicitation of confidential opinions of members of the bar in the area in which the attorney practices.

How to Prepare for Your First Meeting with Your Attorney

After you have found an attorney and made an appointment, new questions often arise. "What am I supposed to do? What does my attorney do? Should I bring any documents or information? How much is this going to cost?"

If you are meeting with your attorney for the first time, he or she needs to know something about you. You should be able to tell your attorney about yourself, your family, your property, and your planning objectives. Some attorneys have a printed information form that will be sent to you before the first meeting. Others prefer to obtain the necessary information on a person-to-person basis. If the attorney you choose does not have a form to provide you, Appendix A shows you what a typical questionnaire looks like, and you may find it useful in preparing for the first meeting with your attorney.

If you have an existing will, trust, buy-sell agreement for your business, antenuptial agreement, divorce decree, or other similar documents, you should take them, as well as copies of any gift tax returns, to your initial meeting. Having this information immediately available will be helpful in the planning process. Although your attorney may not expect you to bring deeds, stock certificates, or life insurance policies for a simple will, you should have these documents available if needed. All documents of title may need to be reviewed for more complex estate planning.

Legal Fees

Lawyer's fees differ widely and depend on a variety of factors, including the complexity of your estate plan, the value and nature of your assets, the possibility of family conflicts or future litigation, the attorney's volume of estate planning practice, the attorney's expertise, and the city in which the attorney practices. However, it is a safe generalization that the cost to have a qualified attorney prepare a simple will is one of the best bargains going. Many attorneys charge less than it costs them to actually prepare the will. They recognize the need of individuals in our society for a simple will and they lower their fee to make this service available to a greater number of people. They may also provide this service in order to attract new clients or with the hope of handling the estate. Whatever their reasons, you benefit. Take advantage of the opportunity.

Now that you have started your estate planning experience, let's see what your simple will could look like.

In this chapter, you will learn:

- how to make cremation and burial arrangements
- how to handle debts and taxes
- what tangible personal property is
- how to make specific gifts
- the importance of describing real estate
- what "rest, residue and remainder" means
- what a personal representative is
- what powers a personal representative should have
- how to handle real estate outside Tennessee
- the advantages of a self-proving affidavit
- how to make your will and store it safely

2

THE SIMPLE WILL KEPT SIMPLE

The best-known and most used estate planning device is the simple will. A will is a written statement of an individual's directions for the distribution of his or her property, to take effect after his or her death. In order for the document to be effective as a valid will (admitted to probate), it must be signed as required by law. These laws haven't changed much during the past several centuries, regardless of your state of domicile, but it is important to take advantage of a relatively modern innovation, the self-proving affidavit to a will. But, let's write your will first.

Everyone who has assets should have a will, whether or not those assets have significant value. Remember, the State of Tennessee has, in effect, written a will for every Tennessean who dies without a valid will. As occasionally happens when the government steps in, the procedure becomes more time-consuming and more expensive and usually doesn't produce a result everyone likes. A simple will is the way to avoid this problem.

Printed will forms are available at stationery stores, and through television and newspaper advertisements and similar sources. These forms generally result in a very poor will. A document intended to be used by a large segment of the public addresses only those matters most common to all, in the manner most suitable for all. Just as one size of clothing does not fit all, one form of will does not fit all. The individual too frequently has to conform to the form.

The best choice is to have a reputable attorney prepare a will for you. Attorneys use a variety of form wills also, but your attorney begins with the form that is generally right for you and then revises that form to do what you specifically want it to do. More importantly, you will have the opportunity to ask and to be asked questions you need to consider. Remember, almost everything in your name will be tied up in this document. Mistakes and omissions, discovered after the will takes effect, can't be corrected.

A simple will only looks simple. Numerous options and alternatives can, and often should, be considered during the drafting process. Initially, you should realize that the designation "simple will" is not a legal term, though it is generally understood to mean a will that leaves everything directly to specified beneficiaries. No trusts, special tax provisions or complex formulas for dividing the estate are included in a simple will. Typically, a simple will might leave everything to the spouse, if surviving, and, if not, equally to the children. What should the simple will, or for that matter any will, say? What should be omitted?

Introductory Clause

The initial paragraph is ordinarily a single sentence. "I, John Smith, a resident of Knox County, Tennessee, declare this to be my Last Will and Testament and revoke all prior wills and codicils." (A "codicil" is the legal term for an amendment to your will.)

If you are commonly known by a name other than or in addition to your legal name, you should include both names. For example, Diana Davison Lambert Jones, also known as Dee Jones.

Naming Tennessee and the county of your residence is considered an indication of your intent to be a Tennessean, and helps establish domicile. This statement also helps determine the county in which your estate will be probated.

On the other hand, your assurance that you are "of sound mind and body" does not prove anything and is generally omitted. You must be of sound mind and at least 18 years old to have the "testamentary capacity" that entitles you to make a will in Tennessee, but this traditional affirmation has been discarded along with "heretofore," "aforesaid," and other legalese as excess verbiage. If your mental ability at the time you executed your will could become an issue, because of advancing age, illness, duress, or other reasons, then more aggressive and effective measures than a self-serving statement are necessary. Your attorney may prepare a record establishing your "sound mind." Such a record might include written statements from friends and your doctor. The attorney may document the reasons you chose to dispose of your assets in a particular way. This should be done at the time your will is signed.

There are important rules concerning what should not be included in a will. Neither praise nor recrimination belong in a will. Words of appreciation are best shared during life. Moreover, an intended gift to "Shirley McGaha, my devoted secretary whom I could never adequately repay for all her invaluable assistance to me over the years" may be treated as additional employment compensation to Shirley, and as such, be subject to income taxes imposed on wages. Unnecessary facts and personal opinions rarely serve any valid purpose. Not naming a person as a beneficiary usually has the effect of disinheriting that person. If you want to clarify your intention, particularly in the case of a child, it is desirable and sufficient to say, "I make no provision for my oldest daughter, Linda Jane." Linda Jane may be a multi-millionaire, a drug addict, or an adult child from whom you are presently estranged. Feelings and circumstances change, so don't explain, at least not in your will. When you die, your will becomes part of the public records in your county. If you insist on having the last word or "setting the record straight," you may subject your estate to unforeseen red tape, expense or even a will contest.

A new will generally revokes all prior wills and codicils automatically, even though you don't specifically say it does, but it is best to be very clear about your intention.

Cremation and Burial Instructions

Instructions for your funeral and burial generally do not belong in your will. After all, the will generally is not read until after the service. If the arrangements were not in accordance with your wishes, remorse, guilt, or bitterness may result. There is one exception. A statement of your intention to be cremated is helpful, particularly in those situations where there is no close family member or there are family members who disagree on this issue. If the person in charge of your estate (named the "personal representative" or the "executor" in Tennessee) arranges for cremation according to the instructions in your will, your living will, or in a written contract you signed, that person is protected if sued for allowing the cremation. A simple, direct sentence, "I desire that my body be cremated," is sufficient. Whatever your preference may be, talk with your clergy, family, or close friends so the appropriate persons are aware of your choice. Leave the specifics in a letter with these individuals or make arrangements with a funeral home.

Debts and Taxes

Many wills contain some instructions concerning payment of "my just debts" and taxes. Generally, it is best to omit any reference to your debts and to let your attorney worry about the technicalities of apportioning taxes (identifying who should pay how much of what tax). A saying survives from old English law to the effect that one must be just before one can be generous. Rest assured, valid creditors will file their claims and be paid. Specific instruction should be included in your will if you want your personal representative to pay any charitable pledge or other moral obligation that you are not legally obligated to repay, or to pay off an existing mortgage before the mortgaged property is transferred to the designated beneficiary.

Tangible Personal Property

Next, generally, comes a section distributing your tangible personal property. Tangible personal property is a legal term and is much preferred to general, vague terms such as personal effects. There are three general categories of property: real property (real estate), intangible personal property (stocks, bonds, partnership interests, money, promissory notes, and other pieces of paper or similar items which are not valuable, but which represent something that is valuable), and tangible personal property (everything else). The last category includes things such as pots and pans, jewelry, furniture, boats, airplanes, paintings, stamp collections, tools, shotguns, silver and crystal — all the things you own personally, even if you use them in your business. Give some thought to these items. This is one of the areas where many problems occur. There is a saying among estate planners that people get angry over the tangible personal property, then fight over the money. There are four common ways to give away tangible personal property: (1) the general statement; (2) the family letter; (3) the legal separate writing; and (4) an enumeration of items in the will. Each has its pros and cons. Think about which would be best for you and talk with your attorney.

The General Statement

The general statement has no detailed enumeration of the tangible personal property, so it is the simplest way to give away ("bequeath") tangible personal property. Beth's will could provide: "I give all of my tangible personal property to Michael, my husband, and if he is deceased then equally to my children, Luke and Margaret, who survive me to be divided between them as they agree. My personal representative shall sell any property as to which there is no agreement within sixty days after the date of issuance of Letters of Administration concerning my estate and shall add the proceeds to the residue of my estate."

Consider including a "tie-breaker," a method of dividing the property if the beneficiaries can't agree. Common solutions authorize the personal representative to make the division in the event of a deadlock or to sell the disputed property and distribute the proceeds.

There are numerous variations of the general statement. This version limits the beneficiaries who will inherit the property. For example, if Mike dies before his wife, Beth, the tangible personal property will go to their children who are living when Beth dies. The children of a child who has died will inherit nothing because of the clause "who survive me." The purpose of limiting beneficiaries to living children is to avoid the possibility of a deceased child's share passing to a grandchild who is not yet 18 years old (a "minor"). Having a minor inherit a fractional share of the furniture is an undesirable result. Having a minor inherit property valued in excess of $10,000 may necessitate a guardianship for the property, an even less desirable result. If Beth wants some items to go to the children of a deceased child, she can provide for such gifts in other ways. It is better not to do it in the general statement disposing of tangible personal property.

Suppose it is not a grandchild but a child who is a minor. Here the problem may be more immediate. There are a number of alternatives which can be used. Sometimes it is decided that the minor's interest in the tangible personal property should be held by an individual. In such instances, the gift of the minor's interest in the tangible personal property is given outright to an individual. Then a letter or note is left to be given to the person at the time that the tangible personal property is distributed which says, in effect, "Please sell any of the items of tangible personal property that are part of my child's share in which my child would have no interest and save those items that you think are significant, and give them to my child at the time that he or she will be better able to appreciate them." This idea frequently works well where there is a close friend whom you know will share the silver, the grandfather clock, or similar family items.

Sometimes, if there is no person to whom you feel comfortable in just giving the items of tangible personal property in the hope that they will do "the right thing," then the person named as guardian for the minor child will hold the assets and, after getting an appropriate court order, sell those assets that are not appropriate to keep until the child comes of age and will keep those items which the guardian feels are appropriate. The advantage to a guardianship is that the value of the assets will always go to the minor child. However, guardianships are expensive. Having to deal with items of tangible personal property with small value such as furniture, pots and pans, and similar items, frequently outweighs the benefits.

The Family Letter

Frequently, the testator (the person making the will) wants to leave all or most of his or her tangible personal property to one beneficiary to be distributed to others in accordance with personal instructions in a letter. In his will, Scott gives all his tangible personal property to Laura. However, he has also written her a letter, which he has put in their safe deposit box with his will. This letter says that, even though he made her the legal owner of all items of tangible personal property in his estate, he wants her to give certain items to particular people and to select at least one special memento to give to each grandchild and a few items to go to close personal friends. There are no special phrases or legal requirements for the letter because *it has no legal effect.* Scott can include any instructions he wishes. The risk is that Laura may not comply with Scott's instructions, possibly for reasons beyond her control. She may be in poor health and not competent to make gifts. There is *no legal obligation* on the person who inherited these assets to share them with the intended beneficiaries. If you choose this method, you are relying solely on the good faith and good intentions of the beneficiary and on the beneficiary's ability to carry out your instructions, so choose wisely and be clear in your instructions.

Two Additional Warnings

If any of the gifts to be passed on to others by the person who is given the family letter has a value in excess of the annual exclusion from gift tax (currently $10,000), there will be undesirable tax consequences unless the transfer can be made over several years or otherwise be made to fit within the exclusion. Also, if the beneficiary named in your will has any outstanding debts or obligations, creditors may be able to make claims against the property regardless of the beneficiary's good intentions.

The Legal Separate Writing

Under Tennessee law, a person making a will can also make a signed, separate written list of specific items of tangible personal property and the intended beneficiary of each item. If that person follows a few simple rules, the list will be enforced as part of the will. Betsy, a widow with no children, wants to use the separate writing. Her will must specifically refer to the separate writing, so it contains this provision:

> There is a separate writing signed by me and in existence at the time that I sign my will, and if such writing is delivered to my personal representative within thirty days after the issuance of the Letter of Administration, then I give the items of tangible personal property listed in the separate writing to the persons named therein. I give all my tangible personal property, other than the items contained in my separate writing, if any, to my sister, Susie.

Upon Betsy's death, the separate writing becomes, in effect, a part of the will. The separate writing does not require witnesses or the formalities of the signing procedure required for a will to be valid. However, the simplicity of this method is also its peril. Too frequently the separate writing is treated casually and, if so, it eventually causes trouble.

Three Common Pitfalls in the Legal Separate Writing:
(1) Your Signature and the Date Should Be on the Separate Writing

Your separate writing must be signed by you to be valid. While the law does not require it to be dated, it is a very good idea and sometimes essential. The separate legal writing must be in existence at the time your will is signed, so the date on the writing must be on or before the date of your will. Your will must refer to the separate legal writing (as it was in the provision quoted above). Holly had a will that referred to a separate writing. During her life, she had prepared two different lists. When she died several years ago, both separate writings were found, both signed by Holly, neither dated. Both documents listed almost identical assets, but different beneficiaries. Needless to say, both sets of beneficiaries thought the particular separate writing that named them was the true separate writing referred to in her will. Only after a great deal of time and effort was it determined that one list included assets acquired later than some of the other assets and, therefore, was probably the later list. It seemed most likely that a new list was prepared to include recently acquired items.

(2) Accurate Descriptions Should Be Used

When preparing a separate writing, always describe both the items and the beneficiaries very specifically. It is a poor idea to say, "Grandmother Murphy's wedding present is to go to Bob." Not everyone will necessarily know or agree on what Grand-mother Murphy gave you on your wedding day some fifty years ago. Describe each item so that even a stranger could identify it. Assume that, given half a chance, someone will misinterpret what the writing says.

Several years ago, two attorneys called me. They were stuck. Before her will was signed, Betty had made a separate writing listing various items and the friends who were to receive them. Her china was given to Susan. Mary was given the balance of the tangible personal property. Susan and Mary, good friends, went to the house of their deceased friend, in the presence of the personal representative, and began to gather up the items left to each of them. Susan went into the kitchen and began to carefully pack the bowls, plates, cups, saucers, and other items of china. When she finished, she went into the living room with empty boxes, talked briefly with Mary, and began to wrap the Hummel figurines. Mary stopped her packing and said, "What are you doing, Susan?" She replied, "These are made of china, so I am taking them." Susan and Mary probably have not spoken a civil word to each other since that hour.

Mary felt clearly that Betty had always wanted her to have the Hummel figurines because she herself had a collection and Betty knew how much she loved them. Susan thought Mary was being a little too emotional. Besides, the law was on her side, wasn't it? After all, they were made out of china. It was determined that, yes, the Hummel figurines were made out of china, but no, they were not "china" under the separate writing. "China" is generally thought of as a generic term for dinnerware, not as a reference to the chemical content of a particular object. In a document such as the separate writing, the usual and customary meaning was probably intended. The Hummel figurines belonged to Mary. Susan put up quite a fight before the resolution was reached, and to this day thinks the lawyers and judge unjustly deprived her of part of her rightful inheritance of china.

(3) Safekeeping of the Separate Writing is Essential

The remaining concern is to insure that your separate writing is available to be probated with your will. It should be kept with your will or with your important papers or in some other safe location so that it is not lost or destroyed without your knowledge. Additionally, your personal representative must be able to locate this precisely written, signed, and dated list. Tell your attorney, your personal representative or a responsible family member that you have made a separate writing and where you keep it, or leave a note in your safe deposit box with your will (don't write on your will!) disclosing the location of the separate writing. The will may say to ignore any separate writing that is not delivered to your personal representative within a specified period following your death. This provision is intended to avoid the problems that would otherwise result when your list is discovered in the bottom drawer of your desk after the desk and all your tangible personal property have been distributed to beneficiaries under your will (beneficiaries who are not the same ones set out in your separate writing).

If you want the option of making a separate writing, talk with your attorney at some length. Be sure that you understand exactly what you are supposed to do concerning the tangible personal property list, and be sure to do it.

Enumeration of Items in the Will

This is the most formal, most rigid, and most certain way of disposing of tangible personal property. If you have special items of great intrinsic value or of great personal value to you or to family members, it may be wise to list them in your will. You do not need to worry about the gifts being invalidated as a result of the technicalities and potential problems of the separate writing. Your attorney will incorporate your instructions as specific gifts in your will. These items will be inventoried and the court will see that each item goes to the beneficiary to whom it is bequeathed.

Specific Gifts

We have been discussing how items of tangible personal property can be specifically given to beneficiaries. The disposition or giving of tangible personal property above is really a form of specific gift. However, specific gifts can encompass more than just gifts of tangible personal property.

Wills routinely contain gifts of specific property or cash amounts to an individual or organization. Frequently, real estate is specifically willed. As with tangible personal property, each item must be accurately and clearly described, taking into consideration whether the property may change during the years after the execution of your will.

Intangible Personal Property

Occasionally, an attorney is asked to include a specific gift of a stated number of shares of stock, such as "I give my 100 shares of IBM to my granddaughter, Allison." This bequest may cause problems. IBM has split and split, and can be expected to split again. If there is a two-for-one split after you execute your will and your estate owns 200 shares, who gets the extra 100 shares? Or, what happens if you sell the stock? Does Allison get nothing, or the equivalent value? If equivalent value, is it value at the time you signed the will or at the time of your death? Generally, avoid the gift of a specific number of shares of stock in your will. Your attorney can help you avoid this and other pitfalls commonly occurring with property descriptions.

Real Estate

If you want to make a specific gift of real estate, find the deed. Your attorney will need a correct legal description of the property, and the deed is the best source. The legal description on a tax bill tends to be casual and sometimes inaccurate. Use your deed, or perhaps your title insurance policy. Your attorney will want to review the deed to confirm how your title is held. Your attorney will also need the tax ID numbers from your real estate tax bill.

Consider who should receive the tangible personal property, if any, located on the property. Gay may leave the vacation home she received from her parents to her daughter, intending that the furnishings remain with the home. But Gay's will gives all her tangible personal property to her brother, John. John gets the furniture, the pots and pans, and the yard and pool maintenance equipment in the vacation home.

Rest, Residue, and Remainder

Now that you have distributed all the tangible personal property and made specific gifts of certain property, what's left is the residue. The residue may comprise the bulk of your estate or it may be nothing. Even if you think you have given away all of your property, your will should always include a provision giving away the residue in order to catch any property that otherwise would not be covered and would fall into intestacy (be treated as if you did not have a will). You may have forgotten something, you may acquire additional property which does not fit into any other category in your will, a beneficiary may turn down your bequest (disclaim it), or you may fail to make sufficient alternate bequests if a beneficiary dies before you. In these cases and others, that property will pass under the intestacy laws unless you include a residuary clause. The residuary clause is a broad general statement: "I give and devise the rest, residue, and remainder of my estate to _____." No items of property are named, only the beneficiary or beneficiaries to whom the broad category of property will be given.

If you didn't consider it before, think now about who should get various items in your estate if the named beneficiary is deceased. Should the item go to the beneficiary's spouse or children? Should it go to another beneficiary? Should it be included in the residue? Your attorney can draft your will following your specific wishes.

Per Stirpes

Often, somewhere in a will, you may see the words *"per stirpes."* *Per stirpes* means the property that would have gone to a beneficiary who is deceased passes down that beneficiary's family tree, generation by generation. Let's think about William and his three children: Elizabeth, with two children, Brad and Bonnie; Robert, with one child, Robert, Jr.; and Blake, with two children, Blake II and Liz. William, a widower, leaves his estate to his children, *per stirpes*. William's son, Blake, dies in a car accident while his father is living. When William dies, his estate will be distributed one-third to Elizabeth and one-third to Robert. Blake's one-third will be automatically divided equally between his children, Blake II and Liz (*per stirpes*). If Robert had died also, Robert, Jr. would get his dad's entire one-third interest, even though his cousins, Blake II and Liz, would receive only one-sixth each.

Selecting Your Personal Representative

Your attorney will ask you whom to name as personal representative. That is the generic term for executor, executrix, administrator *de bonis non*, and the whole Latin panoply for the person (or persons) responsible for administering your estate. Administration includes locating and managing your assets, determining which claims against your estate are valid debts, paying those claims, paying taxes, and distributing the remainder of your estate to the proper beneficiaries.

You should give serious thought to choosing your personal representative. Most of the time, it is a spouse or a responsible family member. Like some other states, Tennessee does have a few restrictions on who can serve as personal representative: in general, the person must be either a resident of Tennessee, one of a specified group of relatives, or a trust company having trust powers in Tennessee. The out-of-state relatives who may be named to serve as the personal representative of an estate include the spouse, parent, grandparent, or direct descendants of the person making the will, as well as the spouses of all of those people. To serve, a person must be mentally and physically able to act as personal representative and must be at least 18 years old.

Appendix B is a genealogical chart which shows the relationship of individuals to each other.

If you have an existing out-of-state will which names an out-of-state bank or business associate as personal representative, it is unlikely either will be qualified to act in Tennessee. A few out-of-state banks have qualified in Tennessee and could be named personal representative through their Tennessee offices; however, for the most part, your former bank and nonfamily members outside Tennessee will not be qualified. Even if your nonresident personal representative is a family member and qualified to serve in Tennessee, reconsider your choice. All other things being equal, it may be preferable to name a responsible Tennessean because it is easier to administer a Tennessee estate from Tennessee.

Often, in a simple estate, it is good to select a personal representative from among the beneficiaries of your estate. These are presumably the people closest to you and, since at least part of the assets belong to whomever you chose, he or she is more likely to be attentive to the management of the estate. However, if you think that naming one beneficiary as personal representative may create friction among any of the beneficiaries, don't do it. Go to a neutral party in whom you have trust and confidence.

Powers of a Personal Representative

The law imposes certain obligations on your personal representative (in general, to settle your estate and distribute your assets in accordance with your will and applicable law), and grants certain powers to enable your representative to accomplish these tasks. Typically, a will provides additional powers so that your personal representative will have considerable authority over your estate. After all, you have carefully selected your personal representative for this position of trust. Give this person the power needed to fully manage your estate. Even in a simple will, it is advisable to give your personal representative certain powers in addition to those granted under the law. The personal representative should be able to make certain decisions regarding tax matters, sell or otherwise deal with the real estate, and generally manage the property with broad authority to get the job done with the least amount of delay and expense. If the personal representative is not empowered to do something that needs to be done, then he or she will have to ask the probate judge for authority and explain why the particular action is necessary. It is better to provide in the will a general, broad authority, supplemented by any specific powers you anticipate may be needed, so that this additional step can be avoided, unless you believe close judicial supervision is desirable. Tennessee law allows you to give your personal representative a list of powers by referring to Tennessee Code Annotated Section 35-50-110 in your will; that list of powers is found in Appendix C.

Real Estate Outside Tennessee

Special clauses are needed in the wills of Tennesseans who own real estate outside Tennessee. In such cases, it is necessary to have an *ancillary administration*, which is a probate proceeding in the state where the real estate is located. Laws vary among the states, but an ancillary administration may also be required if you own personal property in another state. This probate proceeding is in addition to the probate proceeding in Tennessee. It is an abbreviated proceeding limited to the specific property subject to the jurisdiction of the other state. Despite this limitation, some states generate a lot of red tape if the matter of ancillary administration is not sufficiently covered in the will. The best way to handle the situation is to name a specific person to serve as your personal representative for the ancillary administration. Select a person who is qualified to act as personal representative under the laws of the other state and give that person the same powers and authority as your personal representative in Tennessee and waive bond. Your ancillary personal representative and your Tennessee personal representative may be the same person as long as that person is qualified to act in both states.

Meeting with Your Attorney

Having given careful thought to the basic contents and requirements of a will, you are now ready to see your attorney The attorney may have other questions, suggestions, or comments. Particularly if your attorney has considerable experience, take advantage of that experience: You are paying for it. Books and television shows may address particular matters of concern to you, but have no way of addressing, or even knowing, the factors that make your estate unique. An experienced professional who has talked with you is your best source of advice. Just as it is important for you to listen to your attorney, your attorney needs to listen to you. Tell your attorney what you want and ask questions when you don't understand. Remember, your attorney wants your estate plan to go as smoothly and simply as possible. If your estate has problems, your attorney will have problems.

Self-Proving Will and Affidavit

After your will is written and you are reading it, you may notice that there are two separate places for the witnesses to sign. This means your attorney is trying to make things as easy as possible for you and your personal representative. The first time the witnesses sign, they are signing as witnesses that you signed the document as your will.

The second time the witnesses sign, they are signing an affidavit. A will becomes self-proving by having this special affidavit added after the end of a will. The affidavit is a notarized, sworn statement by the witnesses that you signed the document as your will, that the witnesses signed your will as witnesses, and that each of you signed the will in the presence of all of you. At the time of your death, it is not necessary that the witnesses actually appear in person before the probate court. Their testimony is already incorporated in the self-proving affidavit. This allows the will to speak for itself. The process of opening administration of your estate is quicker and greatly simplified. This is especially true if one or more witnesses are out of town, have deceased, or are otherwise unavailable at the time of your death.

Where Should I Keep My Will?

Now that you have made your will, what do you do with it? You might leave it with your attorney, but you may feel more comfortable keeping it yourself. Many people prefer to be responsible for their own papers. If you choose to keep your will, it is best to keep it in a safe deposit box located in Tennessee. Your will can be kept with other important documents at home, in a locked box, file cabinet, or special drawer, but it could be inadvertently thrown out or misplaced if mixed with a number of other easily accessible papers. There is also the possibility of fire or water damage. Also, it is not unheard of that a relative may find the will after death and destroy it if the will doesn't give that person what he or she would receive without a will.

You may have read or heard that putting your will in a safe deposit box is a bad idea because the box will be sealed upon your death. Tennessee law does require banks to seal safe deposit boxes after the death of a box holder, whether the box is owned separately or jointly with someone else. However, after your death, your spouse, parents, adult children, or the person you have named as your personal representative can open the box in the presence of a bank officer. The bank officer and the personal representative will remove the will and see that it is sent to the court.

Extra Copies

You should sign only the original of your will. This signed document is your will. Your attorney will make a copy of your will for you to keep at your home. The attorney will also have a copy at his or her office in your personal file. These copies let you review the contents of your will without having to remove the original from its safe location. If you have questions or want to make a change, your attorney will have a copy readily available and can prepare any necessary revisions without the original. Don't ever sign any copies.

Reviewing Your Will

The question is frequently asked, "How often should I review my will?" It depends. Has there been a significant change in your life or your finances? Has the life of any beneficiary or family member changed? Have you simply had second thoughts about a prior decision? If the answer to any of these questions is "yes," your will may need to be revised. For example, Tennessee law provides that if you are divorced, any provisions of your will in favor of your ex-spouse are automatically null and void as soon as the final decree of divorce is entered on the court record. That may be exactly the result you want, but it is usually a good idea to take a look at your will as soon as you become involved in divorce proceedings and to discuss any changes you want to make with your attorney as soon as possible.

If your estate plan includes a more complex will, trusts, or other documents containing specialized tax provisions, your will and these related documents should be reviewed every several years. Tax laws change constantly, and a document with significant tax language can easily go out-of-date. Simple wills, by virtue of their simple nature, are less easily outdated by changes in the law, but are just as subject to changes in personal circumstances. If children die, marry, divorce, have grandchildren or fall in with the wrong crowd, or if you marry or your spouse dies, it is time to look at your will and see what changes are needed.

Additionally, you need to keep in mind the initial premise under which the will was written. A 30-year-old man with a wife and two young children cannot possibly foresee how he would want his property distributed 50 years from now. He should consider and plan for his death to happen within the next five years. Then, at age 35, he should review his will and consider the next five years. A 57-year-old married woman with independent adult children may know how she wants to leave her property even if she lives to be 100. The need for regular revisions is less likely, but this doesn't mean she can put her will away and forget about it.

Now that we have done a simple will, let's turn to one of the other most used estate planning tools — the durable power of attorney.

In this chapter, you will learn:

- what a durable power of attorney is
- who should be given your durable power of attorney
- what powers should be given
- who should give a durable power of attorney
- how to revoke a durable power of attorney
- when not to give a durable power of attorney
- whether to give more than one durable power of attorney

3

THE DURABLE POWER OF ATTORNEY

Many people worry that age or infirmity may cause them to become unable to manage their assets. The durable power of attorney — simple, inexpensive, and effective in a wide range of circumstances — is typically the solution, or part of the solution, for this special need. General and special powers of attorney have been in existence for a long time. A general power of attorney is a written document giving another person (referred to as your attorney in fact) broad authority to act for you with respect to your property. A special power of attorney gives another person (your attorney in fact) limited authority to perform a specific task for you. You may be familiar with these documents empowering someone to act on your behalf, but let's review how these work.

A durable power of attorney is a general power of attorney which endures. To quote from the Tennessee Statutes, "This power of attorney shall not be affected by subsequent disability or incapacity of the principal." What this means, in plain English, is that if the person who signs the durable power of attorney later becomes ill, incompetent, or otherwise unable to act, the power of attorney keeps on working. The person to whom the power is given (the attorney in fact) can assume control of the assets for the incapacitated owner.

Ordinarily, if a person is unable to manage his or her own financial resources and no one else has the necessary authority, the only solution is a conservatorship. There is a court hearing to allow a judge to decide whether the person is really unable to manage without help (the judge would make an adjudication of disability or incapacity) and, if so, appoint a conservator. In the past, conservatorships have been awkward, burdensome, expensive, and slow. Today, conservatorships are more complex, more expensive, and less responsive to many of our needs. As conservatorships become increasingly less desirable, the durable power of attorney becomes increasingly more significant.

Tennessee law provides that a durable power of attorney remains effective until the person giving the power revokes it or dies. Even if a person is clearly incompetent, the durable power continues to work. In fact, the document giving the durable power of attorney may specify that, if someone files a petition asking the court to determine competency, the court should consider appointing the attorney in fact as conservator. However, if the arrangements a person has made for the management of his or her assets prove adequate, there should be no need to have the court intervene and impose a conservatorship. Nevertheless, a durable power of attorney cannot guarantee against conservatorship. The document may not provide sufficient authority to permit the attorney in fact to fully manage the incompetent person's property, the person named as attorney in fact may be unable or unwilling to continue to serve, or some family member may be dissatisfied with the attorney in fact and want to have a conservator appointed. These situations, among others, may lead to a competency hearing.

Tennessee law permits the durable power of attorney to be given to any person, whether or not he or she is related to the giver or is a Tennessee resident.

In the past, powers of attorney dealt primarily with financial matters, the handling of assets, signing of legal documents, and other actions involving management of property. Since 1990 in Tennessee, a durable power of attorney for health care may authorize an attorney in fact to make health care decisions for the principal, including the authority to consent or to refuse or withdraw consent to "any care, treatment, service, or procedure to maintain, diagnose, or treat an individual's physical or mental condition." (The "principal" is the person who gave the durable power.) This durable power of attorney for health care may be given to anyone, and that person may be authorized to make important health care decisions for you. You can give power of attorney for health care to the same person to whom you give power of attorney for financial matters, or you may choose different persons to act for you in these different capacities.

The durable power of attorney for health care will be discussed further in Chapter 4. There is another document provided for under Tennessee law to specifically deal with health care issues — the living will — and that document is also discussed in the next chapter. It seems wisest to address medical decisions separately from financial decisions. For this reason, the form of a durable power of attorney appearing in Appendix D of this book does not contain language specifically relating to medical, therapeutic, or surgical procedures. The grant of authority for medical powers is contained in the durable power of attorney for health care form found in Appendix E. This form works in conjunction with the living will form found in Appendix F.

Who Should Be Named as Your Attorney in Fact?

The authority granted in the durable power of attorney typically is broad in scope because it is intended to provide a stand-in, another individual to act in your place with regard to your property when you are unable to do so. It should be given to a person who has exhibited maturity of judgment and wisdom in handling financial affairs and who has earned your unreserved trust and confidence. Remember, your attorney in fact can exercise all of the broad rights and powers set forth in the durable power of attorney. You give that person the right to sign your name to legal documents relating to your property. (If you haven't already done so, turn to the durable power of attorney form in Appendix D to see what powers are typically included.) Of course, your attorney in fact has a legal obligation to use the durable power of attorney in good faith and only to serve your best interests. (This is known as a "fiduciary" obligation.) He or she is not authorized to use the powers for personal gain or contrary to your intent or your best interests.

What Should the Durable Power of Attorney Say?

Under the law, the property subject to a durable power of attorney includes all property that you own, whether real estate, stocks and bonds, bank accounts, or any other kind of real and personal property, including your personal residence. Even your interest in any jointly held property is subject to the durable power. The specific language of your durable power of attorney determines what authority your attorney in fact may exercise over this property. You are trying to cover all major bases here. Many unforeseen factors can arise in your financial life and, ordinarily, you want your attorney in fact to be able to address these matters if you cannot. Tennessee law allows you to give your attorney in fact a comprehensive list of powers simply by referring to Tennessee Code Annotated Section 34-6-109. That list of powers is reproduced for you in Exhibit A of Appendix D.

One power which you want to consider and which is not included in the form in Appendix D is the power to make gifts. Gift making by an attorney in fact is a very difficult subject. When should the holder of the power of attorney make a gift of your assets if you are incapable and unable to express your own wishes? How much should be given away? To whom should gifts be made? What assets should be given? Clearly this can be a fertile area of controversy. The person who holds the power to make gifts may make gifts to himself or herself (unless the power of attorney specifically prohibits such gifts). Such gifts can be challenged by other interested persons on the grounds that the gifts were not part of the overall estate plan, but were made simply to benefit the recipient. The court may void the challenged gifts if it determines that the holder of the power of attorney abused his or her power or if it finds that the holder cannot show that his or her acts benefitted the person who gave the power of attorney.

The power to make gifts should be included in a durable power of attorney only when it is clear that the gifts will be advantageous to the donor and the donor's estate plan and that they are unlikely to cause major controversy within the family or with other beneficiaries. If it is desirable to permit the holder of the durable power to make gifts, then the document must include language specifically granting that right.

Revocation

The person who gives the durable power of attorney can revoke it at any time. It can also be revoked by court order. It is always revoked by death. Upon death, the will, a trust, or whatever documents provide for the disposition of assets come into effect. (One important exception to the rule that death revokes a durable power of attorney is that any action taken after the death of the principal by the attorney in fact in good faith and without knowledge of the death of the principal will be upheld and binding upon the heirs of the principal.)

You may revoke the durable power of attorney either by having the durable power of attorney document returned to you and destroying it or by giving your attorney in fact a written statement that you are revoking it. As a practical matter you may wish to do more. You may even send a copy of the notice of revocation to everyone who knew about the durable power and might otherwise assume your former attorney in fact still has authority to act for you. If the durable power may be used in any manner affecting real property or if it was recorded for any reason, and if you are concerned it still might be used, record a copy of the revocation in the county in which you own real estate or where any prior power of attorney was recorded.

Who Should Give a Durable Power of Attorney?

While the durable power of attorney can be a valuable estate planning tool, it is not necessary in all situations. It grants broad powers and should not be used indiscriminately. For a young couple with little likelihood of incapacity, the durable power of attorney is probably unwarranted. However, even young couples may need a durable power of attorney for special circumstances, as when one spouse is going to be out of the country for an extended period of time, perhaps serving in the military or working for a multinational corporation. Here, the durable power of attorney can be extremely helpful in letting the spouse who remains at home transact the financial affairs of the couple without relying on the slow, overseas mail. In today's world, even with our modern communications, it can take an extended period of time for written documents to go overseas and come back. The financial world moves much faster than overseas mail. Facsimile machines quickly transmit pages of information over long distances, but you can't get an original executed document over the fax line. Many transactions require the real thing, not a copy. Without a power of attorney, any check that requires both spouses' signatures has to travel between spouses. Faxing a check for the absent spouse to sign and deposit, or sign and fax back, won't work.

For the older couple, the durable power of attorney is almost essential. Faced with the increasing likelihood of incapacitating illness and the delay and expense involved in conservatorships, the durable power of attorney should always be considered. This document is not always the right choice, however.

When Not To Give a Durable Power of Attorney

There are instances where a durable power of attorney won't work well. Often this is because of the individuals and their relationships with each other, or it may be the situation itself which requires other solutions. Trying to operate an active business for a long period of time under a durable power of attorney is not ideal, nor is managing properties located in several states. A more common example occurs in many second marriages made late in life. Either or both spouses may have adult children from a prior marriage. They may have signed an antenuptial agreement in which both spouses limit or waive their respective marital rights in the other's assets. Giving each other a durable power of attorney in this situation is usually not wise. If one spouse (Kristy) becomes incapacitated, the other spouse (Bob) is in a difficult position. Even if Bob is a capable, fair individual who previously got along well with Kristy's children, exercising his authority as attorney in fact can be a burden on him and a source of conflict. The children feel protective toward their mother. They may be suspicious of Bob's motive, and, not infrequently, they will disagree with his decisions. These conflicting opinions can lead to misunderstanding, family friction, and in some instances, outright rifts. For these reasons, it is frequently better to give the durable power of attorney to an older son or daughter rather than a new spouse.

Should You Give More Than One Durable Power of Attorney?

The durable power of attorney is nondelegable. This means that if you give the power of attorney to someone, that person may not in turn pass that power of attorney on to someone else, not even if he or she becomes unable or unwilling to act for you. Only the person who receives the power of attorney from you can exercise it.

Nondelegability is one reason it may be desirable to give more than one person your durable power of attorney. There is no provision in the law that would prohibit this. It is possible to give the durable power of attorney to both a spouse and a child, or to two children, for example. Dividing responsibility, pooling business judgment, instituting a system of checks and balances, or simply avoiding a choice between qualified close family members are additional reasons for not limiting your choice to a single individual.

Bill and Marge are getting on in years. They have two sons, Bob and Charles, and a modest estate. Marge is concerned about what will happen if she is no longer able to manage the family assets. Bill has never wanted to deal with any of the financial aspects of their life. He doesn't even like to write checks. Bill and Marge have a great deal of confidence in their sons and know that Bob and Charles will want to help if something should happen to either of them. Bill and Marge decided they should each sign a durable power of attorney appointing the other as attorney in fact. Each of them is now able to act for both of them in any transaction concerning their property. If Bill's signature is needed, Marge can use the durable power of attorney to sign his name as his attorney in fact. Perhaps Bill is concerned about assuming responsibility if Marge becomes unable to manage the family finances; he is pleased that the durable power of attorney will make the transition easier. Additionally, Bill and Marge thought it was a good idea to give durable powers of attorney to their sons. If Marge becomes seriously ill, Bill will want to spend his time with her, not coping with their financial affairs. Bob and

Charles could use the durable powers of attorney to help their parents during this period. Either of them could raise money for their mother's medical expenses or change the investments to produce a higher income stream or just attend to routine financial matters.

A durable power of attorney could have been structured to require *both* Bob and Charles *to act together* to exercise its authority. This serves as a check in that each one must get the consent of the other before the durable power of attorney can be used. If one person exercises bad judgment, the other can refuse to go along. However, there is a negative side. An obstreperous co-holder of the durable power of attorney can block good decisions. From a practical standpoint, it may be inconvenient to require the holders to act together, since both must sign every document. You can best decide whether the holders of your durable power of attorney should be required to act together, or whether you want each to have the power to act individually.

There is another side of this question of multiple powers to be considered. Many banks, stock brokerage firms, and other institutions have their own durable power of attorney forms that they require to be used. Even if you only want to name one individual as your attorney in fact, you may need to sign several different forms to insure that the individual can completely manage all of your property without unnecessary complications.

Summary

The durable power of attorney, combining simplicity and broad authority, is one of the most frequently used estate planning tools. It is also one of the least expensive. Most Tennessee attorneys who handle estate planning have a standard form, possibly preprinted, for a durable power of attorney. They also keep a file of optional provisions which are commonly used. Even custom-tailoring a durable power of attorney to address a special concern or asset that you own is rarely time-consuming. The document is created by selecting appropriate provisions from the existing collection of alternate provisions and adding or substituting them into the standard form. The power to make gifts is one example of an optional provision. The power to consent to medical, therapeutic, and surgical procedures is another.

Whether the attorney uses a printed form or a tailor-made power of attorney, the power of attorney is very inexpensive for what it does. It is easy to understand and easy to implement. When you start your estate planning, the durable power of attorney should always be considered.

In this chapter, you will learn:

- what is included in a written living will
- how to give instructions about feeding tubes
- how a living will works
- if a living will covers you outside Tennessee
- how a living will is signed
- how to revoke a living will
- the durable power of attorney for health care
- who should and should not be named as your attorney in fact for health care

4

LIVING WILLS

Few decisions are more difficult, more traumatic, or more painful than the decision a family must make for the medical care of a loved one who can only be kept alive by artificial means. In one of the most well-known cases in American law, the New Jersey Supreme Court wrote:

Medicine, with its combination of advanced technology and professional ethics, is both able and inclined to prolong biological life. Law, with its felt obligation to protect the life and freedom of the individual, seeks to assure each person's right to live out his human life until its natural and inevitable conclusion. Theology, with its acknowledgment of man's dissatisfaction with biological life as the ultimate source of joy ..., defends the sacredness of human life and defends it from all attack.

In re: Quinlan (1976).

The dramatic dilemma faced by law, medicine, and the family of Karen Ann Quinlan was played out as our society and that family sought to find their way through what is now known as the "right to die."

Responding to this case and cases within its borders, Tennessee adopted the "Right to Natural Death Act," a policy statement on an adult's right to die. The law permits an adult to make the written declaration commonly known as a living will.

Tennessee believes that "every person has the fundamental and inherent right to die naturally with as much dignity as circumstances permit and to accept, refuse, withdraw from, or otherwise control decisions relating to the rendering of his or her own medical care ..." Each individual's right is subject to society's interest in protecting human life. However, while recognizing the sanctity of life, Tennessee also recognizes that artificially prolonging the life of a person with a terminal condition may provide only a precarious and burdensome existence and may not provide what is medically necessary or beneficial for the patient.

The Written Living Will

The Tennessee statutes provide for written, not oral, declarations. People who feel strongly about terminating medical care should prepare a written declaration before the need arises. The law offers a suggested form for the written declaration which is shown in Appendix F.

How a Living Will Works

You may wonder if the hospitals and doctors in Tennessee really recognize the living will. The answer is yes. The medical care providers must determine that the person is terminal. Once the determination is made that a person is terminal, that there is no reasonable medical expectation of recovery and that, as a medical probability, death will result, the living will becomes part of the medical record. The response in almost every case is to follow the law which provides for withdrawal of medical procedures to prolong life. In fact, if a physician chooses not to comply with the living will, then the physician is required to make every reasonable effort to transfer the patient to another physician. In practice, a transfer is not needed very often. A physician usually accepts the living will unless there are circumstances which cause him or her to feel that it is not a valid document, or that the person is not terminal or that there may be some expectation of recovery. "Terminal" as defined in the statute means "any disease, illness, injury or condition, including, but not limited to, a coma or persistent vegetative state, sustained by any human being, from which there is no reasonable medical expectation of recovery and which, as a medical probability, will result in the death of such human being, regardless of the use or discontinuance of medical treatment implemented for the purpose of sustaining life, or the life processes."

What if I Become Ill Outside Tennessee?

Although the Tennessee living will is valid here, not all states may recognize Tennessee living wills. While most states have some form of law providing for living wills, the language and the requirements vary from state to state. Nevertheless, the Tennessee living will should provide guidance as to the wishes of the terminally ill person. Most health care providers, even outside Tennessee, will consider such wishes.

Feeding Tubes

One of the most troubling areas has been whether to withdraw water and food artificially provided through nasal or gastric tubes. The Tennessee law authorizes the withholding or withdrawal of "medical care," which is currently defined as any procedure or treatment rendered by a physician or health care provider and designed to diagnose, assess or treat disease, illness or injury. The Tennessee definition of "medical care" includes: surgery; drugs; transfusions; mechanical ventilation; dialysis; cardiopulmonary resuscitation; artificial or forced feeding of nourishment, hydration, or other basic nutrients, regardless of the method used; radiation therapy; or any other method used to diagnose, assess, treat, sustain, restore, or supplant vital body functions. Tennessee law further provides that the term "medical care" will not be interpreted to allow the withholding or withdrawal of simple nourishment or fluids so as to condone death by starvation or dehydration *unless* the provisions of the living will include a statement such as the following: "I authorize the withholding or withdrawal of artificially provided food, water or other nourishment or fluids." The living will law in Tennessee recently added the above provisions related to artificial or forced feeding of nourishment (water and food) when the United States

Supreme Court ruled in the dramatic and touching case of *Nancy Cruzan.*

Nancy was a young woman who suffered traumatic injuries in an automobile accident. She was placed on a feeding tube for many years, until her fate came before our highest court to be decided. The Supreme Court held that each individual has the constitutional right to the freedom to determine the manner in which he or she will die, and if the individual chooses to have feeding tubes withheld or withdrawn, the medical care providers must follow the individual's wishes. The Tennessee statutes, at the time the *Cruzan* case was decided, did not permit feeding tubes to be withheld or withdrawn pursuant to a living will or any other document.

When the U.S. Supreme Court announced its decision in the *Cruzan* case, the Tennessee legislature rapidly wrote new laws concerning health care for people who are incapacitated and unable to express their wishes. The result was two legal documents in the statutes that govern when a person is unable to express his or her own wishes. They are the living will and the durable power of attorney for health care.

The law was amended in 1991 to cover those who wished to authorize the withholding or withdrawal of a nasal or gastric tube. Tennessee law in regard to living wills is still evolving. It is not fixed in place, but is a living, growing response to society and its perception of what is proper and ethical. Tennessee is recognizing that people have a valid constitutional right to express their wishes concerning their health care if they are terminal, and to reasonably expect that those wishes will be honored when the time comes.

Formality of Signing

The living will must be notarized. It also requires two witnesses who are not related or married to the person signing the living will, nor can the witnesses be employees of a health care facility providing care to the person signing the living will. You should sign several copies of your living will. (This is referred to as "making multiple originals.") Keep one signed original at home and give one to your physician. A signed copy should be given to a sibling or an adult child, and an additional signed copy may be kept in an easily located place.

Revocation

You may revoke your living will declaration. This is done with a signed and dated revocation or by an oral expression of intent to revoke the living will when communicated to the attending physician. In Tennessee, the law requires that you be competent in order to sign a living will; however, you may revoke the living will at any time, regardless of your mental state or competency.

From a practical standpoint, if a person does not want heroic or extended life-prolonging procedures to be used, that person should execute a living will. If the statutory form expresses your wishes then follow the form. Departure from this form might, in some instances, cause the declaration to be invalidated and, in almost all instances, will cause the care providers to proceed more slowly and more carefully than they would with the familiar statutory form.

No one should ever feel obligated to sign a living will declaration. It is a very personal, individual decision. Many people, when considering the prospect of medical care during a terminal illness, want everything to be done for as long as possible. Someone else may say, "Don't put me on those machines." Another will respond, "I have no intention of dying and I think the whole question is irrelevant and I refuse to consider it any further." The decision can be difficult because it involves contemplating one's own mortality. As one of the sages said, "It's not so much death I fear, as the prospect of dying."

The Power of Attorney for Health Care

The Tennessee legislature has also provided that you may designate someone to make unforeseen or on-the-spot medical decisions for you if you are no longer able to make those decisions for yourself. This designation is known as a power of attorney for health care, and the person you name is your "attorney in fact" for health care. The difference between a living will and a power of attorney for health care is that the living will represents your own personal declaration about what you desire in the event that you have a terminal condition; whereas the power of attorney for health care is the appointment of someone else to "speak for you" concerning your medical care whenever, for whatever reason, you are unable to communicate for yourself. You need not be in a terminal condition for the power of attorney for health care to be used.

What Can the Attorney in Fact for Health Care Do?

The power of attorney for health care normally gives the attorney in fact for health care the power to give advance directives concerning medical, therapeutic, or surgical procedures, including the administration of drugs. Unless you limit the powers of your attorney in fact for health care, he or she will be authorized to make medical decisions which cover almost every conceivable question or situation that may arise. Not only can these individuals make medical care decisions, but they can consult with health care providers and give what is known as "informed consent." They are specifically authorized to sign medical consents, authorizations, or releases, to access any clinical records or other medical information, to apply for benefits such as Medicare and Medicaid, and to transfer an individual to or from a hospital, hospice, nursing home, or other care facilities. The attorney in fact for health care cannot, however, authorize the withholding or withdrawal of artificially provided food or water unless either the living will or the power of attorney for health care specifically states that this can be done.

The attorney in fact for health care usually has the right to receive information concerning the diagnosis, prognosis, alternative treatments, risks versus benefits of treatment, side effects of any medication, financial impact of proposed treatment, and the likely outcome if consent is not given to suggested treatment.

The person who designates another as his attorney in fact for health care may revoke the designation at any time. Like the power of attorney for financial matters, this power of attorney can be revoked in writing or orally. Notification of a revocation should be given to your health care providers as well.

Who Should Be Given Power of Attorney for Health Care?

The person or persons you name as your attorney(s)-in-fact for health care should be those you would want to make medical decisions for you, usually a spouse or a child. It is possible to name a number of people in series so that if one were unable to make medical decisions for some reason, another would be named as the alternative. It is also quite common to name two persons simultaneously. This is done to avoid hard feelings or questions as to why one person was named and not another.

Who Can Be Designated as Attorney in Fact for Health Care?

A person does not have to be related to you to be your attorney in fact for health care, but he or she must be at least 18 years old. Also, the attorney in fact for health care must be someone other than your doctor or other health care provider, or any employee or relative of your doctor or health care provider. If you give power of attorney for health care to your spouse and you are later divorced, the final judgment of divorce automatically revokes the power of attorney, and you should designate someone else as your attorney in fact for health care.

What Happens If You Don't Name an Attorney in Fact for Health Care?

If you do not name an attorney in fact for health care and you become incapacitated, then someone must begin what is known as a conservatorship proceeding, and a court will appoint a person to act on your behalf. Usually, this will be a spouse, child, parent, or someone closely related to you. Conservatorships are usually time-consuming and expensive, and you must remember that the judge does not know you and has not had the opportunity to talk to you about your wishes for medical care. With the power of attorney for health care, you can make many medical care decisions in advance and consider what you do or do not want in the event you can no longer make health care decisions for yourself.

The Form for Designation of the Power of Attorney for Health Care

Included in Appendix E is a form which is used for a power of attorney for health care. This is just one of many forms this document might take. You should also know that many health care providers and medical care facilities have forms that you can fill out and sign or adapt to your own use.

Summary

The difficult, confusing, and highly emotionally charged area of medical care when a person is incapable of making medical decisions has been the subject of considerable attention from the courts and from the legislature. Gradually, the courts and the legislature, as well as society in general, seem to be moving toward a feeling that people may clearly express how they wish medical decisions to be made for them if, at some later date, they cannot make such decisions for themselves. Starting with *Karen Ann Quinlan* and the case of *Nancy Cruzan*, federal and state courts and legislatures are setting standards as to what should be contained in so-called "right to die" documents.

The Tennessee legislature has responded to these court opinions by providing guidelines for how a person's statements are to be set forth and recognized. The legislature has set forth two legal tools for giving advance medical directives. One, the living will, expresses a person's wishes if he or she is terminal, whether death is imminent or not, and even if the individual is in a persistent vegetative state. The other tool is the power of attorney for health care. This is a document which designates another person to make medical decisions, and the nature and extent of the powers authorized can be as specific or general as you desire. Both of these documents respond to society's feelings concerning medical care and each gives us the right to determine how we want our medical care to be handled in the event we cannot clearly express our own wishes.

In this chapter, you will learn:

- the pros and cons of trusts
- how incompetency is determined
- the disadvantage of conservatorships
- how to avoid probate
- what fees to expect
- how to save on estate taxes
- what income taxes to expect after death
- what marital rights are
- the dangers of undue influence
- how to make gifts from a trust
- deeding real estate into a living trust
- whether trusts are private
- what the living trust document provides
- how distributions are made
- what powers a trustee has
- what a successor trustee is
- what a corporate trustee is
- how to fund your trust
- how to decide if a living trust is right for you

5

LIVING TRUSTS

For many years, living trusts have been used by thoughtful estate planners in constructing estate plans for Tennesseans. It has been more than 25 years since Norman Dacey came out with his now famous book entitled *How to Avoid Probate*. That book, and the thoughts expressed in it, struck a responsive chord in many. Since that time, the living trust has been increasingly popular. Living trusts are known by several names: *inter vivos* trusts, revocable trusts, revocable living trusts, or self-declaration trusts. A living trust may generally be described as a trust that is set up by an individual while he or she is alive. The individual frequently names himself or herself as trustee, but alternatively may name a bank or another individual to serve as trustee. Under the terms of the living trust, the person who creates it is to receive the income and as much principal as he or she may request at any time. The trust is completely revocable and may be changed by the person who set it up. In short, the person creating the trust has lost no control over his or her assets, but has placed most if not all of the property into the trust. The income remains the same and the principal is available at any time. While there are many types of trusts, this is the pattern most living trusts follow.

By the time we finish this chapter, you will have a good idea about what a living trust is and whether it would be a good idea for you. Not all people, and certainly not all attorneys, will agree with everything expressed in this book. Certainly many will disagree with the opinions in this chapter. Nevertheless, if you remember that a living trust is neither a cure-all nor a complex, expensive, frustrating fraud, you will be able to make your own decisions, and those decisions will be the right ones for you.

Unfortunately, many laypersons view the living trust as a panacea for all estate planning problems. They believe it will save estate taxes, reduce the cost of probate, and speed up administration of the estate. They believe it will keep creditors from claiming against the estate, and protect the estate against will contests, greedy heirs, and overreaching attorneys. Conversely, many attorneys, even some in the estate planning field, view the living trust with suspicion. They overreact to the unwarranted expectations of the public by telling their clients that living trusts are unwise, inefficient, expensive, clumsy, difficult to deal with, full of red tape, illegal, and confusing.

The living trust will not solve all ills, but it can be most beneficial and even essential in many estate planning situations. The following is a summary of fact and fiction about living trusts:

Let's look at some of the reasons for using a living trust. The living trust may provide a good vehicle for current management of assets. Many people, for various reasons, do not want to manage their own assets. They may be elderly or infirm, or their lives may be so occupied by their jobs that they do not have time to spend on managing these assets. Professionals may find themselves in this situation, as do entertainers and people who are required to be out of the country for extended periods.

Many times someone will ask a trust department to manage assets in an investment program. The trust department may do this through an investment management account. The person remains his or her own trustee, or at times the corporate investment adviser may be asked to become the trustee under the terms of the trust agreement to buy, sell, and otherwise make investments.

The Living Trust

What is it? As defined earlier in this chapter, the living trust is an agreement set up while the person is alive. The trust agreement defines who the trustee is and what the trustee's obligations will be. Assets are put in the trust, and the trustee follows the instructions written in the trust agreement. The trust agreement actually is a contract between two people. One is the person who puts the assets in the trust and the other is the trustee. Some living trusts are 40 pages. Others are 15. The length depends upon the complexity of the estate planning situation and the feelings as to what is most appropriate. This changes from one client to another and from one attorney to another.

Ingredients

Let us consider the typical ingredients of a living trust. First, the trust agreement reveals the person who is putting assets in the trust. Generally this person is known as the grantor, the settlor, and, sometimes, the trustor. This is the person creating the trust; typically, this would be you.

The trustee is the person who receives the assets, invests them and distributes the income and principal according to the grantor's (your) wishes. The trust is revocable. The trust must specifically provide that it can be altered, amended, or revoked in any way that you as the grantor see fit.

COMPARISON OF WILLS AND LIVING TRUSTS

	WILL	LIVING TRUST
Estate tax savings	Same as a living trust	Same as a will
Income tax savings	Slight income tax savings after death	No income tax savings
Costs to settle the estate	Usually 1%-2% more than with a trust	Usually saves 1%-2% over a will (probate)
Distributions to beneficiary	Distributions can be made as promptly as with a living trust	Distributions can be made as promptly as with a will
Confidentiality and privacy of documents	Private before death, public after death	Semiprivate both before and after death
Confidentiality of assets	Private before death, semiprivate after death	Private before and after death
Incompetency	No benefit if incompetent	Considerable benefit if incompetent
Creditor Protection	No protection during life; substantial protection six months after death	No protection during life; less protection after death than with a will
Costs to create document	Cheaper than a living trust	More expensive than a will

Distributions

The trust normally will provide that all the trust income will be distributed to you and that you may take out as much principal as you wish on demand. The trust will provide that if you become incapacitated, the successor trustee has the power to distribute income and, if necessary, principal to others on your behalf. In the event you become incapacitated, the trustee can use funds to pay for nursing care, nursing homes, extended-care facilities, hospitals and physicians, as well as day-to-day living expenses. Some trusts go further and provide that the trustee may distribute principal or income to a spouse. The thinking here is that if all the assets of the family are in the trust, and all income will be held by the trustee for the benefit of the grantor, this may leave the grantor's spouse and family in a difficult situation. Fortunately, Tennessee law is not that harsh, but it probably is a wise idea to have a clause in the trust saying that the assets in the trust may be used for the benefit of either the grantor or the grantor's spouse.

Upon the death of the grantor, the trust typically says that the trustee is authorized to pay the debts of the deceased, pay any estate taxes, transmit funds to the personal representative for the purposes of these costs or other expenses, and hold the remaining assets in the trust according to specified terms and conditions.

The terms and conditions of a living trust, upon the death of the person creating the trust, may be as broad as human imagination can be, subject to a few limitations. These limitations are imposed chiefly as a matter of public policy. Frequently, a living trust provides that the income will go to the surviving spouse. If the spouse is dead, the trust may provide that the principal will go to the children. Sometimes, if the children are young, the trust provides that the trustee will continue to hold the income or principal in the trust and to distribute only as much income or principal as is necessary for a child's health, support, maintenance, or education, taking into consideration other assets which may be otherwise available to the child. The distribution of the principal would occur in stages specified by the grantor.

Trustee Powers

What is income? What is principal? What types of investments are permissible for the trustee to use? Giving a trustee wide latitude usually turns out to be better than setting narrow limits. Each person, considering what trust powers the trustee should have, naturally is inclined to be conservative, and conservatism is generally a desirable thing in the area of estate planning. Here, however, too much conservatism can be a problem. It is impossible to look into the future and see what types of investments, opportunities, or problems will occur during the lifetime of the trust. Because of this, it is generally wiser to give much broader discretion to the trustee than might be considered appropriate initially.

There are two other reasons why it is desirable to give a trustee broad discretionary powers. One is that, because trustees are required by Tennessee law to manage trusts in a conservative fashion, they will be naturally conservative. Secondly, trustees are required to adhere to what is known as a fiduciary responsibility. A fiduciary responsibility is the highest kind of responsibility that can be imposed on an individual. Because the fiduciary responsibility is so strong and the courts are so strict on any trustee's misdoings, the trustee will naturally gravitate toward the safe ground. Usually, problems arising in the trustee's powers are a result of too narrow rather than too broad a grant of authority.

Successor Trustee

When a trust is created during the lifetime of its creator, it is common for the trustee of the living trust to be the person who created the trust. Successor trustees should also be named in the trust. If the grantor becomes incapacitated through age, illness, death, or misfortune, someone else can manage the assets in accordance with the terms of the trust. Generally you, as the person creating the trust, will know who will be best able to manage your assets if you are unable to look after them yourself. Sometimes it is a spouse. Sometimes it is a trusted friend, professional adviser, or a trust company. Frequently, it is a child, or maybe two of the children. After all, there is no requirement to have only one trustee. If you have more than two trustees, however, things are going to be more complicated. It can be inefficient and clumsy if, for example, each check must be signed by all trustees.

Corporate Trustees

Corporate trustees fulfill a very necessary function in the field of estate planning. Their trust officers have special knowledge about how to administer trusts and interpret instructions given in trust agreements. However, not all corporate trustees are created equal, nor are all trust officers created equal. In fact, the corporate trustee you name today may be owned by another corporation next year.

The banking industry has changed a great deal over the past 20 years, and according to analysts of the banking industry, it is likely that change will continue over the next 20 years. These changes directly affect the trust departments and the administration of the trusts in terms of efficiency, responsiveness, operating procedures, and expenses. You may want an individual and a corporate trustee to serve together, each with special skills: the individual for the personal touch and the corporate trustee for technical knowledge and assistance.

Fees for Corporate Trustees

Some trust departments quote their fees based on the amount of principal plus a different percentage of income depending on the services requested. Others choose to give a more generalized rate. Still others choose to charge for each transaction that occurs in the trust. A general rule of thumb is that, when all is said and done, it is probably going to cost about 1% of the value of the principal to have the trust run by a corporate fiduciary each year. If you consider 1% of all the assets that might be in the trust and consider that this figure will be taken out of the trust each year for as long as the corporate trustee will serve, you can see that it can become very expensive over the long term. Yet the corporate trustee is usually a stable financial institution. Corporate trustees also argue that they have better investment results and keep better records than individuals. Many do; some do not. Most corporate trustees are here to stay, meet a special need and provide much service to their customers.

Funding Your Trust

Once you have set the terms of the trust and it has been prepared, reviewed, and signed, you need to place your assets in the trust. The importance of putting assets in the trust cannot be over-emphasized. All too frequently, people will spend considerable sums of money for a trust and fail to put assets into it. This is not unlike the person who buys a very expensive automobile and never puts any gas in it. See Appendix G for instructions on funding a trust.

Incompetency

It is desirable to consider an *inter vivos* trust as an alternative to conservatorship for future management of the assets if incompetency should arise. Tennessee law concerning conservatorships has changed recently. Many new provisions have been added which greatly increase the cost and "red tape" in conservatorships. Because of the possibility of accident, old age, or illness, you may be concerned about managing your assets. You can set up a living trust which provides that you will manage assets as long as you can. If you are unable to do so, you have already named a successor trustee to take over. If a successor trustee has not been named, the court probably will appoint a conservator of the property. By having a trust that specifically names a successor trustee, you can be sure the question of "Who shall manage my assets if I am incapacitated or incompetent?" is settled.

Suppose Frank is in his 70s and is wondering how he should set up his estate plan. He speaks with his attorney who recommends a living trust. Frank, having considered the benefits of a living trust, agrees and the attorney prepares a trust. Under the terms of the trust, Frank is his own trustee. He can alter, amend, revoke, or change the trust in any way he wishes as long as he is alive and competent to do so. He receives all the income under the terms of the trust and receives as much of the principal as he wishes.

As trustee, he controls the investment decisions completely. If he becomes incapacitated, Frank has named his son, Bill, in the document to take over as his successor trustee. The successor trustee, of course, would have the responsibility of paying the income and, if necessary, the principal, to or for Frank's benefit. If Frank were severely incapacitated, he might be in a nursing home. His son, Bill, could pay the income directly to the nursing home. If Frank had to have a significant operation, Bill could pay the doctors and hospital as well. It would not be necessary, because of the assets being in the trust, to appoint a formal court-supervised conservator for Frank's assets. His son, Bill, could just take over managing these assets as Frank's successor trustee. Bill, however, would not have the power to alter, amend, or revoke the trust. That is reserved only for the creator of the trust.

On Frank's death, the assets that are in the trust are distributed by Bill to the beneficiaries. The assets are still subject to estate and inheritance taxes; such taxes are not increased or decreased by the trust. The distribution of Frank's assets will not be speeded up or slowed down because of the trust if the assets are over $600,000 because the IRS will not permit an estate to be closed or a trust to be terminated until they have reviewed the estate tax return and issued their "closing letter." The Tennessee Department of Revenue will often perform an inheritance tax audit (independent of the IRS) for persons whose assets are over $600,000, and state inheritance taxes are also not affected by whether the assets are held in a trust or in Frank's name alone at the time of his death.

On the other hand, if Frank's assets are under $600,000, then Bill may choose to distribute the assets in the trust promptly. He might decide to hold off until all the bills are in, or he might distribute part of the assets and then hold back a small reserve in case unexpected expenses came in.

If Frank did not feel that his son, Bill, was the right person to handle funds due to Bill's age or lack of experience in handling assets, Frank could designate some other person or, if there wasn't any other person Frank felt was appropriate, Frank could name a trust department. The trust department would take over paying Frank's bills and handling the investments, and ultimately the distribution to the beneficiaries that Frank had chosen.

All in all, this is a fairly simple process and one which is used in Tennessee every day.

Conservatorships

There is another advantage to a living trust when it comes to the future management of property. Not only does the living trust provide *who* shall serve as the person to manage these assets, but, more specifically and more importantly, it sets out *how* these assets shall be managed. The alternative to the living trust is a conservatorship. There are few attorneys today who would advocate a conservatorship over a living trust. Conservatorships in Tennessee are very expensive and time-consuming. The process involves the testimony of at least one physician, friends and family, and a considerable amount of attorney time, court time, expense, and perhaps family embarrassment.

Once the determination has been made by the judge that the person is unable to manage his or her affairs, the court appoints an individual or a corporation to serve as conservator. This person is subject to a great number of restrictions and requirements. Each one causes more expense, more delay, and more red tape. Under a living trust, on the other hand, assets are easily administered by the successor trustee. If there is a situation where there is a reasonable likelihood that a person may become incapacitated, it is wise to consider a living trust for the future management of assets.

Avoiding Probate

The most common reason offered for a living trust is to avoid probate. The perception of many people concerning probate in Tennessee is based on what they have experienced in other states. Tennessee probate is as different from the procedures in New York, Massachusetts, Michigan, and other states as our Tennessee accent is as different from their local dialects. Tennessee probate functions relatively quickly and with a minimum of expense compared to most northern states. An example of the differences may be seen in the fees charged by trust departments, depending upon whether the assets are administered through a trust or through a probate proceeding.

Fees

The difference in cost of probate versus trusts is generally far less than many people think. After estate taxes are considered, the difference may be less than 1% of the value of the estate assets. One of the largest trust departments charges 3% as personal representative and 2% as trustee. After estate taxes in the 37% to 55% range or income taxes in the 30% range are considered, the difference may be one-half to two-thirds of 1%. You should take the opportunity to discuss the savings with your estate planning attorney. Frequently the savings for a trust will be far less than predicted by well-intentioned stock brokers, life insurance salesmen, or other people purporting to have some knowledge of these matters.

Avoiding the Delay of Probate

As we will see in Chapter 17, probate is a process whereby assets passing under a will through court supervision are distributed to beneficiaries. Executors passing assets through probate may encounter delays due to several factors. One is the process of determining assets and beneficiaries. Occasionally, problems arise in determining what assets are in the estate and who is to receive them. This kind of delay can occur in either a will or a trust. However, if the assets and beneficiaries are clearly identified, these problems can be avoided whether the assets are passing under a will or passing through a trust.

Another type of delay arises when the personal representative does not want to distribute assets until the creditor's claim period or the period for contesting the will has elapsed. The creditor's claim period is usually six months after the probate process has started, and the period for contesting the will is two years following the date when the will is first filed for probate. Trustees frequently will distribute assets within these different periods. But some problems that arise in wills are also being seen with trusts as the trusts grow in popularity. For instance, people are taking exception to the disposition of assets in trusts just as they take exception to the disposition of assets in wills. As a result, trustees are becoming more cautious about distributing assets. In fact, some trustees are now publishing notices to creditors, just as personal representatives do, to avoid unforeseen claims arising after assets have been distributed through the trust. Personal representatives frequently can be encouraged to give partial early distributions from an estate rather than waiting for the full six-month period. Thus, some estate planning professionals feel that there is a gradual merging of the probate process and the trust administration process after death. It is too early to tell whether this is a trend or not.

Still another type of delay in settling estates arises because of estate and inheritance taxes. Here there is no difference between the estate and inheritance tax treatment of wills and trusts. The IRS and the Tennessee Department of Revenue will review the estate or inheritance tax returns for all estates exceeding $600,000. The final closing of a person's estate, whether passing via a will or a trust, does not occur until the IRS issues what is known as a "closing letter." In it, the IRS says that it has examined the estate tax return, is satisfied with the return, and has determined that all assets have been reported and all taxes due have been paid. This letter comes just as slowly whether the estate is passing under a will or a trust. Similarly, final closing of a person's estate does not occur until the Tennessee Department of Revenue has issued its certificate stating that all inheritance and/or estate taxes have been paid to the Department's satisfaction.

On balance, it seems as though assets are distributed more promptly under a trust than under a will. Whether this will continue to be the case will depend on future circumstances as they arise. It may well be that trustees, seeing litigation against other trustees, will be a bit slower to distribute assets shortly after the death of the decedent and that personal representatives acting under wills will be more responsive to the wishes and needs of the beneficiaries than they have been in the past.

Saving Estate Taxes

Occasionally, people will be encouraged to enter into a living trust to save estate taxes. The statement that the living trust will save taxes over a will may be clearly and simply answered: "Horsefeathers!" Living trusts do not save estate taxes any more than a will does. The IRS does not care whether assets are inherited via a living trust or a will.

Income Taxes after Death

When it comes to income taxes, the living trust is neutral. Occasionally, people think that living trusts will save them income taxes. Actually, the contrary is true because the Internal Revenue Code considers the probate estate to be a separate tax-paying entity: separate from the person who died and separate from the beneficiaries.

A living trust is not considered for tax purposes to be such a separate entity. All the income earned up until death is taxed to the person who died, and all the income earned after death is taxed to the beneficiaries. There is not a third entity, as there is in a probate estate, with which to share the tax obligation. So, the tax obligation is increased on those persons who actually have to pay the tax. In short, living trusts do not save income tax; in fact, they cause a small amount of additional income tax to be paid.

Marital Rights

Sometimes living trusts are suggested as a way of avoiding a spouse's rights. As we will see in Chapter 6, under Tennessee law a surviving spouse who is unhappy with a will is entitled to take as an alternative approximately one-third of the estate as well as several other important benefits. This is true unless the parties have entered into a valid prenuptial or postnuptial agreement. However, the protective provisions giving the spouse these benefits in relation to the assets passing under a will do not seem to apply to assets held in living trusts. A spouse, either through anger, misunderstanding, or some other human frailty, may make provisions in a living trust that are extremely difficult for the widow or widower to swallow. Because there is little protection under Tennessee law for the surviving spouse when it comes to living trusts, the surviving spouse may find himself or herself in a very bad situation — even disinherited.

Will Contests

Sometimes living trusts are suggested as a way to avoid will contests. Technically, of course, this is correct, because if there is a living trust, most of the assets will not be passing under the will; they will be passing under the trust. If assets pass under the trust, then the contest would not be a will contest — it would be a trust contest. Also, any person who has an interest in the trust, either claimed or real, can contest the trust up until the time the assets are distributed. Under a will, the period during which there could be a will contest by heirs or beneficiaries is limited to two years from the time the will is admitted to probate. With a trust, this period remains open.

Undue Influence

Under Tennessee law, a person may make a will and may understand the effect of that will and be perfectly oriented in terms of assets and the natural beneficiaries, and yet be so under the influence of some third party as to be incapable of making a reasonable, independent decision about who is to inherit the assets. In such a situation, Tennessee law says that the will procured through undue influence is void. In all likelihood, the next prior will would be the one that would distribute the assets.

A case in Florida illustrates that courts may not provide as much protection from undue influence if a living trust is used instead of a will. In Palm Beach, a 76-year-old widow created a living trust. Several months later she married a 32-year-old man. Not totally surprisingly, the marriage did not last very long, and they were divorced within a year. As part of the divorce proceedings, the court ordered the husband to return to the woman a number of assets that he had obtained as gifts from her through undue influence.

However, the story does not end there. Several months later, the couple remarried. The woman sought to make certain changes in her living trust. The trustee, in this case a bank, was concerned that she was acting under undue influence of her husband again. The bank properly raised an issue concerning these changes. After a considerable amount of litigation, the Florida Supreme Court ruled that the undue influence rule, which would have protected her from making such poor decisions had she been writing a will, did not apply to her trust. The provisions she made, which benefitted the husband 44 years her junior, still stand.

This story illustrates that, in Florida as in Tennessee, much of the law which has developed on wills has not yet been applied to living trusts, and many questions that the law has answered concerning wills remain unanswered concerning living trusts.

Sometimes people feel that if they have a trust, they don't need a will. This is not the case. Whether you have a trust or not, you should always have a will. In the case of a living trust, the will is generally a very short one known in the estate planning field as a "pour-over will" because it takes any assets which should be in the trust, but were not in the trust at the time of death, and "pours them over" into the trust. The trust may have some estate tax apportionment language in it to say which assets bear the burden of estate taxes. It is the will that usually controls tax apportionment. For these reasons, it is always necessary to have a will, even if there is a living trust.

Gifts from a Trust

The IRS may have an unpleasant surprise awaiting someone who makes gifts from a trust. Robert wishes to make gifts of $10,000 to his children and grandchildren, and does so by directing the trustee (which may be himself) to make these gifts from the trust which contains the bulk of his assets. But he must live at least three years after each of these gifts. If he dies before three years, the gifted assets may well be included in the estate for tax purposes, even though he gave them away two or three years before his death. This should serve as a strong warning to someone who may be contemplating gifts from an *inter vivos* trust.

Deeding Real Estate into a Living Trust

Any deed which is effective to transfer real property to another person can effectively transfer real property to your trustee and into your trust. Legally, the transfer of title to your trustee gives the trustee every power over the property that is granted in the trust agreement. Very few people know what your trust agreement says, so most people don't know what authority your trustee has.

If the issue doesn't arise sooner, verification of the trustee's authority ordinarily will be required when the property is sold. Before insuring that the buyer is receiving good title to the property, the title insurance issuer will want assurances that the trustee has the power under the trust agreement to sell the property. If a typical real estate deed was used to transfer property to the trust, the only document that contains all the powers of the trustee is the trust agreement. It is likely that the title insurance issuer will require that the entire trust agreement, or at least substantial parts of it, be recorded so that the powers of the trustee are in the public records.

To avoid making public a document intended to remain private, many careful attorneys use a short-hand version of the trust known as a "Declaration of Trust," which is designed to be recorded and which specifies the powers the trustee has been given in the trust. Another approach is to prepare a special deed that recites the authority of the trustee. In fact, many attorneys will take an additional precaution. They provide for a successor trustee in the trust agreement and include the name of that successor trustee in the Declaration of Trust or in the deed. If the current trustee has died or resigned when it is time to convey the property, and if the successor is acting as trustee, there will be no need to examine and record the trust agreement to confirm the trustee's identity.

Some people do not object to having their living trusts recorded, but most do. When a trust is recorded, it becomes part of the public record. Anyone can read the document and see who is to receive what property.

Privacy

Privacy is always an important issue. There may be a loss of privacy while you are alive with a trust and a loss of privacy after your death with a will. The will is recorded after death and therefore the will is open to all persons. Conversely, the trust (or the short-hand Declaration of Trust) frequently must be shown to persons while you are alive. It is unlikely that stock transfer agents will transfer assets into the trust or out of the trust without being given the opportunity to photocopy either the Declaration of Trust or the trust itself. Because of this, there may be a loss of privacy while you are alive because the trust might be shown to persons in order to have them recognize the validity of the trust. One argument occasionally made for trusts by people who do not know better is that your assets passing under a will must be open to inspection by anyone wanting to find out "what you were worth." This is not necessarily true. Under Tennessee law, inventories listing all assets passing through the will are required to be filed with the probate court. However, these inventories can be waived under the terms of the will or, if all the will beneficiaries are adults, they may agree to waive inventories after the will has been admitted to probate. Most careful estate planners include a provision in the will which eliminates the necessity of a public inventory of the assets of the deceased, as well as certain other requirements of Tennessee probate such as the posting of a bond and the preparation of periodic accountings.

Is a Living Trust Right for You?

Frequently it is, but many times it may not be. When all assets are held jointly, the living trust will not save probate costs, since there is no probate. Rather than doing two trusts while both spouses are alive, it may be cheaper and wiser to do just one trust later when there is just one spouse and the property is no longer jointly held. However, if there is concern that one of the parties will be incapacitated or unable to manage the assets at that time, it may be wisest to do a living trust each for the husband and for the wife when the estate planning is being done.

Generally speaking, the older a person is, the more important and beneficial the living trust becomes. The reason is that as a person grows older, the chances of being incapacitated increase. This time of incapacity is when the trust benefits arise. Younger persons are less likely to be incapacitated and to realize these benefits of the living trust.

The size of the assets in the estate also helps in determining whether a living trust will be useful. Persons with quite modest estates will feel that they do not want the expense of a living trust. Conversely, persons with very large estates frequently choose not to go to a living trust. The expenses of settling their estate frequently will be the same whether the assets are passing under a will or under a trust, and, in some instances, they will be able to save money by having their assets pass under a will instead of a trust. Besides the slight income tax benefit to a will, it is usually easier to support deductions on a federal estate tax return for the personal representative's fee than it is to support deductions on the estate tax return in the same amount for trustee's fees. Persons with medium to medium-large estates generally will see some benefits in having a living trust. A broad generalization, and one subject to debate, is that people with an estate of several hundred thousand dollars or less usually benefit less from living trusts. Persons with assets over this amount probably should consider the merits of a living trust. In any case, if you are discussing the advisability of a living trust with your attorney, talk about the pros and cons noted in this chapter. Your attorney may have some additional suggestions or comments.

Inter vivos trusts can be extremely useful for some estates. They are essential tools in estate planning, particularly if there is concern about loss of ability to manage assets in the future. They provide privacy after death and frequently save money on moderate-sized estates. While *inter vivos* trusts frequently cost two to three times more than a will to set up, they usually make up this difference by the savings in costs of administration after death.

In this chapter, you will learn:

- what happens when there is no will
- who is entitled to inherit from your estate
- why it is so expensive
- who will be appointed to handle your estate
- what happens to your children
- what assets are not affected if you die without a will

6

DYING WITHOUT A WILL

Lawyers will often tell you that, just like everyone else, you do have a will (even though you may not be aware of it): Their rationale is that if you have not signed a will of your own, the state legislature has made one for you! Each state's laws governing inheritance rights are a little different, and in most cases the laws of the state in which you live at the time of your death determine the persons who will be entitled to inherit your property. When you die without a will, it is said that you have died "intestate," and the people who inherit from you in that situation are called the "heirs of an intestate estate." In Tennessee, the laws covering intestate estates are called "statutes of descent and distribution." The easiest way to explain how Tennessee's laws apply when a person dies intestate is to give examples of the situations that may arise and describe how the property must be distributed.

Rights of the Heirs of Your Intestate Estate
If You Leave a Surviving Spouse

If you die intestate and your spouse survives you, his or her share of your estate will depend upon whether you have also left any children, grandchildren, or more remote direct descendants who have also survived you. If you have left no direct descendants, then your surviving spouse will be entitled to receive all of the property you owned in your name alone at the time of your death.

This will be true even if you left surviving parents, brothers, or sisters.

If there are children or other direct descendants who survive you — even if they were born to a previous marriage — then your surviving spouse will receive either one-half or one-third of all of your property, depending upon how many children survive you. The surviving spouse receives one-half of your property when only one child survives you, or when the persons who survive you are the living descendants of only one child of yours. Your child (or his or her descendants) will take the other one-half share. If two or more of your children survive you, or if the descendants of two or more of your children are living at the time of your death, your surviving spouse is entitled to receive one-third of your estate, and your children must share the remaining two-thirds equally. The living descendants of a deceased child will take their parent's share of your property. Another way to say all of this is that your surviving spouse takes a child's share or one-third, whichever is greater.

Tennessee law governing the inheritance rights of children and their descendants apply to adopted children, and the rules uphold the inheritance rights of a child conceived before the death of its parent but born after that parent's death. A child born out of wedlock is always entitled to inherit from its mother, and from its father if the natural parents ever marry each other or if the father's paternity is established in court either before or after the father's death.

If You Leave Descendants but No Surviving Spouse

If you are not survived by a spouse, but you have had children, they will each be entitled to take an equal share of all of the property which was in your name alone at the time of your death. If one of your children dies before you, leaving no direct descendants of his or her own, then no share is created for that child. However, if any of your children predeceases you leaving direct descendants who are living at the time of your death, those descendants will share equally in their parent's portion of your estate. When this happens, the descendants are said to take "by representation."

Let's see how taking by representation works. Suppose you have four children: Anne, Martin, Leila, and Liza. Neither Anne nor Martin has had any children, but Leila has two children and Liza has one. If Anne predeceases you, but the other children survive, only three shares will be created and those shares will be divided equally among Martin, Leila, and Liza. If only Leila predeceases you, then Anne will take one-fourth, Martin one-fourth, Liza one-fourth, and Leila's two children will take one-eighth each. This is what happens when Leila's children take by representation. Similarly, if only Liza predeceases you, her child will take a full one-fourth (Liza's full portion) of your estate.

However, there is an oddity in Tennessee's law of taking by representation. Suppose that you lived a very long time and, sadly, all four of your children (Anne, Martin, Leila, and Liza) predecease you. In that case, you would have three grandchildren living: Leila's two children and Liza's one child. You might think that Leila's children would each take one-fourth of your estate (Leila's share) and Liza's child would take one-half (Liza's share), but under Tennessee law, if *all* of your children are deceased, the descendants at the next level will all be treated equally, so that each of your three grandchildren will receive one-third of your estate. (Most grandparents are pleased with the way that Tennessee's law of taking by representation works.)

If You Leave No Descendants and No Surviving Spouse

If you die without a will and you are unmarried, with no surviving children or their descendants, then all of the property in your name alone will be distributed to your parents, equally. This is true even if they are divorced and haven't spoken to each other in years. If you only have one surviving parent, he or she will receive all of your property.

If neither of your parents is living, your property will be divided equally among your brothers and sisters. If any one of your siblings has predeceased you, leaving descendants who survive you, those descendants will take by representation. If you have a half-brother or half-sister, he or she will be treated exactly as a full brother or sister.

But what if you die without surviving parents, brothers, sisters, or their descendants? What happens to your property then? Tennessee law requires that we examine your genealogy: we search for your grandparents and analyze whether there are any living descendants of either your maternal or paternal grandparents. If we find descendants from both family branches, then the descendants of your maternal grandparents will take one-half of your estate (by representation), and the descendants of your paternal grandparents will take the other one-half. If only one of the branches of your family tree contains any living descendants, they will take your entire estate by representation.

And finally, you may ask what will be done with your property if, when you die, we learn you were absolutely the last living descendant of all four of your grandparents? Alas, then the state of Tennessee will take your estate into its coffers, and when this happens we say that your property "escheats to the state." (It sounds as bad as it is, doesn't it?)

Who Handles Your Intestate Estate?

If you die intestate, you (obviously) have not selected anyone to take the responsibility of gathering your assets, paying your last bills and debts, filing your tax returns, paying any tax obligations that exist, and distributing what is left of your property. The person who takes on this responsibility is called the "administrator" of your estate. Another more generic term for the administrator, used more and more these days, is "personal representative." Who is entitled to be the administrator (or personal representative) of your estate for the benefit of your heirs?

Tennessee law gives to your surviving spouse the right to handle ("administer") your estate when you die without a will. If you die without a surviving spouse, or if your surviving spouse does not ask the probate court for permission to administer your estate, then your next of kin will be entitled to do so. The probate judge decides who among your next of kin will be appointed. If you have no spouse or next of kin who survives you, or if none of them asks the court for an appointment to serve on behalf of your estate, then your largest creditor (often the funeral home) has the right to handle the administration of your estate. After the court chooses the proper person to take on this responsibility, there are certain potentially expensive and definitely tedious duties to be fulfilled by your administrator before he or she can be excused from any further responsibility. Chapter 17 provides a more detailed explanation of the responsibilities of someone who handles an estate (whether there was a will or not), but certain of these responsibilities are nearly always required when a person dies without a will.

Requirements of Bond, Inventory, and Accounting

When you die intestate, Tennessee law requires that the person who is appointed by the probate court to handle your affairs must post a bond which is set by the court in an amount at least equal to the value of the assets in your name alone at the time of your death (but no greater than double their estimated value). The bonding requirement satisfies the court's concern about what would happen to the heirs if your administrator wastes or absconds with your money and other property without properly fulfilling his or her duties, because if this happens the bonding company will be called upon to make sure that none of the heirs of your estate will suffer financially from your administrator's lack of honesty.

Within 60 days after your administrator is appointed, he or she must file a sworn affidavit which details all of the assets you owned in your name alone at the time of your death, including a description of each property and its value. Therefore, within a short time after your death, anyone who cares to take a look at your probate file will have a good idea of the size of your estate and the nature of your assets at the time of your death.

Then, over time, as the administrator handles your affairs, he is required by law to file detailed periodic accountings with the court, reporting the funds received and the expenditures incurred in handling the estate. The preparation of these accountings can be time-consuming and costly, because most persons who are appointed as administrators have never been required to compile such a report in the past and so they have difficulty in maintaining the necessary records, and they must often hire an attorney or an accountant to assist them.

If all of the beneficiaries of your estate are adults and if they all agree, the requirements of posting a bond and filing an inventory and periodic accountings can be eliminated. All of the persons who are entitled to inherit from your estate must sign a document excusing the administrator of the estate from these obligations, and the probate judge, in his or her discretion, may then eliminate any one or all of these normal requirements. However, if any part of your estate will be distributed to a minor child, then in most cases these requirements cannot be avoided.

Who Will Raise Your Children?

As you can see, the courts are quite protective of children, especially when their parents have died while the children are still very young. One of the most difficult estate planning decisions for parents to make is the naming of a guardian to raise their children. However, it is usually much better for the parents to choose the proper person to fulfill this very important duty than it is for a Tennessee probate court judge to try to determine what is "in the children's best interests." If the parents never get around to making a will, and if they die before their children have reached age 18, the judge will be forced to decide who should be responsible for the truly tough decisions about braces and dates and car keys and so on. Often family members on the mother's side find themselves engaged in a bitter legal battle with family members on the father's side (and *vice versa*), and the children usually suffer the most when the war is finally ended. This is one of the most obvious situations in which dying without a will is fraught with negative consequences for everyone.

Assets That Are Not Affected
When You Die Without a Will

You must keep in mind that it may make no difference to anyone if you die without a will. If all of your property is owned jointly with your spouse (with the "right of survivorship" which will be explained in Chapter Seven), then all of your property will belong to your spouse automatically the moment after your death, regardless of whether you died with a will or without one.

There are other categories of assets that are not affected when you die without a will: for example, if you own a life insurance policy and you have named a beneficiary to receive the proceeds upon your death, the person you have named will be able to make a claim directly to the insurance company after you die and it will not matter whether you left a will or not. Similarly, if you have a pension plan or an IRA or Keogh account, the balance remaining upon your death will be paid directly to your named beneficiary, and his or her entitlement to the pension, IRA, Keogh, or other plan proceeds will not depend upon whether you leave a will. Of course, if your named beneficiary dies before you do and you have not named a "contingent" or "secondary" beneficiary, in many cases the money must be paid to your "estate," and this means that it will indeed make a difference whether you die with or without a will.

Another example of property that is not affected when you die without a will is found in the living trust. As you may recall from our discussion in Chapter Five, any assets that you have placed in a living trust before your death will be distributed exactly as you have directed in the provisions of the trust, and it will not be necessary to consider whether you had a will when you died. However, if an attorney prepares a living trust for you, do not be surprised if he or she also prepares a will as a "companion" to the revocable trust. Too often when people create such a trust, they forget to add *all* of their assets to the trust. If you do not put everything you own into your living trust before your death, then your heirs will have to find a way to get the property you held in your name alone into the trust to be distributed as you wanted. Attorneys use what is termed a "pour-over" will to take care of this potential problem.

Summary

If for whatever reason you choose to die without a will, you can expect that your heirs will spend more money on legal and probate matters than they would like (and more than would otherwise be necessary). When you fail to take the opportunity the law affords you to make a will, you permit the state of Tennessee to determine who should receive your assets after you are gone, and our state's plan for the distribution of your property may bear very little or no resemblance to your true preferences. A judge who knows little or nothing about your family history, your personal values and standards, or your goals for your children will attempt to determine the best person to raise the children, perhaps for many years. That same judge will appoint someone to manage your property and handle your estate, and an attorney will almost surely be required to help that someone fulfill all of his or her many obligations. Although not all of your assets may be affected by the existence of a will, you can never be absolutely certain that there will be no requirement for you to have one, and the chances are very good that your heirs and the probate court judge will thank you sincerely if you do.

In this chapter, you will learn:

- what "joint tenancy/right of survivor ship" means
- how it is different from "tenancy in common"
- what "tenancy by the entirety" means
- which states are community property states
- how gift taxes are affected when a joint tenancy is created
- what happens when joint accounts are terminated
- what to do upon the death of a co-tenant
- what property should be held jointly
- whether or not the marital home should be jointly owned
- how death taxes are apportioned
- how joint safe-deposit boxes are handled after death
- how you can have too much joint property

7

JOINT PROPERTY

Joint property simply means that more than one person owns the same property at the same time. Any type of property can be owned jointly: real property (real estate), tangible personal property (such as cars, paintings, and jewelry) or intangible personal property (such as stocks and bonds).

Joint ownership comes in two general varieties. One is the type that automatically passes to the surviving persons in the event of the death of one of the people whose names appeared as co-owners of the joint property. This is called "joint tenancy with right of survivorship." In the other type of joint ownership, when one of the owners dies, the property does not pass to the surviving joint owners. This is called tenancy in common. The deceased owner's share of the joint property passes to the beneficiary named in his or her will or trust or, if none, under the intestacy (no will) laws of Tennessee.

Joint ownership of property is used by estate planners because it offers many advantages although, as we will discuss later, it can create problems and certainly is not a substitute for a will.

Joint Tenancy with Right of Survivorship

A joint tenancy with right of survivorship means that property is owned by two or more persons and that when one person dies, his or her interest will pass to the remaining person or persons who are the co-owner(s). (For simplicity's sake, we will assume that only two people hold the joint property.) If one person dies, the property passes to the surviving co-owner (or co-tenant, as the attorney frequently calls joint owners). The property passes free of any probate and need not have been in any type of trust. Passing free of any probate offers advantages.

When creating a joint tenancy, it is always desirable and many times necessary to provide in the documents setting up the ownership that the joint tenancy is with right of survivorship. Failure to include the words "*with right of survivorship*" or similar words may mean the property will become a tenancy in common.

Tenancy in Common

A tenancy in common differs from a joint tenancy with right of survivorship in that the interest of a deceased owner in a tenancy in common *does not pass* to the co-owners. The interest of the co-tenant or co-owner in property held as a tenancy in common passes to whomever the deceased co-owner has directed in his or her will. What this means is that property held in the tenancy in common usually passes through probate and will wind up in the hands of the heirs or beneficiaries of the deceased.

Tenancies in common are frequently used when people purchase property for a business purpose, combining their capital and time or talents. The owner does not wish his or her interest go to the other owners on death, but rather to the heirs such as the spouse, children, or other family members. Tenancy in common, therefore, is more frequently seen in business ventures. Sometimes it is used for estate-planning purposes when the intent is to pass the ownership in a specialized fashion and not to the co-owners.

Tenancy by the Entirety

A type of joint property with right of survivorship is called a tenancy by the entirety. "Entirety" comes from the concept in early English law that a husband and a wife were one. The two married people made up one entire person, "an entirety"; therefore, a tenancy by the entirety can never be between persons who are not married to each other. There will always be one man and one woman, and never more than two people, in a tenancy by the entirety. Tennessee automatically provides for survivorship with a tenancy by the entirety. If you own property in a tenancy by the entirety, your spouse will always receive this property if he or she survives. Under Tennessee law, a tenancy by the entirety *automatically* arises when a husband and wife take title to real estate as husband and wife. Therefore, if the deed to your home says "to John Jones and wife, Mary Jones," this automatically, under Tennessee law, creates a tenancy by the entirety because the parties have been identified as being husband and wife on the deed. The real estate will pass to the surviving spouse on the death of one of them.

This is also the case in tangible personal property such as paintings, automobiles, and other possessions. With tenancy-by-the-entirety property, there is no probate and very little red tape. Types of property such as homes, which are essential to the operating of the family unit, are usually joint tenancy with right of survivorship or are a tenancy by the entirety.

There is no difference between tenancy by the entirety and joint tenancy with right of survivorship when it comes to the question of who will receive the property if one of the spouses dies. The answer will always be the same: the surviving spouse will receive the property. If your deed to the home provides tenancy with right of survivorship instead of husband and wife, or husband and wife as a tenancy by the entirety, do not fear; this still means that the property will pass to the surviving spouse if either of you dies.

Community Property

Community property is a concept which comes to us not from the law of England, where most of our legal heritage arose, but from what is known as civil law. Civil law developed out of the Roman laws, was incorporated into the laws of France and Spain, and came to the United States along with persons from those countries. In the United States, there is one state founded by French émigrés, Louisiana, and there are seven states with a strong Spanish heritage: Arizona, California, Idaho, Nevada, New Mexico, Texas, and Washington. These eight states are community property states. The state of Wisconsin has also recently become a community property state.

Community property is property acquired during marriage through means other than gift or inheritance. The concept is confusing to many people because of the power of community property law to change the ownership of property even though the title to the property reads in a different way. For example, in California, community property in the form of stocks and bonds may be in the name of just the husband or just the wife. Nevertheless, even though the title may be in just one spouse's name, because it is community property, the other spouse automatically has a one-half interest in the property.

Suppose the couple moves from California to Tennessee. The title doesn't change. The property is still in the name of the husband only. But the owner of the property is still the husband *and* wife. Under the community property, the ownership does not change when the couple crosses the Tennessee state line. It remains community property no matter where they move. If you have been a resident of the Spanish-heritage states named above, Louisiana, or Wisconsin, and were married at the time that you lived in these states, you may well have community property, even though you now live in Tennessee.

What is Community Property?

Earnings, while living in a community property state, are community property. Property purchased with community property earnings is community property. For instance, if community property earnings from California are used to purchase a lot in Tennessee, the real estate investment may be titled in one person's name, but it in fact is community property owned equally by the two persons. As a rule of thumb, and only that, property acquired before marriage or before living in a community property state is usually not considered to be community property. The same holds for property acquired during marriage by gift or inheritance. Property in the form of compensation for a personal injury is generally considered to be the property of the individual who was injured, and in most instances it is not community property.

People coming to Tennessee from Puerto Rico or the Hispanic countries should note that their ownership may be community property. Puerto Rico, with its Spanish heritage, shares the community property concept with the western states.

Ending Community Property

Tennessee provides that people may sever, divide up, or "erase" the community property aspects when they come to Tennessee. Each person can sign a document stipulating that whatever community property they had is now divided in whatever fashion they agree upon. A lawyer doing the estate plan in Tennessee can look at the title to the property and know for certain who the owner is. If it were still community property, one person's name might be on the title, but the ownership might be equally divided between the two persons, causing confusion and perhaps undesirable results in the estate plan.

Gifting Joint Property

We have talked about general types of property co-ownership: joint property with right of survivorship, tenancies in common, and tenancies by the entirety, as well as the peculiar species of co-ownership known as community property. With these basic building blocks in place, let's take a look at some of the state and federal gift tax aspects and, later, the estate and inheritance tax aspects of joint ownership property. We'll discuss the advantages, disadvantages, some pitfalls, and some of the unusual benefits that can arise through the proper use of joint property.

Gift Taxes When a Joint Tenancy Is Created

When a joint tenancy is created between a husband and wife, there is no federal or state gift tax. A husband and wife can make gifts to each other free of such gift taxes. When a joint tenancy with right of survivorship (more easily referred to as a joint tenancy) is created between people not married to each other, the question of whether there is a gift depends upon the contribution of each of the parties. If each of the parties contributes equal amounts, neither has more than the other and there is no gift. When one person contributes more than the other, a gift is created and gift tax liability arises. However, there are exceptions in the case of United States savings bonds, joint brokerage accounts and joint bank accounts. Here, the gift is considered made not when the joint tenancy is *created*, but when assets in excess of what one person contributed are taken out. Thus, if two people have a joint bank account — say a mother and a son — and the mother puts in all the money, there is no gift until the son takes money out. But this is an exception to the general rule that, in a joint tenancy, a gift will arise when one puts in more than the other.

In the case of joint property, income tax rules are similar to the gift tax in that each joint tenant must report his or her share of the income on his or her own separate tax return. Again, however, note the exception when it comes to a joint bank account. In this case, all the income from the account is reported to the Social Security number of the sole contributor to the bank account, and this person reports all the income on his or her income tax return. This is true even though another person's name may be on the account as a joint tenant. Remember, there is no gift on a joint bank account until one of the people takes out more than he or she contributed. The situation is similar with joint brokerage accounts and United States bonds.

In joint property (other than United States savings bonds, joint accounts, and certain types of brokerage accounts), the income is considered to be owned equally by all persons on the account. Income tax savings through the use of joint tenancies are usually nominal. After all, most husbands and wives file joint tax returns. Other co-owners are likely to be in the same income tax bracket. In the case of children, because of the "kiddie tax," it is not possible to effect significant income tax savings if the child is under age 14.

The kiddie tax is a relatively new provision in the income tax law which says that children under the age of 14 who have income (such as interest on bank accounts) must pay income tax at the parent's income tax bracket. The parents and the young child must pay at the same income tax rate so there is no tax savings.

Termination of Joint Accounts

Joint bank accounts with right of survivorship and tenancies in common can be terminated at will. All that is necessary for one of the parties to terminate the account is to take the money out. It can be done unilaterally without the consent of the other or others.

This is not the case, however, in a tenancy by the entirety. A tenancy by the entirety can be terminated only by mutual consent of the husband and wife. It would be terminated by a divorce decree. Just as there was no state or federal gift tax when the joint account was created between the husband and wife, so there are no gift taxes due when the joint account between husband and wife or the tenancy by the entirety is terminated.

But what if there were a joint tenancy with right of survivorship, and the two people were not married to each other? The question becomes a bit more complex. If the property is jointly owned between persons not married to each other and it is not in the exception category that includes United States bonds, brokerage accounts, or joint bank accounts, the question deserves some thought before a clear answer can be given. For example, suppose a grandmother and a grandson created a tenancy in common with right of survivorship in a parcel of land (the state of Tennessee has "abolished" joint tenancies with right of survivorship *in the ownership of land*, and the term "tenancy in common with right of survivorship" is generally used as a substitute). The grandmother was 80; the grandson 25. A gift arose when the co-ownership was created. The gift was made by the grandmother, who furnished all the funds for the property to her grandson. The grandmother owned half and the grandson owned half in the co-ownership of the real estate. What was the value of the gift from the grandmother to the grandson? It would probably be treated as half the value of the property, since the grandson owned half and the grandmother owned half, and she furnished all of the consideration. Therefore, she would be making a gift to her grandson of one-half of the value of the property. The grandmother would only have to pay gift taxes on half of the property — the half she gifted to her grandson.

When the property is sold and the proceeds divided, if the grandson receives one-half and the grandmother keeps one-half, there would be no gift taxes due. The taxes would already have arisen when the grandmother gave a half interest by putting her grandson's name on the deed. The likelihood of the grandson surviving his 80-year-old grandmother is considerable. This fact offers an interesting opportunity to make a gift and pay less gift tax than you would expect.

Income Tax on Termination of a Joint Tenancy

Just as the income followed the ownership of the joint tenancy, so the income tax consequences on termination follow the joint tenancy. If one co-owner in a bank account has been reporting all the income, he or she will be subject to any income tax consequence on termination.

On the other hand, if the ownership is of improved real estate, the question becomes more complicated. If the joint tenancy is being terminated because the property is being sold, then the gain or loss will be reported to the person based on his or her fractional interest in the property. This will be adjusted for depreciation and other adjustments that naturally occur when improved real property held for investment purposes is sold. If the property was inherited, the basis will be the date-of-death value plus any cash contributions for improvements made by the co-tenants (co-owners), less depreciation. Let's look at some of the tax consequences on death and see how joint tenancies are treated for estate and inheritance tax purposes. The results in some instances can be surprising.

Death of a Co-Tenant

If a co-tenant of a joint tenancy dies and the co-tenancy is a tenancy with right of survivorship or tenancy by the entirety, all the property goes to the surviving co-tenant. In the case of a tenancy by the entirety, there is no estate or inheritance tax because of the tax-free right to transfer property on death between a husband and wife (unless the spouse is not a U.S. citizen). If the parties are not married to each other, then the deceased co-tenant will be considered, for federal estate tax and Tennessee inheritance tax purposes, to have transferred the value of his or her interest to the surviving tenant. This value will be the value of the party's interest at the moment of death.

What About a Joint Bank Account?

If the co-tenant furnished all the money in a joint bank account, there would be no gift made when the joint tenancy was created because of the exception for such accounts. The deceased, for tax purposes, would be considered the sole owner of the joint bank account. The full amount of the joint bank account would be included in his or her estate for estate and inheritance tax (or "death tax") purposes, and the full value of the joint bank account would be taxed in that estate.

On the other hand, if the assets were owned in the form of property such as real estate, a gift of one-half the value of the property is considered to have been made when the joint property interest was created. If there were two owners, the deceased would be considered to own one-half of the real estate at the time of death. His or her one-half would go to the surviving co-tenant. Estate and inheritance taxes would be due on the one-half interest transferred at death. The obligation to pay these death taxes will be governed by the will of the person who died. Frequently, the will has a provision that, if there are any death taxes due because of property passing as joint property with right of survivorship, these taxes should be paid from the residue of the estate. That is to say, the money passing under the will or trust will pay the tax, and not the joint property. The death taxes are actually being paid by the beneficiaries of the residue of the estate.

If the will is silent as to who pays the death taxes, the rule is that the joint account pays its proportionate share of death taxes. If the joint account represented one-quarter of the total estate, it would pay one-quarter of the total death taxes. Application of this simple rule is complicated by deductions, exempt property, and other qualifications.

Uses of Joint Property

Thus far, we have talked about the types of tenancies, their creation, their termination during lifetime, and their termination on death. Now it is time to think about some of the uses of these tenancies, to develop some general rules, and to compare and contrast joint tenancies with solely owned property.

What Property Should Be Held Jointly?

It is a good idea for married people to have a joint checking account and perhaps a joint savings account. The reason for having checking and savings accounts in both names is to have ready funds available in case one of the spouses dies. It can be a source of comfort for the surviving spouse to know that he or she can continue writing checks or drawing funds and have a ready source of cash.

Also, from a practical standpoint, there are expenses associated with death. It is sometimes necessary to advance funds to buy airplane tickets for children or relatives, pay funeral bills, and perhaps pay medical bills. Having a joint account that the surviving spouse can immediately draw upon can be a real benefit, both psychologically and financially.

The Marital Home

When it comes to the house, opinions differ, but in a stable long-term marital relationship, having the house owned jointly is a good idea, especially if the total value of all of the assets owned by the couple is less than $600,000.

One of the most common reasons for changing the marital home from joint to separate ownership is to gain a savings in death taxes for a couple whose assets exceed $600,000 in total value. All of the proper tax questions, including income, estate, and inheritance tax considerations, should be carefully examined in deciding whether the property should or should not be held jointly. Nevertheless, for combined estates worth less than $600,000, it usually is best to have the house jointly held. It meets many emotional needs. It facilitates the administration of the property. It causes no estate or inheritance tax to arise and the income tax problems, if any, are nominal. Joint spousal owner-ship of the house usually makes things easier for all concerned.

If the parties are not married to each other, the question of what should be held as joint tenancy with right of survivorship can be answered very simply. What do you want to pass to this person if you die? If you want your interest to go to that person, you may create a joint tenancy with right of survivorship; however, you will want to consider whether there will be any Tennessee or IRS gift tax consequences involved before you make your decision. On the other hand, if you want your interest to pass to your beneficiaries under your will, then do not create a joint tenancy with right of survivorship. Instead, hold the property in a tenancy in common. More than one person's estate plan has been frustrated because "someone" decided to have the property held as joint tenants with right of survivorship when what was really intended was a tenancy in common — or because "someone" decided that the property should be held jointly to avoid probate. Do not let other people make the decision for you concerning how the title is to be held. Look at titles to property, real estate, stocks, and bank accounts. If the title is held jointly, ask yourself, "Is this where I want this property to go?"

Death Tax Apportionment

There is another significant question when you are considering whether to have property owned jointly. "Are there any estate or inheritance taxes to be paid?" If the answer is yes, be sure to ask who should pay these death taxes on the joint property. In the case of small joint accounts with right of survivorship — perhaps that of a grandmother with a grandson's name on it, or a parent with a child's name on it — it may be a perfectly good result that there should be no taxes charged to that joint account. What is intended is a ready source of funds. Any taxes that might arise can be paid from the residue of the property under the will.

On the other hand, if there will be estate and inheritance taxes, if the value of the joint account is significant, and if the person whose name appears on the joint account is not the sole beneficiary of your estate plan, there may be a problem. It may not be entirely clear to everyone why one child is to receive a substantial amount of money from the joint account and yet the death taxes on the asset held jointly with just that one child must be paid by all the children from the residue of the estate.

Joseph has three daughters; two of them live outside Tennessee, but one daughter, Margaret, lives nearby. Joseph decides it "would be nice" if Margaret's name were on the joint account. A substantial bank account which Joseph owns is made joint with Margaret. On Joseph's death, Margaret receives the money by right of survivorship per the account contract. However, Joseph's will says that all death taxes shall be paid from the residue of his estate passing under his will. Therefore, all three children must share equally in paying the death taxes since the taxes come out of the residue of Joseph's will that is divided among all three children. Margaret, in effect, will benefit substantially by having the other two daughters pay two-thirds of the death taxes on the money which she receives in the joint account. The other daughters are already miffed by the fact that Margaret is receiving this money that they feel should belong to them equally. When they find out they also have to pay estate and inheritance taxes on this money that Margaret is receiving, they are going to be calling their lawyer.

The clause in the will which says that all death taxes are paid from the residue of the estate may need to be changed. Since the children are the beneficiaries of the residue of the estate, they are paying the tax for this other child. Is this the desired result? The answer probably is to say, in Joseph's will, either: (1) that he intends the joint account to pass to Margaret free of any death taxes, which should be paid instead from the residue of his estate; or (2) that a *pro rata* portion of the death taxes must be charged to the joint account.

Totten Trust

There is a peculiar type of ownership that really isn't joint property. It isn't a trust. In fact, it is hard to legally pigeonhole exactly what it is. The name of this strange type of ownership is a Totten trust. It takes its name "Totten" from the name of the people who first created this type of account and the word "trust" because the word trust appears in the documents creating it. It really is not a trust at all. A Totten trust is a type of account typically found in a bank or savings and loan which identifies a particular individual as the owner of the account; after this individual's name, the words "in trust for" appear.

These Totten trust bank accounts function in an interesting and very useful way. While the person who created the trust is still alive, that person can add funds to the trust or take them out. No questions asked. No restrictions. No problems. Upon the death of the creator of the trust, the person whose name appears after the phrase "in trust for" can take the funds in the Totten trust with no questions asked so long as a death certificate is provided showing that the person who created the trust is deceased. "Payable-on-death account" is another term for a Totten trust, and these types of accounts are favored when a person wants a moderate amount of money to go to a particular individual.

The assets in the trust do not go through probate, although certainly they are still subject to federal estate and Tennessee inheritance tax. No gift taxes arose when the account was created because the person who opened the account could take out the money as long as he or she was alive. Thus there was no completed gift.

Totten trusts are frequently used by grandparents who want to provide "a little bit of money" to go to grandchildren. A grandmother can set up an account in her name and a grandchild's name. If the grandmother needs the money, she can always take it out. On the other hand, if she does not take it out, then upon her death, the money will pass to the grandchild with no strings attached. It is not uncommon to find a number of these accounts, each with a different grandchild's name on it.

Sometimes a child's name will be put on the account, although frequently accounts with the child's name on them are held in a joint tenancy with right of survivorship. Remember, with a joint tenancy with the right of survivorship, the child can take the money out if necessary to help out the parent if the parent is incapacitated and cannot sign. With the Totten trust, no one other than the creator of the account can take the money out until the creator is deceased.

Joint Safe-Deposit Boxes

If a safe-deposit box is jointly held, whether between a husband and wife or other parties, the box is jointly held but the *contents* are not. Ownership of the contents is dependent upon how the contents are titled. All that is jointly held is the box itself. The making of the box joint does not in some magical way transform the contents from solely owned to jointly owned.

Too Much Joint Property

There can be too much joint property. Not infrequently, people say, "Make everything joint; avoid probate. You don't need a will and you don't have to worry about anything." Common sense tell us that nothing can be that simple.

Let us look at a problem that occurs with too much joint property. Jim and Karen have been married to each other for many years. Their financial adviser tells them that they should have wills and do some estate planning. On the other hand, their neighbors, Hugh and Charlotte, say, "That's crazy. You don't need to spend that kind of money. All you need to do is have everything joint." So Jim and Karen make everything joint. They save a lot of money — probably $1,000 or so in estate planning fees.

Jim dies and now Karen owns everything. Karen dies and the children look to see what they have to do in order to pay any estate and inheritance taxes due and divide up the property. They find they owe the federal and state governments a combined total of $235,000 in death taxes! It turns out that after Jim's death, Karen did a simple will giving everything to the children equally. With Jim's IRA that (appropriately) names Karen as his beneficiary, together with Jim's life insurance, their home and the money they accumulated, the $600,000 worth of property he had left her had grown to $1,200,000 by the time Karen died.

All this could have been avoided and the children could have been saved this $235,000 in death taxes, but the trap of joint property has already been sprung. The government is the beneficiary and the children are the losers. This could have been avoided if Jim and Karen had each set up a *bypass trust* type of estate plan. Up to $600,000 of that total property could have gone into a trust known as a "bypass trust," estate and inheritance tax-free. That trust would have been for the surviving spouse. In addition, the surviving spouse could have been the trustee. Under the terms of the bypass trust, all the income would have been paid to the surviving spouse. In fact, principal could have been available to the surviving spouse if necessary for health and maintenance. When the surviving spouse died, the trust property would have "bypassed" taxation in the estate of the surviving spouse, and all the property would have been distributed to the kids — tax free. The inheritance would have passed tax-free at the death of the first spouse *and* at the time of the death of the second spouse. When Karen died, the first $600,000 from Jim would have been sheltered in the bypass trust, together with all the appreciation on the original $600,000 that occurred after Jim's death. Karen's death would not have caused any taxes to arise because her estate would have been under $600,000. Because her estate was under $600,000, it would pass to the children free of tax. We will talk more about this type of trust in Chapter 12.

Jim and Karen did save a little money by making everything joint, but not much, especially when you consider the $235,000 in death taxes. This simple mistake is repeated again and again in the state of Tennessee. You can have too much joint property! This is possible because of the tax law which says that on the death of the surviving spouse, the federal government and the state of Tennessee will tax everything over $600,000. Be sure you use the bypass trust on the death of the first spouse (putting the first $600,000 into the trust) if there is any possibility that on the death of the surviving spouse the estate could ever exceed $600,000. If you add up everything you own and then factor in inflation, it is surprising how often the surviving spouse's estate could exceed $600,000. Because of the high rate of estate and inheritance taxes, be sure you don't walk away from that $600,000 exemption that the first spouse has. The exemption can be used through a trust created in a will (a testamentary trust) or in a trust created during a lifetime (a living trust).

Frequently, there will be other considerations. When Bill and Vivian discussed this with their estate planner, they looked at each other and said, frankly, "We worked for this property. We have been a partnership. The kids can be glad of getting anything. Let them pay the tax. We made the money in the United States and we'll pay the tax gladly." This is a conversation repeated many times, but many times more people say, "What? You mean to tell me by having everything joint that my kids are going to have to pay an extra $235,000 in estate and inheritance taxes? No way."

In this chapter, you will learn:

- about the Revolution of 1976
- the definition of a gift
- who pays the gift tax
- about the annual exclusion
- the equivalent exemption or equivalent deduction
- gift tax deduction
- Tennessee gift taxes
- gifts with a spouse
- making gifts today
- when a gift is a gift, with no strings attached

8

GIFT TAXES IN A NUTSHELL

Most people are aware that there is a federal estate tax; fewer people know that there is a federal gift tax; and almost no one, except tax professionals, understands much about either of them or the way they interact with each other. To complicate matters even more, Tennessee has an inheritance tax, an estate tax, and a gift tax. As with the federal estate tax, almost all Tennesseans are aware of the Tennessee inheritance tax. However, like the federal gift tax, fewer people know that there is a Tennessee gift tax.

The good news is that Tennessee's estate tax doesn't cost you anything, as it consists of the federal credit for state death taxes (meaning that if you don't pay it to the state you must pay it to Uncle Sam; thus it costs you nothing more than you must pay anyway). The bad news is that both Uncle Sam and Tennessee demand not only gift taxes but also death taxes, and both governments have lots of complicated rules and tables for figuring who owes what and when. Even though many similarities exist between the federal estate and gift tax statutes and the Tennessee inheritance and gift tax statutes, there are many important differences. For simplicity, the Tennessee gift taxes will be discussed in a separate section in this chapter.

The Revolution of 1976

In 1976, a revolution occurred in estate planning. The tax reform act adopted that year completely changed the federal taxation of gifts and estates. Previously, each individual, during his or her lifetime, could make gifts totaling not more than $30,000 without being subject to any federal gift tax liability. Additionally, each individual, during each calendar year, could make gifts totaling not more than $3,000 per year to an unlimited number of recipients. The federal estate tax laws permitted only $60,000 of assets to be given away at death free of estate tax. Because the gift tax rate was lower than the estate tax rate, it was more advantageous from a tax standpoint to make lifetime gifts than it was to pass property at death. Since 1976, there is no difference in tax rates. A uniform transfer tax ended the favorable federal tax treatment for gifts. In fact, the federal gift tax and estate tax are ,frequently referred to together as the transfer tax.

What Is a Gift?

Let's look at what is included in the term "gift" in terms of gift tax. Any time a person makes a transfer to another person without receiving full value for the transfer, the Internal Revenue Service considers that a gift has been made. This statement may not be perfectly accurate in some unusual circumstances, but it serves as a good statement of the philosophy governing the question of whether a person has made a gift or not. The obvious examples of gifts of money, stocks, or real estate are easy, but people make much more complex gifts, and sometimes are not even aware that they have made a gift.

Sometimes the opening up of a joint account can be a gift. Usually, however, this is not a gift until someone actually takes the money out of the joint account. While this may be the rule for joint bank accounts, a different rule applies if a person has real estate deeded to himself or herself and another person. Having the other person's name appear on the deed is a gift. Sometimes it is never intended to be a gift. It is intended to be a matter of convenience. The thinking may be, "I want him or her to have this when I pass on." Nevertheless, placing another person's name on a deed with your own is going to be viewed by the Internal Revenue Service as a gift.

Who Pays the Gift Tax?

It is important to note that when a person receives a gift, he or she usually does not have to pay the gift tax. The transfer (gift) tax is charged to the giver of the gift, not the receiver of the gift. The tax is not on the property itself; it is on the right to make a gift. The federal tax rates for transfers by gift and transfers through an estate are exactly the same. With the unified transfer approach to federal estate and gift taxes which we now have, there is no advantage from a tax-rate standpoint in making gifts while a person is alive versus passing property on death. As we will see later, however, there are some very significant economic advantages to transferring property by gift rather than waiting to do it on death.

Let's now look at how gifts are actually taxed. Remember, with the unified transfer approach to taxes, the tax rate for federal gift taxes and estate taxes is the same.

The federal gift tax is computed by determining the total lifetime transfers in excess of $10,000 per year per beneficiary. That total lifetime transfers figure is then multiplied by the tax rate found in the IRS tax tables, which yields a tentative tax. From that tentative tax is deducted the unified credit of $192,800 and the amount of any prior gift taxes paid by the individual. The tax tables are found in Appendix H. Before turning to these, it is important to see how they work. This complicated formula can be broken down into meaningful concepts so taxes can be readily computed. The formula will serve to determine not only the federal gift taxes, but also the federal estate taxes. For the Tennessean concerned about paying federal gift or estate taxes, it is essential to master this formula, however intimidating it may seem at first. Let's walk through the formula, starting with some of the simpler concepts.

The Annual Exclusion

Every person can give away up to $10,000 per year per beneficiary free of federal gift tax. This means that gifts under

$10,000 per year per beneficiary fall into the birthday gift category and are not going to cause a gift tax to arise or even require that a gift tax return be filed. If it's under $10,000 and an outright gift, the federal government considers this too small to be reported. Therefore, none of these annual exclusion gifts of $10,000 per year or less per recipient enter into the formula above. However, for Tennessee gift tax purposes, these rules are not the same. See "The Tennessee Gift Tax" later in this chapter.

Two Considerations on Annual Exclusion Gifts

When contemplating making an annual exclusion gift for either Tennessee or federal gift tax purposes, it is important to remember that the gift must be of a "present interest." Gifts that are not of a present interest do not qualify for the $10,000 annual exclusion for either federal or Tennessee gift tax purposes and must be reported on a gift tax return. Present interest means that the beneficiary must have the present right to the gift. A gift of $10,000 in which the beneficiary gets the income or principal five years from now is not a gift of a present interest. There is another very important consideration. No one, through eagerness to be generous or to avoid estate taxes, should so deplete his or her own estate as to become dependent on someone else. The child should never become the parent. The parent should never become the child. The pleasures of giving and seeing the benefits derived from the gifts are wonderful, but financial dependency arising out of unanticipated expense or financial reverses must always be considered.

Let's look at another big tax savings item:

The $600,000 Equivalent Exemption

Note: As of the date of this book, January 1996, the equivalent exemption is $600,000. Recent tax bills have been introduced which would increase the $600,000 gradually over the next few years to $750,000. Remember, the tax laws change. Check with your attorney, accountant, librarian, or other person to be sure the tax law has not changed.

Congress has determined that every U.S. citizen should have the right to transfer up to $600,000 free of any federal gift or estate tax. This $600,000 is in addition to the annual exclusion of

$10,000 per year per beneficiary per giver. Unlike the annual exclusion, however, which renews itself every year, the $600,000 exemption amount is one that may be used either in whole or in part in any way, but does not renew itself.

It is easy to think in terms of a $600,000 deduction because most taxpayers are used to thinking in terms of deductions before the tax is calculated. Actually, in the case of the $600,000 amount, the term "deduction" is something of a misnomer. Technically speaking, there really is no $600,000 deduction, although the law works as though there were. What really happens is that each U.S. citizen has a tax credit against gift or estate taxes of $192,800. Under the tax tables, it turns out that if a person gives away $600,000, the federal tax on this gift is $192,800. Since that person has a tax credit of $192,800 which goes against the tax due of $192,800, there is no actual tax to be paid, because the tax credit has now exactly been eaten up by the tax. Therefore, a person can give away $600,000, either during his or her lifetime, on death, or any combination of these two, and this will produce no actual federal gift or estate tax. This $600,000 is called the equivalent exemption because it is the equivalent amount that is exempt from taxes due to the tax credit of $192,800. For most of our purposes when we are thinking about estate planning for Tennesseans, we will think and talk about a $600,000 exemption rather than the $192,800 tax credit. It is easier to think about the $600,000 as being an amount which every U.S. citizen is born with and can spend during his or her lifetime through gifts or on death in passing property so that this $600,000 worth of transferred property is not subject to any federal gift or estate tax.

Let's see how this might work out when we apply a simple set of facts to these complex tax laws. Tom is contemplating making gifts to his two children, Courtney and Casey. He wants to treat the two of them equally, but he knows that Courtney wants to go into business and will need some extra capital to get her new business started. Therefore, he decides that he will give each of the children $50,000 for a total of $100,000. He realizes that he is over his annual exclusion amount of $10,000 so there will be some tax implications here. He wonders what tax problems he's going to run into.

Tom has not made any previous taxable gifts, so he starts with his full $600,000 exemption. Because of the annual exclusion, he can deduct $10,000 per year per beneficiary. This means he can deduct the $10,000 annual exclusion gift to Courtney and the $10,000 annual exclusion gift to Casey. He will have made, for tax purposes, a reportable gift of $50,000 less $10,000 annual exclusion gift or $40,000 to Courtney and a similar $40,000 gift to Casey. He has a $600,000 exemption which he can use to offset completely these gifts ($40,000 x 2), so he pays no federal gift tax on his gift of $100,000 to the children. However, he has used up all of his annual exclusion that year of $10,000 each, and the remaining $80,000 has been deducted from his $600,000 lifetime exemption, leaving him with a remaining balance of $520,000. If he makes no other taxable gifts during his lifetime, then on Tom's death, his estate would be taxable after the first $520,000 had been distributed rather than the first $600,000. He used $80,000 of that exemption during his lifetime.

The above calculations for federal gift and estate tax purposes are fairly easy. If you remember that every giver receives an annual exclusion of $10,000 per year per beneficiary, gifts to a spouse are free of tax, and anybody can transfer up to $600,000 free of federal estate or gift tax so long as the combined total of federal estate and gift transfers does not exceed $600,000, then you'll have a good working grasp of how the federal gift and estate tax law works.

Deductions

Other deductions are available besides the equivalent exemption of $600,000 and the annual exclusion of $10,000. We'll cover these in more detail, but essentially these are gifts to charities, certain gifts to pay the medical expenses or tuition of another person, and the largest of all deductions, gifts to a spouse who is a U.S. citizen.

The Marital Deduction

The federal government has begun treating a husband and wife for gift tax purposes generally as a single economic unit. This means that, for gift tax purposes, property may be freely transferred between a husband and wife with no gift tax implications. You may transfer as much as you wish to your spouse. There's no tax and, in fact, there's not even a gift tax return required. You simply transfer assets between the two of you as you each consider to be best. The significance of this is great. In estate planning, the ability to shift assets between a husband and a wife without any gift tax arising provides us with many opportunities for changing the management of the assets and for saving estate taxes. We will look at some of these opportunities on a case-by-case basis later on, but for now, it is important to remember that assets can be freely transferred between a husband and a wife without any gift tax consequences. (However, there is a special rule if the spouse receiving the property is not a U.S. citizen, and an unlimited marital deduction would *not* be available in that event.)

The Charitable Deduction

Most everyone knows that if you make a gift to charity, you can take a deduction for this gift. The deduction shows up on your income tax return for the value of the gift that you made to the charity. When it comes to estate planning, however, there's another important rule: you can make a gift to a charity, have it escape taxation in your estate, and yet you can still retain certain rights in the gifted assets. This becomes very important when we want the charity to get the benefit of our gift in the future, but in the meantime, we want to retain the use of the property or retain the right to receive the income. We'll explore this ability to give an asset to a charity with a retained right and how that works under the gift tax, estate tax, and income tax laws with the complex types of trusts known as Grantor Retained Annuity Trust and Grantor Retained Unitrust (see Chapter 14).

Annual Gifting Programs

As we saw earlier, annual gifts of $10,000 or less may be made to any number of beneficiaries for federal estate and gift tax purposes. Each of them may receive up to $10,000. You may do this each and every year. The annual exclusion gifts can mount up when they are given over a number of years and these gifts are given to a number of beneficiaries.

Let's see how this might work in a gifting program. For example, Dan makes annual gifts of $10,000 to each of his four grandchildren. He has given away $40,000, but since these are annual gifts of $10,000 or less, they don't count for tax purposes. They are like holiday gifts or birthday gifts and do not even need to be reported. Dan also decides to make gifts of $100,000 to each of his two children besides the $10,000 to each of his grandchildren. These $100,000 gifts are over $10,000 and so the two $100,000 gifts must be reported. Dan hasn't made any prior gifts, so he started off with his full $600,000 equivalent exemption, but after making the gifts, he's used up part of his equivalent exemption.

What part has he used up? He started off with a $600,000 exemption and he made gifts to his children of $200,000 so you would think that he has $400,000 left. But wait: $10,000 of that $100,000 that he gave to each of his two children would qualify for the annual exclusion. The part that would go against his equivalent exemption would be the $100,000 to a child less the $10,000 annual exclusion amount, leaving $90,000. Because he did this for two of his children, he has used up a total of $180,000 from his $600,000, so $420,000 remains of his equivalent exemption. Remember, the $10,000 gifts to his grandchildren are annual exclusion gifts and don't count. If Dan did the same thing next year, he would use up another $180,000 of his equivalent exemption and he would have just $240,000 left, but he would in fact have transferred two years of $40,000/year and two years of $200,000 for a total of $480,000.

If Dan died after making all these gifts for two years, his exemption, which had started out at $600,000, would have been reduced to $240,000 because of his gifts eating into the $600,000. Dan's estate will be tax-free only on the first $240,000 because this is the remaining portion of his equivalent exemption. You see here how gift taxes and estate taxes have been integrated.

The Tennessee Gift Tax

Tennessee is one of six states which has a gift tax. The other states are Connecticut, Delaware, Louisiana, New York, and North Carolina. Also, Puerto Rico has a gift tax. The state of

Oregon has a gift tax statute, but it applies only to gifts made before 1987.

Tennessee's gift tax statute was enacted in 1939. From 1939 to 1978 the statute remained essentially unchanged. In 1978 and again in 1983, the gift tax statute went through two substantial modernizations. The purpose of these efforts was to align the Tennessee gift tax with the federal gift tax in several important ways.

From the beginning, the Tennessee gift tax has been applied in much the same way as the federal gift tax statute. For example, Tennessee law is very similar to the federal law as to what constitutes a gift. See "What is a Gift?" earlier in this chapter. Also, in Tennessee, the person making the gift is generally the person who pays the tax even though in some instances, the person receiving the gift may be required to pay the tax. The person receiving the gift can be required to pay the tax when the state is unable to collect the tax from the person who made the gift.

The 1978 and 1983 modernization efforts brought several federal concepts into the Tennessee gift tax statute. For example, Tennessee adopted the annual exclusion for present interest gifts, the unlimited marital deduction, split gifts, and the medical and tuition exclusion. Both the federal and state gift tax returns must be filed no later than April 15th of the year following the year in which gifts are made.

However, even though the federal and Tennessee gift tax statutes have many similarities, it is very important for you to be aware of the differences. The primary difference is that the Tennessee gift tax contains two different tax rate schedules which are applied based upon the relationship of the person receiving the gift to the person making the gift. Also, the amount of the annual exclusion allowable depends upon the relationship of the giver to each person receiving a gift.

Another very important difference is that Tennessee gift and inheritance taxes have not been "unified" as have the federal gift and estate taxes. Under the federal law, taxable gifts made during life will reduce the amount of exemption available for federal estate tax purposes. However, taxable gifts for Tennessee purposes do *not* reduce the Tennessee exemption available for inheritance tax purposes unless the gifts are made within the three-year period immediately preceding the death of the person making the gifts. Also, under the unified system for federal gift and estate taxation, once the annual gifts become taxable, the tax amount is cumulative. In other words, for purposes of determining the gift tax payable each year, taxable gifts made in the current year "stack" on top of prior year taxable gifts. The Tennessee gift taxes are recomputed each year without regard to prior year taxable gifts; thus, there is no cumulative effect in the Tennessee inheritance and gift tax system as there is in the federal estate and gift tax system.

The Gift Tax Classification System

Tennessee has two classes of gifts for purposes of determining the amount of exemptions and exclusions allowable and the amount of tax due each year. The classes are defined in terms of the relationship of the person receiving the gift to the person making the gift.

Class A recipients consist of a spouse, child, lineal ancestor, lineal descendant, brother, sister, stepchild, son-in-law, and daughter-in-law. Also, a person who has been legally adopted is considered to have the same relationship to the person making the gift as a natural lineal ancestor or descendant. Class B recipients consist of any other person, relative, association, or corporation not specifically designated in Class A.

While the Class A/B classifications seem simple on their face, many people make gifts to persons thought to have a Class A relationship when they actually have a Class B relationship. It is important to note here that the Tennessee Department of Revenue strictly enforces the statutory provision that any person, relative, association, or corporation "not specifically designated in Class A" occupies a Class B relationship to the giver.

Many of the Class B relationships are obvious. These consist of aunts, uncles, nieces, nephews, cousins, and friends. Some of those not so obvious are various "in-laws" and persons having a "step" relationship to you. For example, your parents are Class A beneficiaries, but your spouse's parents are Class B beneficiaries to you. Another good example is that your brother is a Class A beneficiary to you but a Class B beneficiary to your spouse. Also, you can make a gift to your stepchild, and it is a Class A gift; however, if you make a gift to your stepchild's son (your step-grandson), it is a Class B gift. To avoid making classification mistakes, simply remember that all "in-law" and "step" relatives are Class B except stepchildren, sons-in-law and daughters-in-law.

Classification errors in making gifts can be very costly. The reason is the Class B annual exclusion is only 30% of the Class A annual exclusion, and the Class B tax rates are greater than the Class A tax rates.

The Gift Tax Exemption/Exclusion

From 1939 through 1978, the Tennessee gift tax had only a "maximum single exemption." The Class A exemption was $10,000, and the Class B exemption was $5,000. There were no annual exclusions similar to federal gift tax law.

Beginning with gifts made after December 31, 1978, Tennessee adopted several provisions of the federal gift tax law, including the adoption of the annual exclusion of $3,000 per year per gift recipient for present interest gifts. At this point, some confusion occurred because the maximum single exemptions of $10,000 for Class A gifts and $5,000 for Class B gifts were retained in the new statute.

The confusion with having both annual exclusions and the maximum single exemption occurred because many persons believed they were entitled to *both* the annual exclusions and the maximum single exemption, but this was not so.

Effective for gifts made after 1981, the federal gift tax annual exclusion was increased from $3,000 to $10,000 per year per gift recipient. In a continuing effort to make the Tennessee statute similar to the federal gift tax statute, the Tennessee Legislature adopted the $10,000 annual exclusion by phasing it in over a three-year period from 1984 to 1986. The major problem, and a major point of confusion, was that the increased annual exclusion applied *only* to Class A gifts. The Class B annual exclusion was *not* increased, and it still remains at $3,000 per year per recipient.

Effective for gifts made after 1985, the $10,000 annual exclusion for each Class A recipient effectively eliminated the prior confusion over the annual exclusion versus the maximum single exemption. However, with the advent of the Class A annual exclusion of $10,000 came more confusion as to the application of the Tennessee gift tax to Class B gifts. Many people are aware of the $10,000 annual exclusion for federal gift tax purposes, and they presume that the same exclusion applies to all gifts for Tennessee gift tax purposes. The problem occurs when $10,000 gifts are made to Class B recipients, and it is thereafter discovered that the Class B annual exclusion is only $3,000 per recipient.

Presently, when planning annual gifts, it is very important to consider the relationship of the gift recipient to the giver. If the relationship is Class A, the annual exclusion for the Tennessee gift tax is $10,000 per recipient. If the gift is to a Class B recipient, the annual exclusion is only $3,000 per recipient. Here, a gift planning tip is also important. If the plan is to make only one Class B gift during the year, the gift can be as much as $5,000, because the maximum single exemption would become applicable. However, it must be remembered that if the total gifts to Class B recipients exceed $5,000 in any year, the $3,000 annual exclusions are applicable and the $5,000 maximum single exemption is not applicable.

From a tax planning viewpoint, you can make a significant mistake by ignoring either the federal or state gift tax exclusions. The exclusions represent one of the biggest breaks still left in the tax systems. However, many people do not understand that these are annual tax breaks. If you do not use them each year, they are lost forever. Utilizing the annual exclusions can substantially reduce a taxable estate over a relatively short period of time. For example, a single person making five $10,000 Class A gifts and one $5,000 Class B gift per year over a ten-year period can reduce his or her estate by $550,000 with no Tennessee or federal gift taxes being paid. If that same person is married, the amount increases to $1,100,000 if the person making the gift doubles the amount of each gift and the spouse elects gift splitting, which is discussed next.

Gift Splitting in Tennessee

With the modernization of the Tennessee gift tax laws came another federal concept known as gift splitting. Here the Tennessee law is identical to the federal law; thus, very little confusion has occurred relative to the application of gift splitting by spouses when one of them makes gifts to others. Every married couple should consider the benefits of gift splitting to take maximum advantage of double exclusions and reduction of the tax rates brought about by filing two tax returns. Briefly, the concept is very useful where one spouse makes gifts from his or her separate property, and the other spouse either makes no gifts, or the gifts are to other recipients. For example, a husband who desires to make gifts of $20,000 to each of three children may do so without any Tennessee gift tax if his wife elects to split the gifts. As both the husband and wife are entitled to a $10,000 annual exclusion for each gift to their children, the gifts do not exceed the annual exclusions, and thus they are not taxable.

In order to split gifts, there must be an election made on the gift tax return when it is filed. This is required even if the result of making the election renders the gift nontaxable, because the tax return must be filed in order to make the election. Once the election is made to split the gifts, all gifts made by both the husband and wife to third parties during that year must be split between the two gift tax returns. Also, gift splitting is only permitted if the spouse who makes the gift is married at the time of the gift and remains married to the same person for the rest of the calendar year. (Although if one of the spouses dies during the year and the other does not remarry before the end of the year, then gifts made before the first spouse died can be split as well.)

Even though there has been very little confusion in the application of gift splitting for Tennessee gift tax purposes, there is one area where caution is recommended. When contemplating the use of gift splitting, it is very important to correctly determine the relationship of both spouses to each person receiving a gift from either spouse.

Failure to ascertain the correct relationship could result in Tennessee gift tax when it is otherwise believed no tax would be due. Generally, the error occurs when the gifts are to Class A members of one spouse's family, but the recipient of the gift is a Class B recipient to the other spouse. For example, a sister is a Class A recipient to one spouse but a Class B (sister-in-law) to the other spouse. Another example is where one spouse makes gifts to children and grandchildren from a previous marriage. The children and grandchildren are all Class A recipients to the person making the gift, and the children are also Class A recipients (stepchildren) to the present spouse. However, the grandchildren are Class B recipients (step-grandchildren) to the present spouse.

Generally, when the purpose of making the gifts is to reduce the estate and inheritance taxes potentially due on an estate, it is preferable to make the gifts even though some Tennessee gift tax will be due, because the savings in estate and inheritance taxes is usually substantially greater than the gift tax paid.

The Marital and Charitable Deductions

The marital deduction for Tennessee gift tax purposes is identical to the federal gift tax marital deduction. See "The Marital Deduction" discussed earlier in this chapter. Basically, all absolute gifts to a spouse are deductible and thus, not taxable.

Also, the charitable deduction for Tennessee gift tax purposes is very similar to the federal gift tax charitable deduction. All direct gifts to charitable, religious, and educational institutions are deductible. Also, gifts to the United States, the state of Tennessee, or to any political subdivision thereof, or to any public institution operated exclusively for public purposes are also deductible.

Computing the Tennessee Gift Tax

The Tennessee gift tax is computed at the rates set out in the tables in Appendix H. Generally, the tax is easy to compute even though some computations can be fairly complicated depending on the number of gifts made and the relationship of the gift recipients to the person making the gift.

The first step is to determine the amount of the "net gifts" for each recipient. "Net gifts" is defined as the total amount of gifts made during each year in excess of the allowable deductions, such as the marital deduction and the charitable deduction, and the exemptions or exclusions. The next step is to apply the tax rates depending on whether the gift is a Class A or a Class B gift. Finally, the Class A tax and the Class B tax are added together to arrive at the total tax.

Let's see how this might work when we apply a simple set of facts to the tax laws. Assume that you are a single person, and you have made a gift of $25,000 to your son and another gift of $20,000 to your nephew. Notice that the gift to your son is a Class A gift, and the gift to your nephew is a Class B gift. First, you would determine the net gifts for each classification. Remember that the Class A annual exclusion is $10,000 per recipient, and the Class B annual exclusion is $3,000 per recipient. However, since you made no other Class B gifts during the year, the Class B maximum single exemption of $5,000 is applicable. Thus, the net Class A gift is determined by subtracting the $10,000 annual exclusion from the amount of the gift of $25,000 which results in a net Class A gift of $15,000. The Class A tax is then computed by multiplying the net gift of $15,000 by the applicable tax rate of 5.5%, which results in a Class A gift tax of $825. Next, the Class B net gift is determined by subtracting the exemption of $5,000 from the value of the gift of $20,000 which results in a net Class B gift of $15,000. The Class B tax is then computed by multiplying the net gift of $15,000 by the applicable Class B tax rate of 6.5%, which results in total Class B tax of $925. Finally, the Class A tax of $825 is added to the Class B tax of $925 for a total tax of $1,750.

Now, let's see how this would work using the same facts as set out above except that you are married and gift splitting is elected. Remember that when gift splitting is elected, the spouse is considered as the giver of one-half of the gifts. Thus, you and your spouse would be deemed to have made a gift of $12,500 each to your son, and the $20,000 gift to your nephew would be considered a $10,000 gift by each of you. The first step would be to determine the net gifts made by each of you. As both of you are entitled to exclude $10,000 per year for each Class A recipient, the Class A net gift for each of you would be determined by subtracting $10,000 from the total gift of $12,500 to the son. The result is a net Class A gift of $2,500 for each of you. Multiplication of the net gift of $2,500 by the tax rate of 5.5% results in a Class A tax of $137.50 for each of you. We then determine the Class B net gift for each of you. Subtraction of the maximum single exemption of $5,000 for each of your gifts of $10,000 to your nephew results in net gifts of $5,000 each. As with the Class A computation, the next step is to multiply the net gift of $5,000 by the applicable Class B tax rate of 6.5%. The result is a Class B tax of $325 for each of you. Finally, the total tax is determined by adding the Class A and Class B taxes together. For you, the total tax is $137.50 plus $325 or $462.50. The amount of gift tax due on your spouse's gift tax return would also be $462.50, and the total Tennessee gift taxes due on both returns would be $925.

Notice the tax savings resulting from gift splitting. The amount of tax is reduced from $1,750 to $925. Obviously, a single person is not able to elect gift splitting; however, the benefits of gift splitting are occasionally overlooked by married persons and the gift tax return is filed without making the gift splitting election.

The Medical and Tuition Exclusion

Both the Tennessee and federal gift tax laws include an exclusion that might be called a loophole, and yet it is a very desirable provision for many. If a gift is made for medical care or tuition and is done correctly, there is no gift tax at all. There is no annual exclusion calculation and there is no $600,000 exemption calculation. A person may make unlimited gifts to benefit another person for tuition or for medical care.

Tuition means tuition costs in the more traditional and restricted sense of fees for education. It does not include food, lodging, books, and similar items. Medical care means medical care in the usual sense and in fact is technically defined in the Internal Revenue Code. To qualify for the provisions that say there are no Tennessee or federal gift taxes for payments for medical care or tuition, the payments *must be made directly to the provider of the services.* It will not work if you give a check to the child for tuition purposes. The checks must be made out to the college or university or directly to the health care provider.

Gifts with A Spouse or Split Gifts

As you saw in the section on Tennessee gift taxes, there is a benefit to having a spouse when it comes to making gifts. The same basic rules also apply to the federal gift taxes. The only difference is the federal gift tax is not concerned with classification of the gift recipients as either Class A or Class B. For federal gift tax purposes, the spouse can join in making gifts and thereby reduce the tax effect by half. For both the Tennessee and federal gift taxes, it is necessary, however, to file a gift tax return to indicate a "split gift." The federal gift tax return is a very short gift tax return and is very simple to prepare. The Tennessee return is also very simple to prepare where the effect of gift splitting is to render both tax returns nontaxable.

Making Gifts Today

It is often better from a federal estate tax and Tennessee inheritance tax planning standpoint to make gifts while you are alive. Although the taxable amount of the gift is charged against the total amount that can be given tax free for federal tax purposes, all future appreciation on the gift, including dividends, interest income, capital gains, and other increases in value will occur outside the giver's estate. These increases will belong now to the recipient. Therefore, the value of the gift given during your lifetime is usually much greater than if the same property is passed on at your death. The same is also true as to the Tennessee inheritance tax, but there is also an added benefit. For Tennessee purposes, the taxable gifts made more than three years prior to the giver's death do not reduce the exemption allowable at death.

A Gift Is a Gift, with No Strings Attached

In order for a gift to really be a gift, it is important to make it with no strings attached. It is extremely easy for the Internal Revenue Service and the state of Tennessee to find a way to argue that the giver of a gift kept a string or condition of some type on a gift. The Internal Revenue Service and the Tennessee Department of Revenue will say that it is not a completed gift if the giver still had the right to control the beneficial enjoyment of this gift in any way, to any degree. Since it is not a completed gift, it is still included in the giver's estate and subject to estate tax and inheritance tax. When this happens, things become even more difficult. The person who received the gift doesn't have to give it back. But the estate still has to pay the taxes on the gifted property which is included in the estate because of the string. The people paying the estate tax and inheritance tax may not be the same ones who received the gift. The estate beneficiaries paying this extra death tax will feel that they are being forced to pay the taxes on something they did not get. They then may not feel as generously inclined as the giver of the gift.

Jim and Trixie were married late in life. Trixie promised Jim that, if he would will a substantial part of his assets to her, she would make sure that his kids got his money when she died. Jim died and left a very large estate to Trixie. Jim's children talked Trixie into setting up an irrevocable trust with the property which she inherited from Jim. Under the terms of the trust, she kept the income for her lifetime. On her death, the assets were to go to Jim's children under the terms of the trust.

Trixie died and problems began to surface. The terms of the trust provided for the assets in the trust to go to Jim's children and so they did. On the other hand, Trixie had kept a string. She had kept the income for life. Therefore, the assets in the trust were included in her estate for death tax purposes. A substantial estate and inheritance tax had to be paid from Trixie's estate. The death taxes came out of the assets passing under Trixie's will. In fact, the taxes were so high they ate up Trixie's own small estate. Jim's children came out pretty well. They got all of Jim's property tax free. Trixie's children got nothing. The taxes took everything she personally owned. This example brings into focus the need for effective post-death estate planning as well as effective planning prior to death.

Filing the Gift Tax Returns

If a federal or Tennessee gift tax return is due, almost all individual taxpayers must file the gift tax returns on April 15. The federal gift tax return should be filed in the same place where the federal income tax return is filed. Generally, for all Tennesseans, this is the Internal Revenue Service Center in Memphis, Tennessee 37501. The Tennessee gift tax return should be filed with the Tennessee Department of Revenue, 500 Deaderick Street, Nashville, Tennessee 37242. Alternatively, the tax return may be filed at any regional office of the Tennessee Department of Revenue.

Remember that, in computing the federal gift tax, all prior taxable gifts are taken into account so that the gift tax is cumulative and the $600,000 equivalent exemption will continue to be reduced. However, the Tennessee gift tax is not computed on a cumulative basis from year to year, and the taxable gifts do not reduce the inheritance tax deduction unless the taxable gifts occur within the last three years of the giver's life.

Summary

Each giver can make gifts of $10,000 per year per beneficiary and there is no federal gift tax so long as the gift is a gift of a present interest. There is also no Tennessee gift tax if the gifts of less than $10,000 are made to Class A recipients. However, gifts of $10,000 to Class B recipients will result in a Class B Tennessee gift tax. Making a gift keeps the property out of the giver's estate for federal purposes so long as the giver doesn't attach any strings to the gift. For Tennessee inheritance tax purposes, a gift is not brought back into the estate so long as the giver doesn't attach any strings to it and it is not a taxable gift made within the last three years of the giver's life. Gifts of annual exclusion amounts, whether Class A or Class B, can be very beneficial in reducing the size of the estate and seeing how well beneficiaries manage the property that they are given. It is important always to keep some money aside for unforeseen expenses such as medical care, or changes in personal finances or the economy.

Calculating the federal gift tax is fairly easy. What's necessary is to determine the amount of the gift and then deduct the annual exclusion amount: $10,000 per recipient if just the giver is making the gift, or $20,000 per recipient if the spouse is agreeing that half of the gift will be considered to be a gift from the spouse. The balance is the equivalent exemption amount that is unused. In most instances, this is $600,000 to start with and is reduced as gifts in excess of the annual exclusion amounts are given. Gifts to a spouse who is a U.S. citizen are always free of tax and can be very useful in estate planning, and outright gifts to charities are similarly free of tax and can be quite beneficial in the estate planning process.

Calculation of the Tennessee gift tax is slightly more difficult because of the classification system within the Tennessee gift tax law. As with the federal gift tax, Tennessee gift tax law provides for an unlimited marital deduction for gifts to a spouse.

When making a major gift, it is important to be aware that the gift should be a complete gift without any strings attached unless it is a special kind of gift to a charity. Otherwise, unforeseen tax results could occur which can cause problems. All in all, the gift tax law is more simple than it appears to be at first and with proper utilization, can produce not only excellent gift tax results, but also excellent death tax results. It can also provide the donor with great pleasure in seeing the beneficiaries enjoy the gifts as well as the satisfaction of helping others.

In this chapter, you will learn about:

- federal estate tax in general
- Tennessee inheritance tax in general
- the taxation of specific types of assets
- alternate valuation
- deductions
- funeral expenses and expenses in administering the estate
- debts of decedent, mortgages, and loans
- bequests to a surviving spouse
- charitable gifts
- tax credits
- credit for prior transfers
- unified transfers
- the Tennessee inheritance tax pattern
- federal gift tax + federal estate tax = federal transfer tax

9

DEATH TAXES IN A NUTSHELL

Federal Estate Tax

The federal estate tax works in a way similar to the federal gift tax. Like the gift tax, the estate tax is levied on the right or privilege of transferring property after death. It is not a tax on the property itself.

For tax purposes, the estate is composed of everything a person owns. Uncle Sam throws a very broad net and that net has very, very small holes. Almost nothing escapes his definition of the taxable estate. Not only does it include property and property interests which the person who died (the "decedent") owned at the time of death, but also property transferred during lifetime by the decedent but in which he or she retained any type of interest or string, however small, by way of receiving income or keeping power to change the enjoyment of the property (remember Trixie from the previous chapter). Incidentally, "tax-free assets" means tax-free for income tax purposes. There's no such thing as tax-free when it comes to estate taxes. It is all taxable. Don't be misled into believing that the phrase "tax-free" means it is free from estate tax as well.

Real Estate

In computing the estate tax, Uncle Sam insists that everything that a decedent owned, or had an ownership interest in, be listed on the estate tax return. Assets such as real estate must be listed, and, in almost all instances, appraisals must be done and must show the fair market value.

Stocks and Bonds

All stocks and bonds of any type, including tax-free bonds, must be shown on the estate tax return. They must be shown at their fair market value. In instances such as closely held corporations, the corporate stock is valued using appropriate formulas. In the case of widely traded securities such as IBM and General Motors, the values that are used will be the average of the high and the low of the stock trades during the day on which the decedent passed away. If the decedent passed away on a holiday or weekend, then the average of the high and low values on the trading day before and the trading day after are used for valuation purposes. Some bonds can be a bit difficult to value. In many instances, for example, municipal bonds are difficult to value and require some specialized services. The values for municipal bonds are not usually printed in the newspaper daily as are nationally traded stocks.

Mortgages, Notes, and Cash

All mortgages, notes, and cash must be listed for tax purposes. Any promissory notes due the decedent must be valued at the fair market value. In instances where the interest rate on the note is high, the note may have a value higher than the outstanding principal. Conversely, if the interest rate is very low, then the promissory note may have a value less than the outstanding principal amount. Promissory notes and mortgages may also be discounted if there is a real possibility that the debtor may not pay off the note.

Insurance

Insurance is subject to estate tax and, in fact, it is one of the most easily taxed items by the federal government for estate tax purposes. Any insurance owned by the decedent must be listed. This means that insurance which the decedent owned on someone else's life must also be included on the decedent's estate tax return. Conversely, insurance which was on the decedent's life, but was owned by someone other than the decedent, is reported for informational purposes but is not usually taxed in the decedent's estate.

Jointly Owned Property

Jointly owned property is included in the decedent's estate for estate tax purposes. While joint property may not pass through probate, it is certainly taxed. If the property was owned jointly between the decedent and the spouse, then only one-half of the value of the jointly held property is included for tax purposes because of the marital share rules. If there is jointly held property with persons other than a spouse, then the jointly held property must be included in the decedent's estate. The full value of the property held jointly by a person other than a spouse must be included in the decedent's estate unless it can be proved that the surviving co-tenant contributed to the jointly owned property. If there was contribution by the surviving co-tenant, then the amount included in the decedent's estate is not 100%, but just that proportion the decedent contributed. Joint property means (1) any joint interest which the decedent had either in real estate or personal property (both tangible, such as an automobile, and intangible, such as bank accounts), or (2) any other type of jointly held property in which the decedent had an ownership interest either as joint tenant with right of survivorship or as a tenant by the entirety.

Miscellaneous Interests Included in the Estate

Since there can be other items which would be included in the decedent's estate, the IRS tax return includes a blanket request that anything owned by the decedent that is not reported elsewhere must be included on the miscellaneous schedule of the estate tax return. This would typically include all items such as tangible personal property or any other interests that the decedent might have had. If an item of tangible personal property (such as a painting or an oriental rug) has a value of $3,000 or more, then the item must be specifically listed and described separately on the return. Any collections which have a combined value of $10,000 or more must be individually listed with appropriate appraisals as well.

Transfers During Decedent's Life

Complete transfers made by a decedent during lifetime generally are not included. However, if the decedent made any kind of transfer and retained any type of interest or string, then the decedent's estate must include this transfer. A common example of this is a person who gives away tax-free municipal bonds but keeps the coupons. This is an incomplete transfer in terms of the estate tax law. It is treated as a transfer with a retained income interest. The *entire* value of those tax-free municipal bonds at the time of death would be included in the giver's estate. Earlier we saw, in the case of Trixie, that she transferred her late husband's property to an irrevocable trust, but retained the right to receive the income during her lifetime; thus the full value of those assets were included in her estate, even though she had an income interest only.

Other types of transfers, such as when a person makes a gift but retains the right to direct how the gift will be used, or makes a gift to a group of people but retains the right to direct which members of that group shall enjoy the gift, are also counted at full value in the giver's estate when he or she dies. Any of these retained rights would be a transfer during a decedent's life which would cause the entire value of the property to be brought back into the estate. It's not just the retained right that is taxed; it's the entire value of the property. Certainly assets put into a typical living trust would be included in the decedent's estate tax return and typically would be included under the section reporting transfers during decedent's life with a retained income interest.

The Three-Year Rule and Gifts in Contemplation of Death

It is very difficult to find an asset not subject to tax. Insurance policies are included. In fact, even life insurance policies that the person who died gave away within three years of death are included in this tax. However, the old rule which said that any other gifts made within three years were deemed to be "in contemplation of death" has gone. With the unified federal gift and estate tax tables, the old 25% advantage of making gifts is gone. Under the old rule, *any* gift made within three years of the death of the giver was generally included in the giver's estate.

Powers of Appointment

Sometimes, for estate planning purposes, a spouse will give by will to the surviving spouse the right to direct where the first spouse's property will go upon the death of the second spouse. A couple might decide that the surviving spouse could choose which of the children would receive the assets. This is known as a limited or special power of appointment and is not taxed in the second spouse's estate for estate tax purposes. However, it *is* properly taxed in the first spouse's estate. If the power is broader than this and the spouse can also use the assets to pay his or her bills, or could will the power of appointment property to just anyone, then this is considered to be a general power of appointment and, as such, all the value of the property would be included in the second spouse's estate for tax purposes.

Annuities

Annuities are included for estate tax purposes. The value of the annuity that's included is the fair market value of the right to receive the distributions that remain after the decedent's death. For example, a brother might purchase an annuity with all the income coming to him during his lifetime; upon his death, his sister is to receive the balance of the annuity payments. If the brother dies, his estate must include the value of this annuity on his death since he was receiving the income and there was a remaining value on the annuity which was equal to the payments which the surviving sister will receive over her lifetime, adjusted to reflect that the payments are spread out over some time in the future and therefore should be reduced to equal a current value.

Alternate Valuation

The estate tax law has an unusual provision in it. There are two or three valuation dates that can be used in determining the total value. The date of death is first used as a valuation date. Six months later (on the so-called "alternate valuation date"), the entire estate may be re-valued and, if there is tax due, the new valuation figures may be selected if, taken as a whole, they are lower than the date-of-death values. A third valuation date, the date when an asset is sold, may also be used. It is not uncommon in estates for stocks and bonds to be sold during the course of administration. If these stocks and bonds are sold within the first six months after death, then the valuation date for these securities may be the value on the day that they were actually sold. Unfortunately, the Internal Revenue Service will not let you choose whether some assets can take the date-of-death value and others can take the date six months later. The return must be consistent and show the same valuation date throughout. In other words, if the date-of-death values are used for some of the assets, then the date of death will be the appropriate date on which to value all assets reported on the return. If the alternate valuation date is used for any of the assets, then that date must be used for all assets except those assets which are sold within the six-month period following the date of death. Any asset that is sold within this six-month period is valued at the sale price.

Deductions

We've seen that Uncle Sam includes everything that a person might own at the time of death, even partial interests. In some instances, just retained rights such as income rights could cause the entire value of the income and the principal to be included in the decedent's estate. What are some of the deductions that can be used for estate tax purposes?

Funeral Expenses and Expenses Incurred in Administering the Estate

Funeral expenses are certainly deductible, as are executor's fees, attorney's fees, accountant's fees and miscellaneous expenses incurred in maintaining the property during the time that the estate is being administered prior to distribution to the beneficiaries.

Debts of the Decedent, Mortgages, and Loans

The decedent's debts such as medical bills, mortgages on property, and other debts can be deducted on the estate tax return.

Bequests to a Surviving Spouse

Just as in the gift tax area, assets passing to a spouse are free of estate tax. Any asset that passed to a surviving spouse outright is deducted from the estate tax return, provided the surviving spouse is a U.S. citizen. If the asset does not pass outright to the surviving spouse, then the property may or may not be deductible depending upon certain technical qualifications which we'll discuss in Chapter 12 concerning Qualified Terminable Interest Property (QTIP) and similar advanced concepts, but for now anything that passes to a surviving spouse is free of estate tax and may be deducted on the estate tax return.

Charitable Gifts

As on your income tax return and the gift tax return, charitable gifts are deductible. However, unlike the income tax rules, there's no limitation on the deductions for charitable gifts on an estate tax return. Anything that passes outright to a charity may be deducted at its full market value at the time of death.

Tax Credits

Tax credits are more valuable than deductions, at least on a dollar-for-dollar basis, because the deduction simply reduces the value of the estate, whereas a tax credit is like actual money you can spend. A deduction of $100,000 might be worth $55,000 of real money in an estate that was in the 55% bracket, but a tax credit of $100,000 is worth $100,000. There are two types of tax credits which are sometimes overlooked in preparing estate tax returns. One is a credit for foreign death tax. Taxes paid to a foreign country may be deductible in accordance with treaties between the United States and that foreign country.

Credit for Prior Transfers

The other tax credit is for property which has been subjected to U.S. estate tax within ten years. The government does not think it's fair that it gets two full bites of the (estate) apple within ten years. Accordingly, if estate tax has been paid on property received within ten years before the date of death, then a tax credit for the estate tax paid previously is allowed on the subsequent estate tax return. This tax credit decreases as the interval between the two estate tax returns approaches ten years. For property that was subjected to estate taxes within the last two years, then the estate tax credit allowed on the subsequent return for taxes paid on the prior return is 100%. This drops to 80% for property that was taxed between two and four years earlier, to 60% for property that was taxed between four and six years earlier, to 40% for property that was taxed six to eight years earlier, and finally to 20% for property that was taxed eight to ten years ago. If the property was taxed ten or more years ago, then no credit at all is allowed.

Unified Transfers

As we saw in the prior chapter concerning federal gift taxes, there's a unified rate concerning federal estate and gift taxes. The tax, known as a transfer tax, is usually the same if you pass property by will or if you transfer it as a gift. The tax is computed after adding up all the property which the decedent had together with any interest that would be taxable in the decedent's estate. When all the property that is included in the decedent's estate is added together, then from this are taken the deductions indicated in this chapter. The net result is the property that is going to be included in the measure of tax. If the decedent has made any gifts in excess of the annual exclusion gifts of $10,000 per year per beneficiary, then these gifts will have been reducing the decedent's $600,000 exemption and these reductions must be taken into account. If there have been no gifts in excess of $10,000 per year per beneficiary, then the decedent would of course have the full $600,000 exemption still available.

The Tennessee Inheritance Tax Pattern

The Tennessee inheritance tax pattern is almost identical to the federal estate tax pattern. There is a $600,000 exemption from the inheritance tax. The assets which are included on the inheritance tax return are virtually the same as on the federal return, and the deductions and the credits are substantially the same. The state return is due at the same time as the federal one: nine months from the date of death. The payment for each is due when the return is filed. The state return is filed with the Tennessee Department of Revenue in Nashville. Tennessee uses the same auditing procedures and practices as the Internal Revenue Service, and the two agencies share information occasionally. If the federal estate tax return is accepted by the Internal Revenue Service, that does not mean that the return will be accepted by the state of Tennessee. However, if the Internal Revenue Service challenges the estate tax return on audit and successfully determines that more tax is due, Tennessee will probably increase its tax accordingly. The major differences between the federal and the state tax patterns stem from the fact that the federal system of gift and estate taxation is unified, but the state's gift and inheritance taxes are separate and independent of each other.

Tennessee's Inheritance Tax

Tennessee's tax on estates is based in part on a provision of the federal law which says that, within certain limitations, amounts paid to a state can be credited against federal estate tax. For instance, federal law says that if the federal estate tax on a million-dollar estate is $153,000, the federal government will give a credit of approximately $38,000 on this liability for taxes paid to a state. Tennessee takes advantage of this and says that the Tennessee tax on an estate of approximately a million dollars will be $38,000. The net result is that the estate owes $153,000 by reason of the decedent's death. The federal estate tax is $153,000. However, if $38,000 of this is paid to the state of Tennessee, then only $115,000 need be paid directly to the federal government. It is an unusual kind of tax that doesn't cost you anything extra.

Many times, people will say, "Tennessee has no estate tax; instead, it has an inheritance tax." Technically, Tennessee does have an estate tax for estates from $600,000 to $1,193,548 and for estates in excess of $5,624,000. However, since the Tennessee estate tax is included in the federal tax, you do not have to pay any extra tax; you simply pay part of the overall tax to the state instead of the federal government. So, since you don't pay any extra, it is as though there is no tax. Unfortunately, for estates in the middle range, from values of $1,193,549 to $5,624,000, there is a Tennessee inheritance tax which is *greater than* the amount of the federal credit for state death taxes, so you do pay extra "inheritance" tax to the state of Tennessee for which there is no federal credit available.

Federal Gift Tax + Federal Estate Tax = Federal Transfer Tax

We have talked about gift taxes, both to the federal government and to the state of Tennessee, and about death taxes, both to the federal government and to the state of Tennessee. The important thing to remember about the *federal* transfer tax is that it's unified. It doesn't matter whether you give property while you are alive or on death. The taxes are going to be the same. The first $600,000 is tax free. Annual gifts of $10,000 per person don't count against this $600,000. The federal estate and gift tax rates are the highest rates you are likely to encounter. The important thing to remember about the *Tennessee* transfer tax system is that gift taxes are separate from and independent of the Tennessee inheritance and estate taxes. For the most part, annual gifts made in Tennessee which are greater than the annual gift tax exclusions do not count against the $600,000 exemption available at death, but instead such annual gifts cause an immediate Tennessee gift tax to be due.

The Tennessee inheritance and federal estate tax returns are both due nine months from the date of death unless extensions are granted. For estates worth more than $600,000, the Tennessee and the federal death tax returns are very lengthy and should be completed only by a person who is experienced. The death tax returns for taxable estates will show a great deal of tax liability because of the high rates of tax and because these high rates are applied to everything, not just income. It is important to employ someone who is thoroughly familiar with these complex returns; there is too much money involved to skimp. Ask your tax preparer how many estate tax returns (Form 706) he or she has prepared in the last three years. This will give you an idea of how familiar he or she is with these complex tax returns. For estates worth less than $600,000, no federal estate tax return is due. Tennessee requires only a simple four-page "short form" inheritance tax return for such estates, and no Tennessee inheritance or estate tax will be due.

In this chapter, you will learn about:

- gifts in excess of $600,000
- magic of compounding
- what to give
- property with high growth potential
- business interests
- high basis property
- the step up in basis
- joint property and the step up in basis
- gifts of life insurance
- gifts in contemplation of death
- disclaimers, or, "thanks but no thanks"
- the common disaster

10

BEYOND THE BASICS

We've looked at federal and state gift taxes in a nutshell and estate and inheritance taxes (or "death taxes") in a nutshell. Now it's time to put some of these concepts into use. How can we apply the state and federal gift tax systems and the death tax laws in such a way as to get the best tax result and the best "people" result? We'll start off with some of the federal gift tax approaches to learn how to make tax-smart gifts.

Gifts in Excess of $600,000

In the chapter on gifts, we talked about annual exclusion gifts of $10,000 per year per beneficiary. We noted that gifts in excess of a total of $600,000 (other than the annual exclusion gifts) were subject to federal gift tax. Is it a good idea for a person who has substantial assets to consider making gifts in excess of $600,000? The answer is yes.

Financially successful and generous people frequently make gifts that exceed $600,000. Now the tax begins to be real. The total amount of gifts made in all preceding years is added up and the total amount of taxes due on the total gifts is calculated. Any prior federal gift taxes paid and the unified credit of $192,800 is deducted from the total tax due. The result is the federal tax due for that particular year.

For example, let's suppose that Paul made a taxable gift of $500,000 last year. He would not have paid a federal gift tax because he would have been using up his tax-free $600,000. (Remember, however, that Paul would have paid a gift tax to the state of Tennessee on his $500,000 taxable gift, and the amount payable to the state would have been *at least* $35,900.) Paul has had a good year this year, and he makes a taxable gift of an additional $250,000. Now his total gifts are $750,000. The tax on $750,000 is $248,300. He still has the unified tax credit of $192,800. This is subtracted from the $248,300, so the tax he has to send the federal government is $55,500. A check is made payable to the Internal Revenue Service and the tax return is filed on or before April 15. If Paul has another good year and, after making annual exclusion gifts, he makes another $250,000 gift, he would have made total gifts of $1,000,000. The total federal gift tax would be $345,800, but from that would be subtracted the $192,800 tax credit and the $55,500 previously paid. The tax due on the additional $250,000 would be $97,500. (And in each of these years, Paul would owe a gift tax to the state of Tennessee based on the size of his taxable gifts as well.)

Magic of Compounding

One estate planning idea that works well is that the value of a gift today is worth far more than a gift of the same dollar amount in the future. A gift today has the opportunity to grow and grow, free of any death tax. Property kept will also grow and grow, but then on death can be subject to tax on the final large amount. The amount can be surprising. A dollar given *each year*, assuming a net annual growth rate of 5% over 15 years, will produce a total of more than $21. That's a staggering increase when you think about it.

A $10,000 gift given *each year* for 15 years will compound and grow to $210,000 in 15 years if an annual sustained yield of 5% after taxes can be obtained. Twenty years of such gifts makes the gifts 33 times more valuable.

If the gifts were not made, the retained money and growth occurs in the giver's estate. Since the gifts were never made, the money will be subject to death taxes. The death taxes may be 55%. Because of this phenomenon, people frequently make annual exclusion gifts and wealthy individuals make gifts of $600,000 or more. This is true even though the gifts in excess of $600,000 may cause a tax to be paid. Thereafter, the gifted property can grow and not be subject to death taxes, so that this $600,000 becomes "leveraged." In 15 years, the one-time gift of $600,000 at 5% net growth is worth more than $1,200,000!

Of course, Tennessee's gift tax reduces this magic of compounding somewhat because the state gift tax must be paid immediately as each of these large gifts is made. However, even considering the effect of Tennessee's gift tax, it is still a very tax-smart move for some individuals to give away significant amounts during their lifetimes.

What to Give

If gift giving is such a great idea, what types of property should you give? Deciding what to give frequently can be as challenging as deciding how much to give. One of the easiest things to give is cash, but it is also one of the most expensive. After all, you probably had to pay income tax on the cash. This may have meant selling something and paying capital gains tax on it. Frequently, a gift of something other than cash, such as income-producing property, is better. More often than not, the person who makes the gift is in a higher income tax bracket than the person who receives it. If this is the case, isn't it better to have the income earned in the future paid by the person in the lower bracket rather than the higher bracket?

Property with High Growth Potential

This is a great choice for making gifts. After all, you get it out of the estate at a low rate because it hasn't reached its maximum growth yet. Not only does it come out of the estate at a lower rate, but the growth occurs outside the taxable estate of the giver. At the time of the death of the giver, it may be worth many, many times the original investment and yet there is no tax on it.

Sometimes, however, property goes the other way. Property that is shrinking in value, or property that is technically known as a wasting asset, is not a good choice for a gift. The property, if gifted, would come out at a high cost and have a relatively low value at the time of death, offering little tax savings. Some assets naturally shrink: gifts of copyright interests, patents and interests such as mineral rights. These should be avoided when contemplating gifts. Keep them and let them be taxed at the low value in an estate.

Closely Held Business Interests

Closely held business interests make interesting gifts. They are interesting because (a) they frequently have a considerable value, (b) they have a considerable potential for appreciation, and (c) they can do some unusually positive things in the donor's estate. Let's look at what happens to the owner of a closely held business who decides he would like to make gifts to a number of beneficiaries. Ken has been the sole owner of a very successful car dealership for many years. He really would like to start phasing out of this hectic business and to have the children take over. He decides that he is going to make gifts to the children each year of portions of his interest in the business. Ken is married and so he will be doing some gift-splitting, or having his wife, Jane, join in the gifts. This means that Ken and Jane will be able to distribute $20,000 worth of interest in the business each year to each of his five children. They will be able to distribute tax free to the children $100,000 a year. He does this over a number of years and gradually his ownership in the car business shrinks. As it does, there will come a time when he will have given away a little more than half of the value of the total outstanding stock in the business. Ken is no longer a majority shareholder. This is an emotional time and must be very carefully considered by him, by the children, and by Ken's estate planners.

Once Ken has made the leap and is a minority interest shareholder, he probably will have some sense of loss, but to make up for this, a very beneficial effect has taken place for tax purposes. When Ken dies, the death tax value of his minority interest will be substantially discounted from its numerical value. For example, let's suppose that at the time of Ken's death, he owns 30% of the stock and that the business has a net fair market value of $2,000,000. This means that the numerical value of his stock would be $600,000. But because Ken had a minority interest in a closely held family type of corporation, a very strong argument can be made that his estate should be entitled to a discount because he was a minority shareholder. It is entirely likely that this discount would be 25%.

Therefore, the 25% discount applied to his interest of $600,000 means that, for tax purposes, his stock is valued at only $450,000. In addition, other discounts may be argued for on the grounds that the asset is illiquid and should be discounted because of the lack of marketability. Thus Ken has been able to shift ownership of the business and a tremendous amount of taxability away from his estate over to his children, and he never had to pay any gift tax on the gifted assets. He also was able to push down the remaining value of his stock so that there was little or no tax on that as well.

High Basis Property

Basis of property means the value which the Internal Revenue Service determined to be the basis or value of the property in computing your federal income taxes. For income tax purposes, we are more familiar with how basis works. If a person buys stock for $10 a share and sells it for $15 a share, there is a capital gain of $5 a share. This capital gain is computed on the difference between the purchase price and the price for which the stock was sold. The "basis" is the value originally paid for the stock. Basis may be either higher or lower than fair market value. If the stock had been purchased for $15 a share and was sold for $10 a share, the basis would still be $15 a share and a capital loss of $5 would have been recognized. For gift tax purposes, however, the government's rules are "heads I win, tails you lose."

If a person makes a gift of an asset, the basis in the hands of a recipient is the same basis that the donor owned: if stock were purchased for $10 and, at the time it was given, it was worth $15, the recipient of the property takes the gift with the old basis of $10, but the government *taxes* the gift to the donor at its fair market value at the time of the gift — $15. Therefore, the government collects more gift tax because of the higher value placed on the gift. It also has the capital gains tax still to be collected at some future date when the recipient sells the stock and has to pay capital gains based on the old basis (the donor's basis) of $10. For death tax purposes, it is a little more even-handed.

For federal estate and state inheritance tax purposes, property is valued at its fair market value as of the time of death or in some instances on an alternate valuation date. The basis of inherited property is its fair market value as of the date of death or alternate valuation date. This means that all prior capital appreciation that had occurred in an asset up until the time of a person's death will not be taxed. If, in the example above, a person had bought stock at $10 a share and at the time of death the stock was worth $15 a share, it is taxed for death tax purposes as having a value of $15. In this case, unlike the gift tax, the beneficiary receives the stock at its fair market value as of the date of death or $15 a share, and receives what is known as a step up in basis.

If the proposed gift is of highly appreciated property, it may be better not to make the gift. The reason lies in the provisions concerning capital gains. If a person dies with an asset, it doesn't matter what was paid for that asset. The estate receives a stepped up basis. Anyone who inherits that property could sell the property shortly after receiving it and recognize no capital gains. The person who died would have recognized capital gain had he or she sold the property between the date of purchase and the date of death, but the only capital gain the beneficiary has to pay is on the gain *after* death.

George had a cost basis in Coca Cola stock of $10 per share. Coca Cola was selling for $60 at the time of his death. If George had sold his stock, he would have recognized $50 worth of capital gain on the Coca Cola sale. On the other hand, since George died owning the Coca Cola stock, when his beneficiaries receive the stock, the beneficiaries receive it at a tax basis of $60 — the value as of the date of death. This means that George's beneficiaries of the Coca Cola stock could sell the stock the next day and recognize no capital gains whatsoever. This rule applies to all assets that are inherited, whether by will or by trust.

Conversely, however, if a person is unfortunate enough to have some property that has gone down in value, the same rule applies — that is, all capital loss disappears as well. This leads us to an estate planning insight that may be expressed as a rule: if a person has a terminal illness, it is better to sell an asset in which he or she has a loss and hold on to any assets that have gains. The losses can be recognized for income tax purposes and the gains will disappear and never be taxed on death.

There are some exceptions to this step up in basis. One of the exceptions is on jointly held property. Property jointly held with a spouse may be considered to be only 50% owned by the deceased so there is only a 50% step up in basis. For property gifted to the deceased within one year before his or her death and then inherited back by the giver, there is no step up in basis at all. When considering the lifetime strategies for making gifts, it is a good idea to give income-producing property to beneficiaries who are in low income tax brackets. It is a good idea to avoid selling assets and recognizing capital gains in order to make gifts. It is especially important not to make gifts if the giver has an extremely low basis in these assets and it is likely that the giver will die in the reasonably near future. Making a gift of this type of asset is making a gift to the Internal Revenue Service.

Gifts of Life Insurance

A gift of life insurance also has a peculiar rule. The Internal Revenue Service loves to tax life insurance — so much so that special rules have been passed by Congress making it easier to tax life insurance. After all, life insurance is inherently associated with death. There normally is a large amount of money involved, and it is cash. These factors combine to make the insurance policy proceeds look especially appealing to the tax collector. One of the special rules passed provides that, if a person owns a life insurance policy and makes a gift of that policy within *three* years before death, the full value of that policy is going to be included in the estate, even though the deceased person does not actually own the insurance anymore. This is an echo of the old three-year "contemplation of death" rule, but now the calendar settles all arguments. Did the person own the life insurance policy? Did he or she make a gift of the policy? Did he or she die within three years? If the answer to these three questions is yes, then the answer to the fourth question — "Is that policy subject to estate tax?" — is always going to be yes.

Using Gifts to Change the Tax Basis

Sometimes a close family member is in very poor health. If that family member has a relatively modest estate and if it appears that, although he or she is in poor health, he or she will live at least a year longer, it may be wise to make a gift to that person. This may sound a bit macabre, yet we have to deal with the reality of taxes and death. Under the income tax law, an inheritance has a new income tax basis unless the inherited property was given *to* the decedent within one year of the decedent's death. A gift of property with a very low basis given to a person with a relatively modest estate can produce a significant tax savings. The person receives the gift and lives more than one year. At the time of death, the property receives a step up in basis. All prior capital gain has disappeared. The gifted property can be willed back to the giver with a brand new tax basis and no capital gains tax to pay.

Alternatively, if it appears that the recipient may not live a year, it is still possible to make a tax-wise gift. It is just not permissible to will the property back to the giver. As long as it does not come back to the giver of the property, the step up in basis still applies. The property could then be willed to the children or other persons to be benefitted. How many people's circumstances may fit this and how many people choose to use this device will be a matter of circumstance and timing and, yes, sensitivity, yet it is included because it is something that many people want to consider.

Disclaimers, or a Way of Saying "Thanks, but No Thanks"

The disclaimer is one of the tools used occasionally in estate planning. It is a way of saying, "Thank you, but no thank you," or "I do not wish to receive this inheritance." Disclaimers are frequently used for tax purposes or for other valid considerations. They are recognized under both federal law and Tennessee law. When properly used, they can provide significant tax savings. The disclaimer must be made within nine months from the date of death. Some formalities must be closely adhered to if the disclaimer is going to work for death tax purposes. Let's look at an example in which a disclaimer might be appropriate.

A Typical Disclaimer Situation

Suppose we have a couple, Darren and Autumn. When Autumn dies, the total assets in her estate are worth $600,000 and they are all willed to Darren. Darren has no particular need for this kind of money. He has an estate of $800,000 himself. Because of his inheriting Autumn's property, Darren's total estate will be $1,400,000 or more. The tax on his death would be at least $320,000. That's a whopping amount of tax that the children will have to pay within nine months of Darren's death.

Is there a way to avoid part of this $320,000 in tax on an estate of $1,400,000? The answer is yes. Darren can say, "Thank you, but no thank you" to the property that would pass to him from his wife, Autumn. The $600,000 could go to a trust that would provide him with all the income. The $600,000 owned by Autumn becomes subject to tax, but the tax on $600,000 is zero because of her equivalent exemption.

When Darren dies, how much does he own? Just his own $800,000. The tax on his $800,000 is $75,000. Since Autumn's estate paid no tax and Darren's estate paid just $75,000, Darren and Autumn's family saved $245,000 in death taxes because of a disclaimer.

Simultaneous Death

People frequently think about simultaneous death. "What happens if we're both killed in a plane crash?" The good news is that in many years of practicing law in the estate planning area, we have seen relatively few true common disasters. Few couples die at the same time. Nevertheless, it is an area where there is considerable confusion.

The state of Tennessee has adopted a law entitled "The Uniform Simultaneous Death Act." In essence, what this law says is, "If two people are killed simultaneously or so close to each other that no one can tell who dies first, the law says that neither of them will inherit from the other."

The next question then becomes, "What about joint property?" Here again, logic prevails. The joint property of the husband and wife is divided down the middle. One-half goes under his will and one-half goes under her will. If they have common beneficiaries, so much the better. If they do not have common beneficiaries, then one-half of her property will go to those beneficiaries under her will and one-half will go to the beneficiaries set up under his will.

That is really all there is to the simultaneous death law. In estate planning, however, we can take advantage of other provisions in the law that are a bit more flexible and sometimes can produce some very good results. Under the federal and Tennessee tax law, we can provide that if a beneficiary of an estate plan does not survive 180 days after (or fewer than 180 days if we wish) the death of the person creating the estate, then the beneficiary shall be presumed to have died before the owner of the estate, and will inherit nothing. Now, in fact, the beneficiary did actually survive for a while, but for the purpose of implementing the decedent's estate plan, we treat the beneficiary as if he or she died before the estate owner did. However, we are limited to just 180 days for tax purposes. It is perfectly legal to say in a will, "If any beneficiary does not survive by more than 180 days, that beneficiary shall be presumed, for the purposes of my will, to have predeceased me and shall take nothing." This becomes very useful in reducing death taxes in some instances. If a husband and wife are involved in a car accident and one of them dies instantly and the other dies of injuries in an accident some two months later, we don't have a true simultaneous death. We may have provided in the documents that the now-deceased second spouse is not to inherit anything because the spouse did not survive by 180 days.

From a practical standpoint, it is not critical to provide documents about simultaneous deaths. The statute almost always is going to produce the correct result, which is to say that neither of the people who died will inherit from the other.

If your attorney has not provided for a simultaneous death or provided a survivorship period such as 180 days in your estate planning documents, do not be concerned. Your attorney probably has considered the effect of your assets, the simultaneous death law, and the likelihood of a simultaneous death and made a decision that it is not necessary to provide for survivorship in your will.

Summary

With a working knowledge of the federal and state gift tax laws and the federal estate and state inheritance tax laws and how they interrelate, we've seen how some tax-wise estate planning can save considerable amounts of money. Not only annual exclusion gifts, but gifts in excess of $600,000 for wealthy persons may produce significant tax savings, especially when looking at the magic of compounding and the future growth that can occur when gifts are made.

Gifting of property that has a high basis is usually a good idea, particularly if there is some additional growth potential in these assets. Gifting of life insurance is an area that has some catches in it. Since the life insurance may well be taxable, we have to be particularly careful about the three-year rule which says that gifts of life insurance are going to be included in the giver's estate even if the giver no longer owns the property, if the gift was made within three years prior to death.

Splitting property between a husband and wife can be useful, particularly if it is desirable to take full advantage of each of their $600,000 exemptions. Having all the property joint may cause no tax to arise upon the death of the first spouse. However, all the joint property will be included on the death of the second spouse. The result is that if the second spouse has an estate of more than $600,000 because of the joint property, there's going to be some tax to pay which otherwise would not have arisen if some careful tax planning had taken place before the joint property tax trap had been sprung.

All in all, the basic concepts of the gift and death tax laws are not excessively complicated. It's the exceptions, and the exceptions to the exceptions, and the strange constructions that make it seem so hard. Armed with these few basic concepts, an estate planner can frequently look at an estate and save considerable taxes for the ultimate beneficiaries.

In this chapter, you will learn about:

- the Uniform Transfers to Minors Act
- income and death taxes
- trusts for younger beneficiaries
- the Section 2503(c) trust
- the Section 2503(c) trust after age 21
- the Section 2503(b) trust
- mandatory income distribution
- the Crummey trust

11

GIFTS TO MINORS

We have talked about what to give, how not to give, how the federal and state gift tax systems work and a number of giving techniques. Let's explore how gifts can be made to minors. If you are the impatient type, you can turn to the back of the book to Appendix I and see a table that summarizes advantages and disadvantages of the various ways of making gifts to minors. It would be better, however, to read on first and turn to the Appendix later. Gifting to young people is an area of some confusion. The problems arising from improper gifts to young people can be both practical and financial. There are many ways to give property to minors. We're going to explore some of the best ways, starting off with the simplest and winding up with some of the more complex trust types of gifts.

Gifts to children and grandchildren can be most satisfying and, from a financial point of view, extremely productive. The gift has a chance to compound and, as we have seen earlier, as it compounds it becomes more and more valuable. The gift is also out of the taxable estate and thus avoids death taxes, and you have the pleasure of seeing the beneficiary enjoy the gift. When it comes to minors, things get a bit more difficult. After all, you can't give a minor more than $10,000 without running into pretty serious snags. Under Tennessee law, the child's parents as natural guardians have the right to handle up to $10,000 of the child's money. Once it gets above $10,000, however, there must be a court-

appointed legal guardianship. Court-appointed legal guardianships can be clumsy and expensive. For this reason, modest gifts
to a child or grandchild who is a minor may be a good idea, but
once the $10,000 threshold has been passed, it is necessary to
look at alternatives.

The Uniform Transfers to Minors Act

Tennessee has adopted an updated version of a uniform law
providing for transfers to minors. This law is called the Uniform
Transfers to Minors Act and became effective on October 1, 1992.
This law provides that a person will hold the gifted asset for the
minor beneficiary as a custodian. This is not as a legal guardian or
as a natural guardian or as a trustee in the strict sense of the
word. A custodian is given certain flexibility and powers that legal
guardians do not have. Under Tennessee law, a transfer may be
made for only one minor and only one person may be custodian.
Gifted assets pass to the minor beneficiary when the minor
reaches the age of 21. The assets are registered in the name of the
individual who serves as custodian under the Tennessee Uniform
Transfers to Minors Act. This arrangement avoids the red tape of
the guardianship. It is frequently used for the transfer of stocks
and bonds. In fact, if you were to look at the back of most stock
transfer certificates, there would be a legend for the transfer
under either the Uniform Transfers to Minors Act or the Uniform
Gifts to Minors Act.

Income and Death Taxes

Income earned in the custodial account is taxed to the child.
Because of the so-called "kiddie tax" (discussed earlier), the tax
rate for children under the age of 14 is the same as their parents'
rate. Once the child turns 14, the tax rate is at the child's rate, but
the income is still taxed to the child. For death tax purposes, the
child is considered to be the owner of the property and, as the
owner, the asset will be included in the child's estate. If the
custodian dies, the property is not included in the custodian's
estate *unless* the custodian was also the giver.

If a person makes a gift under the Tennessee Transfers to
Minors Act and names himself or herself as a custodian for the
property, the Internal Revenue Service will cause the gifted proper-

ty to be included in the custodian's estate. The reason is that the giver still retained rights over the property that permitted the giver to determine beneficial enjoyment of the property; in other words, it was a gift with a string attached. If you intend to make an irrevocable gift and do not wish to have the gift included in your estate, do not name yourself as custodian.

Since the giver (donor) should not be the custodian, sometimes the spouse is named as a custodian so that the giver can argue that the gift should not be included in the giver's estate. This may work if the spouse is not also the parent of the child who is the beneficiary of the gift.

In instances where the parent is the custodian of a minor beneficiary, the IRS has argued that the parent has a legal duty to support the minor, and the property could be included in the custodian's estate. While this argument may or may not prevail, it is frequently desirable to name a trustworthy uncle or aunt of the minor. In this way, the problem of the legal duties of support and the unforeseen inclusion of the child's property in the custodian's estate is avoided.

Remember, there is no time requirement that the gift be made at least three years before death in order to avoid having it included in the giver's estate (with the two exceptions of life insurance and the technical relinquishments of certain rights in trusts).

Trusts for Younger Beneficiaries

Having explored outright gifts which, if in excess of $10,000, may cause a legal guardianship to arise, we now turn to two types of trusts that are often used because of their flexibility. The first takes its name from Internal Revenue Code Section 2503(c).

Section 2503(c) Trust

You will recall that a gift must be one of a present interest to qualify for the $10,000 annual exclusion. There is an exception to this when it comes to younger beneficiaries. The exception is found in Section 2503(c) of the Internal Revenue Code. In the case of beneficiaries under age 21, a gift may qualify for the annual exclusion as a present interest if the property can be used for the benefit of the beneficiary before attaining age 21, and, to the extent that the gift is not consumed, it must be distributed to the beneficiary at age 21. If the beneficiary dies before reaching age 21, the property in the trust must be distributable to the beneficiary's estate. By taking advantage of this portion of the law, a trust can be set up which provides that the income and, if necessary, principal can be used for the minor beneficiary's health, support, maintenance, education, or any other good purpose that you, as the creator of the trust, wish to direct at the time the trust is created.

You can name the trustee and set forth what specific powers the trustee is to have, and also include other important conditions that you feel should be set out in the trust. Each year you can put up to $10,000 in the trust tax free. Other people, should they wish, can add their $10,000 per year to this trust. The income does not have to be used and can accumulate. You know who the trustee is because you're the person who created the trust and named the trustee. Once the trust is set up, it is not necessary to do a trust each year. By the time the minor is 21, a considerable sum of money may have accumulated. In fact, if you were to put aside $10,000 in the year a child is born and each year thereafter, and have that gifted money compound at the rate of 7% after the payment of all taxes, that $10,000 would grow to more than $400,000 upon the child's 21st birthday. Setting aside money for a young child clearly has great benefits. The Section 2503(c) trust provides an easy way to do this if a custodian or guardianship is not to be used.

Section 2503(c) Trust After Age 21

Often, someone will look at the amount of money that is going to pass to the beneficiary at age 21 and say: "That's too much money to give a young person" — and it frequently is. To deal with this problem, we have to be creative. One way to be creative is to provide that the trust will comply with the restrictions imposed by Section 2503(c) and that the trust will become available to the beneficiary at age 21; but to provide further that, if the child does not take the money out during a reasonable period after reaching age 21, say 60 days, the trust then becomes irrevocable. This means the assets in the trust are now protected against possible spendthrift tendencies at a young age, and the money can stay in the trust.

The child must have the right to take out the principal without any restrictions after age 21. But after that, the trust can provide that if the child does not take out the funds, then only the income is used for the child's benefit. The principal stays there and is not distributed to the child until perhaps ages 25, 30, and 35. In fact, it is not even a requirement that the income be distributed after a child turns 21 and the 60-day time period has passed. However, many people would prefer to have the income distributed to the child by this time in order to give the child some experience in receiving and handling money.

If substantial sums of money are to be set aside, the Section 2503(c) trust should be considered. There is flexibility in creating the trust document in that it can be crafted, shaped, and molded according to your wishes. Subject only to the requirements of Section 2503(c), the trust can receive large sums of money, invest them, see them grow, and, upon the child's 21st birthday, acknowledge the child's right to the funds. Typically, the child does not exercise the right to take the funds out because the parent has encouraged him or her not to do so. Thereafter, the trust continues to grow and provide income and, if necessary, principal can be available when a child is getting married, buying a home, or having children.

Section 2503(b) Trust

We saw that the guardianship or custodianship has a disadvantage in that assets must go to the beneficiary at age 21. We also saw that the Section 2503(c) trust has an advantage as the trust can be shaped as you wish and if the funds are not taken out after a child turns 21, the trust can continue. Some beneficiaries, however, might exercise their right to take the principal out. To be certain that this will not happen, a Section 2503(b) trust is set up. The Section 2503(b) trust, or current income trust, is a hybrid type of trust. It provides assurance that the principal will not go to the beneficiary when he or she turns 21. This trust, however, requires the giver to give up certain tax benefits.

Mandatory Income Distribution

The Section 2503(b) trust requires a mandatory distribution of all income received by this trust. The way this trust works is a bit complex. What happens is that the entire property transferred to the trust is considered to be a gift, but then that gift is considered to have two components: the income portion and the principal portion. Since the income must be distributed to the beneficiary, the income portion qualifies as a present interest for the annual exclusion. The other portion (the principal portion) does not qualify for the annual exclusion and is required to be reported on a federal and on a Tennessee gift tax return. The allocation between the principal and income is made based upon IRS tables. These tables change frequently because the "deemed rate of return" depends upon the interest rates charged in the financial world.

The Section 2503(b) trust has the advantage that the principal may not be taken out by the beneficiary at age 21. In fact, the principal may never be distributed to the beneficiary if that is what the trust provides. This trust is the most complex of the types of trust typically used for a gift to minors. Many people who want to make substantial gifts to minors prefer to use the Section 2503(c) trust because of the ease in setting it up, and the hope and expectation that the beneficiary will not exercise the right to take the funds out upon attaining the age of 21. Nevertheless, the Section 2503(b) trust does have an important advantage since the principal does not go to the beneficiary at age 21.

Crummey Trust

One of the most used trusts bears a very unimposing name: the Crummey trust. This trust takes advantage of provisions in the Internal Revenue Code by permitting a person to make annual gifts of $10,000 a year and recognizing the necessity that these gifts will be gifts of a present interest.

How can we couple these ideas together with a trust so as to provide a very useful vehicle in making gifts for the benefit of young people? We can create an irrevocable trust which says that gifts may be distributed to the trustee. Each year the trustee, upon receiving the gift, must notify the beneficiary that the beneficiary has a reasonable period of time, say 30 to 45 days, in which to take the asset out. If the beneficiary chooses not to take the money out, then the gift stays in the trust and the beneficiary cannot later have a change of mind and take the money out.

What has happened is that we have made a gift of a present interest because the beneficiary had the right to take the money out for a reasonable period of time, but simply chose not to. If the money is left in, the trust gift should qualify for the annual exclusion. At the same time, we know that the beneficiary cannot take the money out later because that right has been given up.

Let's see how this works in practice. Joe has two daughters, Beth and Debbie. He wants to set aside some extra money for their benefit, but he does not want them to have the money when they turn 21. He is hopeful that there will be a considerable sum of money in the trust. He has thought about a Section 2503(c) trust, but doesn't want to take the risk that either of the girls might decide to take out the money at age 21. Even if they have only 60 days to think about it, one might decide in that time that she really would like to have a red Corvette.

Accordingly, Joe decides to set up a Crummey trust. He is thinking about an irrevocable trust and wants to name his brother, Ben, as trustee. Ben would be authorized to distribute as much income or principal as he deems fit for the girls' health, support, maintenance, or education.

Recognizing that it is possible that one of the girls might have more needs than the other, he decides to set up two separate trusts, one for Beth and one for Debbie. That way if Ben, as trustee, decides to take out some money for one of the girls, the other girl wouldn't be penalized. Each trust provides that the income will start going to the beneficiary at age 21. Distributions of principal will occur with one-third going to each daughter from her own trust at age 25, one-third at 30 and the balance of the trust at 35.

So far, the trust sounds perfect. However, we have not yet dealt with the question of how to make this an annual gift. Joe provides in the trust agreement that at any time his brother receives some funds to put in the trust, he must advise Debbie or Beth that funds have come into her particular trust. Debbie or Beth would have 45 days to direct Ben to distribute the newly added funds to them rather than to the trust.

Note here that neither Debbie nor Beth has the right to take out the principal — just the newly added funds. Also, there is a reasonably clear understanding that, as the girls reach some age of judgment, if they take any of the money out, there will be no more money coming in. This provides a good incentive for them to waive their right to take the newly added money out of their trust. Each year Joe, joined by his wife, Gay, adds $20,000 to Beth's trust and $20,000 to Debbie's trust. Each year, Ben notifies Beth and Debbie that they have the right to take the $20,000 out. For the first few years, Beth and Debbie are very young and could not realistically exercise their rights. Later, as they grow older, they become aware of this but choose not to exercise their rights, knowing that there would be deep trouble around the house if they decide to take any money out.

Joe and Gay continue to add $20,000 to each girl's trust. After 15 years, they will have contributed $300,000 to each of the girls. This invested money has been growing as well. Even if the money has been compounding at the rate of 5%, it should have earned over $100,000. Brother Ben has not been taking any trustee's fees. This means that each girl now has a trust worth more than $400,000. The only red tape has been that brother Ben had to give notice each year when the money was contributed to the trust that each girl had the right to take out the newly added assets. He had to do so in writing and give them a reasonable period in which to exercise this right. Through some clever estate planning, Joe and Gay avoided having this $400,000 available to either Debbie or Beth when they turned 21, as would have happened in the Section 2503(c) trust. In fact, it is even possible to stretch this a bit. When Joe and Gay were still fairly young, Ben decided to buy some life insurance on Joe and hold that in the trust. He kept some of the money for investment purposes, but recognizing that something could happen to Joe, he decided to have $100,000 worth of term life insurance included. At Joe's young age, the term life insurance cost very little and provided some additional assurances that the money would be there for the girls in case anything happened to Joe.

Summary

We've come a long way in looking at gifts for estate planning purposes. In the previous four chapters, we've covered the annual exclusion of $10,000. We've talked about the equivalent exemption of $600,000. We've looked at some loopholes for college and tuition expenses, we've discussed the unlimited marital deduction of property passing to a surviving spouse, and we've even considered a situation where the surviving spouse receives only the income. We've looked at the significance of compounding when gifts are contemplated for death tax purposes. The magic of compounding permits a gift to be given and compounded outside of your estate so that on death, the death tax on the compounded growth has disappeared. We now know that the step up in basis, which is really a capital gains consideration, is a decision maker many times when gifts are contemplated. On the other hand, making gifts of highly appreciated property is not desirable. Making gifts of property with high future growth potential is one of the best ways to make a gift. Gifts such as life insurance, and gifts with certain strings attached, are likely to be included in the estate, yet gifts of life insurance, if done correctly, can be extremely beneficial. Frequently, gifts of life insurance are coupled with gifts of closely held businesses so that the growth in the value of the life insurance policy or the growth in the value of the business is removed. In some instances, the minority discount can be obtained along with other significant death tax-lowering techniques used by reducing the total holdings of closely held stock. If a person dies owning less than 50% of the stock of a small company, he or she has a minority interest, and therefore, the IRS and the Tennessee Department of Revenue will recognize the market value of the stock as less than its mathematical proportion. A 49% share is worth much less than a 51% share since 51 can outvote 49.

When considering gifts for children and minors, it is important to note that gifts in excess of $10,000 are likely to require a guardianship, which is undesirable. It is better to make the gift to a custodian under the Uniform Transfers to Minors Act and have the property go to the beneficiary at age 21. If a significant sum of money will be involved, don't make the gift under the Uniform Transfers to Minors Act, but rather with a

Section 2503(c) trust. Here the trust can provide that if the money is not taken out by the young person, it stays in the trust and can be distributed in portions over an extended period of time to guard against possible spendthrift tendencies of the beneficiary. Better still is the Crummey trust which provides certain protection against the beneficiary taking out all the money at age 21. The principal is protected and set aside so that it will not be distributed until we say it is to be distributed. Gifting in the estate planning area is beneficial from both a financial standpoint and a standpoint of personal satisfaction. All Tennesseeans with significant assets should contemplate making gifts to achieve these significant benefits.

In this chapter, you will learn about:

- the marital deduction
- restrictions on the marital deduction
- citizenship
- the no-strings transfer
- the QTIP marital deduction
- the limited power of appointment of the QTIP — a second look

12:

MARITAL DEDUCTION

L et's look at how property can be transferred between spouses so that significant tax benefits can be recognized.

The marital deduction is the most important of all death tax deductions. The marital deduction is available for property passing from the decedent to a surviving spouse so long as the surviving spouse is a citizen of the United States. Resident alien and nonresident alien spouses are *not* entitled to the marital deduction in most cases. The marital deduction is a dollar-for-dollar deduction for everything that passes to a surviving spouse outright. In instances where property does not pass to a surviving spouse outright, it is necessary to see if the surviving spouse has been given a sufficient power or interest in the property to permit it to qualify as a deduction in the estate. If the surviving spouse can will the property, including any undistributed income, to anyone he or she wishes on death then this will qualify the property for a marital deduction. There are also other types of transfers to a surviving spouse which will qualify for marital deduction on the death tax returns.

Since assets can be freely moved between a husband and wife without state or federal transfer tax being applied, this becomes one of the most frequently used estate planning tools. If a couple has assets and the assets are not equally balanced, especially if one of the spouses has assets significantly under $600,000 and the marriage is a very stable one, it is a good idea to consider transferring assets from the wealthy spouse to the poorer spouse. In this way, the couple can take advantage of the $600,000 exemption which the poorer spouse has as well. While the actual tax savings vary depending on the total amount of assets and the tax brackets, between $200,000 and $300,000 in estate taxes can be saved by putting more assets in the poorer spouse's name (see Appendix J).

Let's suppose that Ted and Sally are a happily married couple and that the marriage has been of some duration. Ted has all the assets, approximately $1,200,000, in his name. If Sally dies, there will be no way to use the $600,000 exemption in Sally's estate. After all, she did not have any assets in her name. Her $600,000 exemption will be lost. Let's look at the tax effect. When Ted dies, his estate would then have assets of approximately $1,200,000. The tax bite on Ted's estate would be around $235,000. On the other hand, if they had split up their assets so that Ted had half and Sally had half, the tax bite on Sally's death would have been zero, because she would have been able to use her $600,000. The tax bite on Ted's death would have been zero because he would have had a $600,000 exemption. They would have avoided the tax of $235,000 and their children would have received that much more from the estate.

Restrictions on Marital Deduction

In order for assets passing to a surviving spouse to qualify for the marital deduction, the law does impose certain reasonable limitations or restrictions on how these assets can pass. The first of these is that the assets must pass to a spouse. It is necessary that the couple have entered into a valid marriage between the two of them. Persons in a same-sex relationship will not be entitled to the marital deduction. Similarly, persons who may have lived together for an extended period of time, and in fact may have lived together as husband and wife to the world, would not be entitled to the marital deduction if they have not entered into a valid marriage either at law or common law. (The number of common law marriages existing in the state of Tennessee is small because Tennessee does not recognize common law marriage. A common law marriage is created when a man and woman present themselves to the community as husband and wife for an extended period of time in a state that recognizes common law marriages.)

Another limitation which the tax law imposes is a requirement that the surviving spouse be a citizen of the United States. This has become increasingly important as Tennessee has received many visitors from outside the United States, some of whom have decided to make their homes, or at least purchase real estate, here in Tennessee. We have many Canadians and people from other nations who, while owning property in the state of Tennessee, are not entitled to the marital deduction. This recent change in the tax law was enacted in order to prevent assets not being taxed upon the death of the first spouse from being exported to the home country, with the result that the United States government would not be able to tax those assets on the death of the second spouse either.

An exception to this limitation was written into the tax law. This exception provides that a spouse who is not a United States citizen may take action to enable those assets to qualify for the marital deduction. This is done by placing the assets in certain types of trusts which will provide assurance to the United States government that, when the non-United States citizen spouse dies, the assets would be subject to taxation by the United States.

Once we have a valid marriage to a person who is a United States citizen, then the qualification of the marital deduction becomes rather easy. All that is necessary to qualify for the marital deduction is simply to pass it to the surviving spouse. Where we run into trouble occasionally is when people start putting limitations or qualifications on the property passing to the surviving spouse.

The No-Strings Transfer

The no-strings transfer will always qualify for the marital deduction, but once strings are put on it, the likelihood is that the marital deduction is going to be lost. A transfer to a husband or wife with, for example, the proviso that if either he or she were to remarry, the property would go to the couple's children, will cause the property passing to that surviving spouse to not qualify for the marital deduction. Therefore, it is usually not a good idea to place strings on the marital gift. There is, however, one type of string which can be placed on the marital deduction that is frequently used and will not cause the marital deduction in the estate of the first spouse to be jeopardized.

QTIP Marital Deduction

The QTIP marital deduction, more formally known as Qualified Terminable Interest Property, is a recent innovation which responds to the wishes of many couples to provide for their spouse and yet, at the same time, to have assurance that the property, upon the death of the second spouse, will pass to the designated beneficiaries, such as the first spouse's children. We see this type of marital deduction most frequently in second marriages, but many times in first marriages as well. Since it offers a new vista of estate planning opportunities, let us take a look in some detail at this particular type of marital deduction.

The QTIP marital deduction essentially is property which is placed in trust for the benefit of the surviving spouse on the death of the first spouse. This property, for the benefit of the first spouse, is usually held in trust. Under the terms of the trust, provision is made that the surviving spouse will receive all the income from the property in the trust. No qualifications or strings can be attached on the right to get the income. The principal, however, need not be made available to the surviving spouse, unlike the traditional marital deduction where the surviving spouse had the right to receive the income *plus* as much of the principal as he or she wished.

Here, the principal is set aside for the next group of beneficiaries. Frequently, provisions are made that permit the principal to be invaded by the trustee for the surviving spouse's health or support, but this provision is not necessary. What is necessary, however, is that the surviving spouse must have the absolute, unrestricted right to receive the income for life. If this is done and the principal is set aside so that it can never be invaded during the spouse's lifetime for anyone other than the spouse, if at all, then the property will qualify for this form of marital deduction known as the QTIP.

It is easy to see why this is such a popular item. After all, in second marriages, many people want to provide for their spouse. They love them very much, but at the same time, they want to be assured that when they die, their property will go to their children and that their spouse will not give it away to perhaps their next husband or wife, or to their own children.

By utilizing the advantages of a QTIP, a husband and wife can set up a trust in the estate plan. That trust will provide that the spouse will receive all the income for as long as the spouse is alive. Further, as noted above, the principal may or may not be invaded for the benefit of the surviving spouse, depending upon the terms of the agreement itself. This provides assurance to the first spouse that when he or she dies, the other spouse will be provided for. On the other hand, they also know that the property which they have worked so hard for during their lifetime, or which they may have inherited from the other parent of their children, will in fact go to the children of the first marriage or at least will not be unwisely spent by the surviving spouse.

While we have been considering the marital deduction and the QTIP in the context of a second marriage in the preceding paragraphs, the QTIP is often used in estate planning for a marriage of a couple of many years' duration who only have children by that marriage. Sometimes, this is utilized because one of the spouses feels that the other spouse should not be burdened with the responsibility of managing the money. In these instances, occasionally a QTIP trust is set up. Sometimes, both spouses agree that the surviving spouse should not be subjected to the requests of children importuning the surviving spouse, perhaps now in declining health, to give them money out of the marital trust. By pointing to the documents and explaining to the children that all the surviving spouse has is the income interest and does not have the ability to invade the principal, the widow or widower will be able to tell the children clearly that he or she cannot invade the trust and cannot give the money to one or more of the children.

Finally, there is a subject that not many people talk about, but it is one that comes up in the minds of many persons considering estate planning, particularly those with a number of years of experience. What if the surviving spouse becomes burdened with years of living? Old age or infirmity creeps in and the discretion to invade is exercised unwisely. By being able to invade the principal, they make themselves vulnerable to fortune seekers, marriages late in life in which the younger spouse may make demands for money, or simply poor investments as a result of high-pressure salesmen. All these considerations are very valid and very human reasons for creating the QTIP marital deduction. The QTIP provides the surviving spouse with a steady income stream from the assets in the trust, but at the same time provides all parties concerned with assurance that the assets in this trust will pass to the designated beneficiaries. The surviving spouse will not be invading the principal of this trust and will not be willing the principal of this trust to persons other than those designated.

The Limited Power of Appointment of the QTIP—a Second Look

Occasionally, we use a variation of the QTIP. Here, the trust is set up with the income going to the surviving spouse. The principal may be invaded by the trustee only for the benefit of the surviving spouse in limited circumstances. Here, however, the surviving spouse is given what is called a limited power of appointment. This provides that the surviving spouse, in his or her will, can direct to whom the principal in the marital QTIP trust will be distributed when he or she dies. However, this discretion as to who will receive the principal in the marital QTIP trust is limited to a class of beneficiaries. Typically, those beneficiaries are lineal descendants of the first spouse.

Why would you want to make this kind of provision? Sometimes, there is a significant change in the family after the death of the first spouse. If the first spouse's estate plan directs that all the principal in the marital QTIP trust will go equally to the children, then that's exactly what will happen. However, by giving the surviving spouse, who is the income beneficiary of the QTIP trust, the power to redirect the property among the children and grandchildren, we have given this surviving spouse a "second look." By giving the spouse a "second look," we have provided flexibility that may be very desirable if circumstances change. One of the children could develop a significant medical problem, for instance. This child would need more assets than the other children. With a second look, the surviving spouse can then redirect more of that principal to the child in need.

Sometimes, a child may be very successful financially and have little or no desire for additional funds. Here, funds can be directed away from that child. Conversely, a child may demonstrate a total inability to handle funds. Here again, funds should be directed away from that child and over to the other children or to a trustee for the benefit of that spendthrift child. By using the flexibility of the second look and yet, at the same time, having the absolute certainty that the property will not go to any group other than lineal descendants, estate planners can provide a very desirable mix of certainty and flexibility.

The ability to freely transfer property between spouses, either during lifetime or on death, is of great importance. This unlimited right to transfer assets to the spouse is important not only because it provides opportunities for estate planning, but it provides assurance to the surviving spouse when the estate plan is in place that neither he nor she will be deprived because of some provisions in the death tax laws. Because of the unlimited transfer of assets, we no longer have to deal with this problem.

While such was not always the case, for today and probably for at least the foreseeable future, there is the unlimited right to transfer assets tax free to a spouse. After all, while we see the tremendous number of changes that occur each year in the tax law, such a fundamental change would have far-reaching impact, both economically and politically. Few politicians are foolhardy enough to stand up and tell the American public that they are going to vote for a law which will tax your assets when you give them to your husband or wife.

In this chapter, you will learn:

- why the durable power of attorney is important
- whether you need a living will
- whether a trust is right for you
- how to make an estate plan
- whether annuities are right for you
- how to arrange for management of the estate
- what prenuptial and postnuptial agreements contain
- what an elective share is
- whether you need specialized estate planning

13

ESTATE PLANNING FOR THE SINGLE PERSON

Let's face it. Being single can be difficult in many ways. There is the loneliness, the lack of companionship, the lack of someone with whom to share. There is the lack of support system — someone not only with whom to talk and share things, but also someone who is there when needed. Being single is also difficult for estate planning.

The death tax laws provide many benefits such as marital deductions for people who are married, and yet it is true that most people die single. After all, even if almost everyone married and never divorced, 50% of the people would die married and 50% would die single. There are large numbers of people who are not married and, therefore, most people will go through some period in their adult lives when they are single. For many of these people, this period will occur toward the end of their life, when they are thinking about estate planning.

Durable Power of Attorney for Financial Affairs

Some of the first things that a single person should consider are, "How are my affairs going to be managed if I am unable to manage? Who is going to make the decisions? What guidance is to be given in making those decisions? What authority should he or she have?" These are important questions, many of which were discussed in Chapter 3.

Under Tennessee law, a person is permitted to make out a durable power of attorney for financial affairs. The power of attorney is said to be "durable" if it contains language which provides that the document will remain in effect even if the person who gave the power of attorney later becomes disabled or incapacitated. For convenience, the term "financial power of attorney" is used here to refer to such a durable power of attorney for financial affairs. (A typical financial power of attorney is included in Appendix D.) It is extremely broad in what it covers and it should be. The financial power of attorney is intended to provide for guidance and authority in managing a person's affairs if he or she is unable to do so.

The financial power of attorney is particularly helpful for the single person. It gives the single person some assurance as to who is going to manage his or her affairs. It also gives the appointed person a broad authority to manage the single person's affairs. The financial power of attorney should be as broad as possible, since people have many types of assets and many different needs.

The financial power of attorney should always be executed before it is actually needed. By the time it is needed, in many instances, it would be too late. A person who, through illness or misfortune, has lost the ability to manage his or her affairs may also be unable to sign and give the financial power of attorney at that critical time.

Sometimes, the financial power of attorney is used in instances when the person who is giving the power of attorney is just going to be out of touch for a period of time. Perhaps he or she is taking a trip abroad for a month and wants to be sure someone will be available to take care of things. In this instance, of course, "taking care of things" means much more than picking up the mail and looking after the home. It means, perhaps, answering questions and in some instances making financial decisions. So, financial powers of attorney are used in two instances. They cover the situation in which a person has become incapacitated and unable to manage financial affairs, and they also cover the times when, by reason of temporary illness or absence, a person is not able to handle things effectively and wishes somebody to take over for a relatively brief period. This type of financial power of attorney is always completely revocable. If for some reason you feel the holder might exercise the power in ways you wish they would not, you can cancel it.

Living Wills and Health Care Powers of Attorney

Living wills and health care powers of attorney are especially important for single people. Although these subjects were covered in Chapter 4, we'll summarize briefly. Living wills provide instructions to health care providers in the event a person has a terminal illness. Health care powers of attorney appoint someone to make health care decisions if a person is unable to make his or her own medical decisions. Tennessee law is not fixed in this area. It seems to be moving in the direction of giving greater latitude to people who want to provide instructions for their medical care.

The single person does not have a spouse to make health care decisions. A family member, such as a child or brother or sister, certainly can do this, but having the living will and health care power of attorney documents gives that person a great deal of legal and emotional assurance as to what steps should be taken and what instructions are to be given. It is more important for a single person to have a living will and a health care power of attorney than for a married person to have them. The married couple may well have spent some time discussing what they would like to do and what approaches they would like taken, so that each knows the other's wishes through this time of sharing. Such sharing may not have occurred with a sibling or a child, or may not have occurred in a long time.

The financial power of attorney, the health care power of attorney, and the living will form a natural trio of documents that the single person should consider.

Trusts

Trusts are also important to the single person. The trust can be a living (also called *inter vivos*) trust, or set up in a will.

For the single person who is over 65, a living trust may be desirable. Of course, it is not going to be possible to have your assets joint with your spouse if you are single. By transferring your assets into a living trust, you have already designated who is to manage the assets and who will inherit them. You have given the person who is acting as trustee, which may be yourself initially and your successor trustee, broad authority in managing these assets. This authority is more widely recognized by many financial institutions than the financial power of attorney.

Since trusts are more broadly recognized, it follows that a trust will be more effective than a financial power of attorney in dealing with assets if you become incapacitated. The trust is more effective than the financial power of attorney because of its greater recognition and broader authority.

The Single Person's Estate Plan

The financial power of attorney, living will, health care power of attorney and will or living trust are the most important documents for the single person. Once these are in place, we should look at the estate plan itself. One of the most important aspects of the estate plan is that there is no marital deduction. We saw in the preceding chapters that the marital deduction provided for the greatest death tax savings. With the single person, death taxes become much more significant. Since deferral is no longer possible through the marital deduction, we need to look at other tax savings possibilities. The living trust *may* not be needed at all then.

Annuities

Annuities have considerable advantages for single people. One advantage is that they provide a guaranteed income for life. This income is greater than that usually earned by investments such as stocks, bonds, or CDs because the annuity ends on the death of the single person. The single person may not be seeking to leave a large estate and may well appreciate the high income stream that the annuity provides. The income is significantly increased over the income that would be recognized solely from the income on investments without a partial return of capital. The single person also appreciates the security of an annuity issued by a large financial institution with very high ratings. It is essential that the issuer of the annuity be among the most highly rated by the companies that rate financial providers of annuities. After all, when you're alone, there's no one to fall back on. There's no safety net. As a single person, you must be conservative in many of your approaches to financial planning. The best investment might not be the one with the greatest yield, but rather the one with the most certain yield.

Antenuptial and Postnuptial Agreements in Tennessee

One of the things about being single is that you can still get married. For the single person who is a Tennessean, getting married significantly affects estate planning. We will cover the more important aspects of estate planning for the single person who is contemplating marriage in the following paragraphs. If a marriage occurs later in life, particularly when there are children of a prior marriage, the question of an antenuptial or postnuptial agreement frequently comes up, because under Tennessee law, a surviving spouse cannot be entirely disinherited. That is, if you were married a second time and you never signed an antenuptial or postnuptial agreement, and you died leaving all of your property in your estate to your children by your first marriage, Tennessee law provides that your second spouse would have the right, within nine months following your death, to take certain property from your estate, including a forced or "elective" share.

The Elective Share and Other Spousal Rights

Tennessee law provides that the following property interests may be taken by the surviving spouse regardless of what the will says: all of the household furniture and furnishings, the tools, musical instruments, family Bible and wearing apparel of the decedent, together with the "family automobile" (all of these items are known as the "exempt property"); one-third of the assets passing through probate (referred to as the "elective share"); cash from the estate sufficient to support the surviving spouse for one year following the date of death (this right is known as "year's support"); and if the house was not jointly owned, the surviving spouse is entitled to a "homestead" right (which is usually settled with a cash distribution of $5,000 from the estate). The spouse can take all of these rights, against the will of the deceased spouse, simply by filing an election.

Antenuptial Agreements

Antenuptial agreements are agreements on property rights entered into before marriage. Antenuptial agreements are favored under the laws of Tennessee because they set forth what the parties wish to have done with their assets. Each party to the marriage is assured that his or her assets will not be taken if he or she dies first. Assets can be set aside for children or loved ones without the possibility of a forced sharing with a spouse under Tennessee law, and all of the spousal rights enumerated above can be eliminated with an antenuptial agreement.

Many people late in life agree with each other that they will not take all of the rights Tennessee affords a surviving spouse, and they sign an antenuptial agreement. Occasionally, the agreement also says that neither will seek any alimony or support from the other. Each person agrees that he or she will not make any claims against the other's estate. Each, however, is free to provide as much as he or she wishes for the surviving spouse. There certainly is no language in the agreement prohibiting a spouse from leaving his or her estate, or any portion of the estate, to the surviving spouse, but neither is *required* to do so.

It is essential that each of the parties to an antenuptial agreement carefully identifies goals, that each has the opportunity to consult with his or her own personal attorney, and that all assets are carefully spelled out and disclosed to the other person. Because the opportunity for pressure by one person on the other is so great, each one should have an attorney.

Joint property would pass to the surviving spouse and would not be adversely affected by the antenuptial agreement. It is important when considering an antenuptial agreement, however, to read the documents carefully. Not all antenuptial agreements say the same thing. Also, there may be provisions in the antenuptial agreement for the husband or wife in the event there is a dissolution of a marriage. Divorces do occur and people need to know what they can and cannot do and what the courts do in the event that this happens.

Generally speaking, it is desirable to incorporate in the antenuptial agreement a financial statement from each of the persons signing the antenuptial agreement. The attorney also may check to see if the client owns any real estate in a state other than the state of Tennessee. The antenuptial agreement will be applicable to all Tennessee assets. Whether it is applicable to assets such as real estate owned outside the state will depend on where the real estate is located. Some states favor antenuptial agreements; others do not. A typical antenuptial agreement is attached as Appendix K.

Postnuptial Agreements

Postnuptial agreements, like their name implies, are agreements on property rights between spouses entered into after marriage. Postnuptial agreements are reviewed very carefully by the courts. In Tennessee, antenuptial agreements are recognized by a specific law which states clearly that such agreements are enforceable in our state. However, there is no such specific law recognizing postnuptial agreements. The concern here is that, subsequent to marriage, one of the parties may exercise undue influence or apply pressure on the other spouse to cause him or her to give up property rights.

The postnuptial agreement can correct oversights or address questions that have come up because of a change in circumstance. Sometimes people want to get married and do not want to think about the financial aspects of their union. Therefore, they will marry and only later begin to consider such items as property rights. Postnuptial agreements function very much like antenuptial agreements. They set forth the financial understandings between the parties and give husband and wife the assurance that their assets will go to their designated beneficiaries upon the death of one of them.

Estate Planning

Estate planning is challenging for the single person. It is difficult, but there are no insurmountable problems. It just takes a little more time, a little more thought, and a little more effort. There is also the satisfaction of knowing that you are doing things on your own; you are the captain of your own ship. There is a certain amount of pride in knowing that you can do it and that you *are* doing it — whether you are a young person who does not expect to marry, or a person who has been married and is now single. Whatever these difficult times might be, you are learning and beginning to do things. The fact that you are reading this book in itself speaks of who you are and what you have been able to accomplish so far.

As a single person, you have some tools to meet these challenges. First, you have the durable power of attorney with which you can give someone control over your financial affairs. Second, you have the health care power of attorney to provide guidance and legal authority to the person of your choice, giving him or her specific rights and responsibilities in dealing with your health care matters. Physicians, hospitals, nursing homes, and other health care providers will be much more responsive to someone you have named in your health care power of attorney. This is particularly true in the case of a single person. Third, you have the living will which gives instructions concerning your medical care decisions when you are terminally ill and/or if you are in a persistent vegetative state.

Finally, you have trusts — those flexible devices that permit you to designate who is to manage your financial affairs if for some reason you are unable to do so. There are almost no limitations as to who can be a trustee, so the flexibility and field of choices is quite broad.

Give some thought to the management of your property while you are alive and its distribution to your beneficiaries upon death. You will see that estate planning for the single person is, in the final analysis, not really that much different from planning for other persons.

In this chapter, you will learn:

- the importance of knowing your charity
- what is deductible
- what the deduction is
- what substantiation and overvaluation mean
- what to consider in estate planning
- what charitable remainder trusts are
- what a pooled income fund is
- how to give gifts of tangible personal property
- what a charitable residence gift is
- whether to give life insurance
- what a charitable lead trust is

14

CHARITABLE GIVING

As a long and honored tradition in estate planning, charitable giving is well established. Indeed, the gifts of individuals and corporations to charities have made our society a substantially better one than it otherwise would have been.

The role of charitable giving in the estate planning area is recognized in the Internal Revenue Code and by careful practitioners as a useful adjunct to formulating a good overall estate plan. While it is not really possible to "make money by giving it away," there are a number of techniques that can be used advantageously to provide the best possible result in making charitable gifts. It will be the best result both in the sense of maximizing financial return and being most productive in a practical and a charitable sense.

We'll look at some of the ways charitable giving works from an estate planning standpoint regarding income, gift, and death tax. Then we'll move into some of the more complex and interesting possibilities of charitable giving.

Know Your Charity

First, let's look at income tax and charitable contributions. The first rule is to know your charity. Charities come in many varieties, some good and some not so good. Some may not even be recognized as charities by the Internal Revenue Service.

The best way to get to know your charity from an income tax standpoint is ask the charity for a copy of its tax determination letter. Any charity should be able to give you this unless it is the type of organization that is not required to have such a letter. Organizations not required to have a tax letter are churches or temples which, by their nature, are recognized as being charitable and do not ask for or receive tax determination letters from the IRS.

Deductibility

For income tax purposes, the IRS assigns two levels of deductibility for charitable contributions. It imposes a maximum on the amount given to all charities cumulatively. You can give up to 50% of your adjusted gross income to public charities and get a 100% deduction for the contributions. These are called 50% charities. In the case of nonpublic charities — that is, private and semi-public charities — the maximum that can be deducted is 30% of your adjusted gross income. Fifty percent charities are those that we typically recognize as being charities: medical research organizations, governments, schools, hospitals, churches, temples, and universities. All these are recognized by the IRS as tax deductible charities. The semi-public and private charities are more likely to be organizations such as nonprofit cemetery associations, private foundations, veteran's organizations, and fraternal organizations that operate under a lodge system.

If you give to a bona fide charity recognized by the IRS as a charitable organization, how much is your income tax deduction?

What is the Income Tax Deduction?

For income tax purposes, a taxpayer is allowed a 100% deduction for property contributed to a charity (subject to the limitations just noted above). The amount of the deduction is almost always the fair market value of the property at the time of the contribution. Cash is the easiest thing in the world to value.

Gifts of stocks and bonds that are traded on a major exchange have a readily determined value, which is the value the security had when it was transferred to the charity.

Substantiation and Overvaluation

There have been some problems over the years with people inflating the values of gifts to charities. This problem became almost epidemic several years ago. There was a cottage industry of unscrupulous individuals who would sell you assets cheaply with the idea that part of their product would be a highly inflated appraisal. You could attach this appraisal to your tax return substantiating a very generous donation to the charity. The sellers claimed you would actually make more money than the cost of the goods. Obviously, this was a violation both of the spirit and the letter of the law. It resulted in new regulations requiring substantiation of the gifts of tangible property. The substantiation is required for gifts of more than $5,000 fair market value. An appraisal must be attached to the tax return setting forth the appraiser's qualifications and asserting that the appraiser has no relationship with the giver of the property.

The IRS, however, went further and set a substantial penalty for significant overvaluation. A penalty of 30% of the tax that was not paid applies if property is overvalued by 150% of its final fair market value. Thus, if an item were listed as a $7,500 charitable gift and in fact its value was $4,000, the overvaluation would be more than 150% and the penalty would be 30% of the tax saved. This is not the end of the story. The IRS may also charge a penalty for negligence. Thus, the scam of significantly overvaluing gifts to charities was ended for all but the most naïve.

Loss Property

Loss property is property with a basis higher than its current market value. It is not a good idea to give this kind of property to charities. The maximum charitable deduction is the fair market value rather than your higher basis. Because of this, it is wiser to sell the property. Establish the loss for tax purposes; lock in the loss on your personal tax return; and then give the net proceeds to the charity and take a charitable deduction for this. In this way, you get *both* the deduction of the amount given to charity and the tax loss when you sold at a loss. If you just give it to the charity, you lose the benefit of your tax loss.

Gift and Death Tax Planning Aspects

Having looked at the income tax aspects of charitable giving briefly, let's turn to the gift and death tax planning aspects of charitable giving. They are similar to the income tax rules for charitable giving, but there are some significant differences.

Making Outright Charitable Gifts

For both gift and estate tax purposes, any gifts made outright to qualified (that is, IRS-approved tax-exempt) charities are fully deductible. In other words, no matter how much money you give outright to a qualified charity, either during your lifetime or upon your death, a complete gift or estate tax deduction will be allowed without limitation, and no gift or estate tax will be due as a result of your charitable gift. (Similarly, there is no Tennessee gift, estate, or inheritance tax imposed on outright charitable gifts.)

Making a Charitable Gift and Keeping the Income

Making a charitable gift, removing the asset from being taxed in your estate and keeping the income sounds too good to be true. But there are some very real, legitimate tax breaks that can be used through sophisticated estate planning and gifts to charities.

Gifts to charities can be made through what are called charitable remainder trusts. There are two types of these trusts. One is an annuity trust and the other is the unitrust. These two types of trusts will shortly be discussed in detail. In general, however, the way these trusts work is simple in concept, although in day-to-day practice, it can get rather complex. Basically, you set aside some money in an *irrevocable* trust. You provide in the trust that you will receive distributions based on a designated percentage of principal each year. This may be 7%, 8% or whatever seems best for you, subject to a few limitations. The distributions are made first from income the trust earns. Upon your death, whatever is left in the trust then goes to the charity. This way, you receive the designated percentage of the trust, like income, and yet you also have the property out of your estate. As an added benefit, you get a substantial income tax deduction in the year in which the trust is set up.

Annuity Trust

The annuity trust is a type of charitable remainder trust and functions like its name, an annuity. The annuity trust is irrevocable. Funds are put in the trust. The income is measured by the value of the trust times the percentage chosen when the trust is created. If you create a charitable annuity trust with $100,000 in it and specify that you receive 7%, the $7,000 per year would be distributed to you each year until your death. The value of the trust may go up or down, but the distribution is always $7,000 per year.

Income Tax on Funds Received from the Trust

The value of the charitable gift is the value of the trust after deducting the right to receive the income for life. The value is based on government tables. These tables define the values of these types of gifts. The tables are generated by computer programs which integrate a number of variables in complex mathematical formulas. The variables are the rate of interest that the person is asking to be paid, his or her life expectancy and the current rate of interest which the federal government deems a reasonable rate of return for investments having an approximate life expectancy equal to the person's life expectancy.

When the $7,000 in our example is distributed to the beneficiary, it is first considered to be taxable income to the extent that the trust has income and capital gains. Finally, it is considered a return of principal or tax exempt income if the trust has either tax-exempt income, or has no capital gains or ordinary income. People frequently want to set up a charitable remainder trust that will earn tax-exempt income in the future. This way, the person not only gets an income tax deduction when the trust is set up for the charitable contribution, but also gets the money tax free which is received in the form of the annuity amount, such as the $7,000.

It is not a good idea to specify in the trust that the trustee shall invest only in tax exempts. This violates IRS regulations. However, there is nothing which says the trustee cannot decide to invest in tax exempts. It might be that the trustee considers the choice of tax-exempt investments is a wise and prudent use of the money you have contributed. The important thing is that nothing in the trust can be construed to prohibit or to require the trustee to invest in tax exempts. For death tax purposes, if a trust ends on your death and distributes to charity, there is no estate or inheritance tax on this property.

Unitrust

The companion trust to the annuity trust is the unitrust. It is like the annuity trust, with two differences. The unitrust is interesting because the value of the percentage of return, such as 7% in our example above, is calculated not just at the time the trust is created, but each year as well. This means that, unlike the annuity trust, if the value of the trust goes up, the actual return increases. Thus, our $100,000 trust might increase to $150,000. If this were the case, the 7% would go to $10,500 rather than just the $7,000 in the case of the annuity trust. Conversely, if you expect a recession, the annuity trust is much more desirable than the unitrust because the amount distributed is fixed at the time the trust is signed and will not go down in a recession.

There is another difference with the unitrust. Funds can be added to the unitrust after it is set up. Funds cannot be added to the annuity trust after it is first funded. Since the unitrust is valued each year, the added funds can be taken into account for subsequent years.

Two Life Trusts

In the case of both annuity and unitrust documents, it is possible to use trusts which are based on not just the life of one person, but on the lifetimes of two people. For example, Linda might want to make a charitable contribution and enjoy the income tax deduction and yet retain some income interest, such as 7% on the value of the contribution each year. She might also want to provide after her death that her sister, Carol, would receive the same 7% for Carol's lifetime. Setting up two life trusts works out well. Linda receives the 7% during her lifetime and an income tax charitable deduction. On her death, the 7% continues on for Carol's lifetime. Upon the death of Carol, the charity receives the money. This "two life annuity trust" or "two life unitrust" functions the same way as the single life trust with the exception that the income period is measured over the lives of both Linda and Carol rather than just Linda. Husbands and wives frequently set up such a trust to be sure each of them will have the income so long as either of them is alive. The deduction will be less than with a one life trust because the period the charity must wait to get the money is longer.

The Pooled Income Fund

There is another way to make a gift to charity and retain the income, and that is through the pooled income fund. Pooled income funds are not run by small charities. They are definitely a large charity project. Here, people contribute funds to the charity and the charity promises to pay them their proportionate amount of income earned by the pooled income fund. It is like a mutual fund run by a charity, except that it is irrevocable and the charity is the manager of the mutual fund. You, as the creator, must retain the income right for your lifetime. If you wish to add other persons, you may do so, but it must be at least for your lifetime.

If the pooled income trust fund has been in existence for more than three years, the IRS will look at the trust's performance on the income investment side. If it has been in existence less than three years, the IRS assumes a rate of return of 9%. Before making a charitable contribution to a pooled income fund, it is prudent to ask how long the trust has been in existence, what its actual yield is, and what type of investment philosophies are followed by the trustees. Since the IRS, for the first three years of the trust, is going to assume that your rate of return was 9%, it would be disappointing if it turned out that your income was substantially less than that.

The charitable annuity trust, the unitrust and the pooled income fund are the three general ways in which you can give property away and still receive an income interest on it. Are there other ways to give away property and still enjoy it?

Gifts of Homes and Tangible Personal Property

A gift of tangible personal property in which you retain the right to use the property for your lifetime is not a charitable gift in the eyes of the IRS. Despite what you may have heard, a gift of tangible personal property with a retained right to use the property or enjoy the property will not qualify as a charitable deduction for income tax purposes or for gift tax purposes. You cannot tell the museum, for example, that you have given them a certain painting on your death, but in the meantime, you are going to keep it for your lifetime. Even if you give the museum a bill of sale or deed of gift legally establishing that they are going to get the painting on your death, this is not a charitable gift for tax purposes.

Charitable Residence Gift

However, there is another exception to the general rule that says you have not made a charitable gift if you retain the right to use the property. The exception applies to homes and farms. If you make a legally binding transfer and retain only the right to live in the home as long as you are alive or for a term of years, you receive a charitable income tax deduction. The gift must be irrevocable in order for you to get the deduction. Personal residence means property used personally, not for investment purposes. It is not limited to the principal residence, but would include vacation homes as well. Farms follow the same rule, even though they are not personal residences.

The Charitable Gift Annuity

Charitable gift annuities have been around for some time. They were never popular, but they are becoming more and more popular now, principally through aggressive marketing. They work this way: Assets are transferred to the charity outright. The charity promises to pay the annuity for a lifetime or a fixed term. The amount of the charitable deduction is computed based upon the charitable gift: the fair market value of the property on the date of transfer to the charity, less the value of the charity's promise to pay you income for life. The payments on the annuity can start immediately, or they can be deferred until some specified age. Interestingly enough, a portion of each annuity payment is considered nontaxable income for the recipient. Compare this to the charitable unitrust and the charitable annuity trust where all, some, or none of the income may be subject to income tax depending upon the income the trust actually earns.

Also, it is very important to understand that the transfer of appreciated property to the charity may cause some tax liability to arise. After all, this is more like a sale than an outright gift. There may be some capital gains when you transfer appreciated property to the charity and receive their promise to give you money. Sometimes gift annuities are set up for a husband and wife. This, of course, reduces the value of the charitable gift because we have two lives and a longer period of time over which the charity will be paying income.

Life Insurance

Life insurance in the charitable area has also received a lot of attention recently and, in this case, the attention is justified. The amount that a charity will get through a gift of a life insurance policy can be very substantial. There is a tax-free "internal" build-up of income or value in a policy. In many instances, this favorable tax treatment helps the charity receive more than if the donor just kept the property and willed it to the charity on death. The charitable gift is considered to be a gift of the value of the policy at the time the policy is given. The same rules apply as in other assets. However, life insurance can be difficult for the layperson to value. A complex approach is used involving what is called the interpolated terminal reserve value. This generally translates into something like cash value. The actual figures must come from the life insurance company.

The charitable gift need not be made more than three years before death, even considering the special rules relating to the taxability of life insurance in a person's estate. When the insurance is given to a charity, the three-year-transfer rule applies, but is not much of a problem. For example, if you transfer the life insurance to a charity and do not live for three years, the IRS will include the value of the life insurance in your estate — but your estate gets a charitable deduction for the full value of the life insurance in your estate. What really have you lost?

Charitable Lead Trust

In the charitable remainder trusts described above, the giver received the income and the charity received the remainder. Is it possible and is it ever desirable to reverse the pattern so that the charity gets the income for a fixed period of time and then the remainder comes back to the donor or his beneficiaries? The answer is yes. There does exist a trust known as a charitable lead trust, sometimes called a front trust.

The charitable lead trust or front trust provides that the charity is to receive a determined income for a determinable period of time. Charitable lead or front trusts are particularly useful for very wealthy individuals or individuals who are charitably inclined and who have a current high income but whose income may decrease substantially in the future (for example, a highly compensated executive). The trust is set up while the person is alive. The charity receives the income for a period of time. With the charitable lead trust, the wealthy person can carry out his or her charitable purposes during high-income periods and still have the assets return later such as after retirement when there may be more need for them.

Charitable Giving and Tennessee Law

As mentioned earlier regarding outright gifts to charities, Tennessee's rules are very much like the federal law, and similar savings in Tennessee gift, estate and inheritance taxes can be enjoyed as a result of charitable giving. However, because Tennessee does not have an income tax, there would of course be no corresponding Tennessee income tax benefit from charitable giving, either outright, in trust, or otherwise.

Charitable Giving is Not a Way to Make Money

Nevertheless, charitable giving receives significant tax breaks, and there is a very real sense of satisfaction in setting aside substantial funds for a charity in an estate plan. You may even obtain a bit of immortality through making a substantial charitable gift and having a special fund bear your name. More important is the pleasure of knowing you have done something good for society that will be of a long-term nature. How that charitable gift is set up depends on many considerations: What types of property should be transferred? Should the transfer be made while you are alive or set up in your estate plan? Do you desire to keep some of the income and, if so, how much? If the income is to be kept, should this income be kept so it continues on for the benefit of a spouse, brother, sister, or other person?

Charitable giving is important to you and to your community.

In 1993, total charitable contributions in the United States were estimated to be $126 billion. Sums such as this materially improve our society when they are given to carefully selected groups that will invest the money wisely, monitor its use, and give you assurance that your charitable contribution is meeting a need you feel is important.

In this chapter, you will learn about:

- defined contribution plan
- defined benefit plan
- individual retirement accounts (IRAs)
- limitations on contributions and benefits
- survivor benefits
- borrowing from the plan
- required distributions
- early withdrawals
- distribution alternatives: lump sum/ installments/rollovers
- five-year averaging
- tax-free rollovers
- spousal rollovers
- excise taxes
- excess distributions
- excess accumulations

15

RETIREMENT PLANS AND IRAs

Retirement plans have become an increasingly impor-tant source of retirement income for the American public — and an increasingly regulated area of tax law. The resulting complexity means that most people don't understand the intricacies of deferred compensation law.

Today, many people have retirement plans. They may have a profit sharing, pension, 401(k), SEP, Keogh, IRA, or another type of plan, setting aside funds for retirement. These types of retirement plans receive certain tax advantages; typically, money contributed to the plan is not subject to income tax until it is distributed from the plan. Deferral of income tax until the money is received (tax-deferred income) should not be confused with the exemption from tax that is given to certain income, such as interest on some government bonds (tax-exempt or tax-free income). When funds come out of a retirement plan, whether in the form of a distribution to you upon retirement or a distribution to the beneficiary of your retirement plan upon your death, the distributions are subject to income tax. In addition, any retirement plan funds you own at the time of your death may be subject to death taxes.

It is surprising to see how much money can accumulate in your retirement plan. Frequently, you forget this employee benefit until you receive notice from your employer telling you how much has accumulated or been contributed to the plan. Then you see that your share is larger than you expected. Individual Retirement Accounts (IRAs) also tend to grow rapidly. Since retirement plans ordinarily pay no income tax currently, the income they earn accumulates and that income earns income. This compounding of income produces a significant amount of money over an extended period of time.

Retirement plans play an important role in estate planning because they are inherently a savings plan for the future, and they are frequently a person's largest asset other than their home. We will look at some of the general rules and approaches to handling retirement plans in the estate planning context. While there are many different types of retirement plans, generally these plans can be broken down into two broad categories. One is the defined *contribution* type of plan and the other is the defined *benefit* plan.

Defined Contribution Plan

The defined contribution plan is based on a fixed contribution. The contribution is made by your employer, by you as the employee, or by either or both of you, depending on the specific plan your employer has adopted. These contributions, together with earnings, forfeitures, and other accumulations, give you a retirement benefit. The amount that the employer contributes each year is fixed and, because of this, the plan is known as a defined or fixed contribution type of plan. On your retirement, you receive the amount that is your share. This amount can either be in the form of a lump sum or in payments spread out over a period of time for you and your spouse. Usually 401(k) and profit sharing plans are defined contribution plans.

Defined Benefit Plan

The other type of plan is the defined benefit plan. Here, the amount the employer contributes is not fixed or defined each year. Rather, the approach is from the other end — that is, the amount you will receive on retirement is fixed. Based on this defined amount, each year your employer determines the amount of that year's contribution to your plan. Since your benefit is usually calculated as a percentage of your final average pay, the contribution varies considerably. Each year the contribution is determined by actuarial methods. The employer's contribution depends upon your age, the number of years you have worked for the company, and the number of years it is anticipated that you will remain with the company.

Individual Retirement Account

An Individual Retirement Account or IRA is one of the most common types of retirement plans. Usually it is an account with a financial institution which is set aside for retirement years. Anyone who works for a salary can have an IRA. However, if you (or your spouse if you file your income tax returns jointly) are already a participant in a qualified retirement plan (including Keogh and SEP plans) or if your adjusted gross income exceeds $25,000 on a single return or $50,000 on a joint return, then the $2,000 contribution to the IRA is no longer tax-free. For couples who file joint returns and have adjusted gross income of more than $40,000 but less than $50,000, only part of the contribution to an IRA is tax-free. A nontax-free contribution to an IRA may be made, but it is made with after-tax dollars. However, the earnings in such an IRA are tax-deferred. If you are not a participant in a qualified plan, you can contribute up to 100% of your earnings or $2,000, whichever is smaller. It is perfectly permissible to have more than one IRA. In fact, in many instances, it is desirable to have more than one IRA. If you have money from a deceased spouse's IRA which you have kept in an IRA, that money should continue to be kept separate from your own IRA. We will talk about spousal rollovers later in this chapter. If you have an IRA to which nondeductible contributions were made, this IRA should be kept separate from an IRA to which you have made deductible contributions. Otherwise the bookkeeping becomes a real headache.

Limitations on Contributions and Benefits

There are limitations on how much can be set aside in retirement plans. The Internal Revenue Code says that the employer's contribution for a defined contribution plan must be the lesser of 25% of your compensation, or $30,000. However, certain types of defined contribution plans do have lower contribution limits. The limitation on defined benefit plans is on the maximum that you can receive after retirement. In 1995, this was approximately the lesser of $120,000 or 100% of your average compensation up to $150,000 over your three highest-paid years. This $120,000 figure changes each year because it is based on cost-of-living adjustments.

Survivor Benefits

Changes in the tax law enacted several years ago require that most employer-sponsored retirement plans give the surviving spouse automatic benefits. Generally, this is done in a "qualified joint and survivor annuity." This means that the retirement plan must be set up in such a way that retirement benefits are paid to the employee and upon the employee's death, the retirement benefits continue to be paid to the surviving spouse. While this requirement is mandated by federal law, it is subject to a number of exceptions and qualifications. The surviving spouse may waive his or her right to receive the benefits. However, any such waiver by a surviving spouse must be done perfectly before it will be accepted. For single people, naming a beneficiary does not constitute a gift since the designation can always be changed. If, however, a beneficiary who is not a spouse were irrevocably designated to be the beneficiary, this would then constitute a gift and gift tax would be applicable. Incidentally, this would be considered to be a gift of a future interest. The $10,000 annual exclusion for gifts would not apply so the first dollar would be taxable for federal and state gift tax purposes.

Borrowing from the Plan

You may want to use the money in your retirement plan without incurring the income tax obligation of a distribution. The government permits certain plans to offer participants loans under certain circumstances. If the applicable requirements are not met, the loan is considered a distribution and income tax applies. The government will insist that the loan not exceed $50,000 or one-half of the current value of your account in the plan. Plan loans must be repaid under most circumstances within five years. Interest payments have to be at a reasonable rate of interest.

Required Distributions

The tax law requires that distributions of retirement plan benefits (including IRAs) begin when you attain the age of 70 years and six months. Failure to take the required amount of money out at this age and each year thereafter will cause significant tax penalties to arise. For persons under the age of 70 years and six months, there are no required distributions.

Early Withdrawals

Sometimes people may want to take their money out ahead of time; that is, before reaching 59 years and six months. This is called early withdrawal. Early withdrawals from a retirement plan or an IRA are subject to a 10% penalty tax to discourage people from taking out the money before retirement. In addition, the regular income tax is also applied to these distributions. As a result of this "double tax," the government can take a significant portion of early withdrawals.

There is an exception to the requirement of being aged fifty-nine years and six months. If a person is no longer employed by that employer (separated from service); under this exception, distribution may be made at age 55. Also, the government permits early distributions for certain "emergency" needs such as medical expenses or payments to a divorcing spouse pursuant to a court order issued in connection with the divorce. There is no similar provision excusing early distributions for emergencies from IRAs.

Lump Sum, Installments, or Rollovers

Deciding how to take the money out of your retirement plan can be a difficult task. There are three approaches. One is to take it out in a lump sum, pay the tax burden, and have the money. Another alternative is to have the retirement plan money paid out in installments over the anticipated lifetimes of you and your spouse (this is often referred to as an "annuity" option). This defers some of the income tax obligation and lets the retirement plan funds continue to grow, but has the disadvantage that you don't have the money. The third alternative is to take the money out of your employer's plan and "roll it over" into an IRA, which you manage yourself. There are two ways to do this. First, you can authorize your employer's plan to transfer your benefits directly to the IRA of your choice. This is the "direct rollover" option. The other way is to have your employer's plan distribute the money to you and then you roll it over into an IRA (an "indirect rollover"). The tax consequences for direct and indirect rollovers are very different, as described below.

Tax-Free Rollovers

Sometimes, it is a good idea to take the money out of your employer's retirement plan when you retire and put it into an IRA that you manage yourself. This movement of funds is called a tax-free rollover. As long as this is done within 60 days from the date of receiving the money, it will be considered to be a rollover from one plan to another. In such case, it is not considered a taxable distribution to the retiring employee. The IRA can be managed by the employee or a money manager and at the same time be tax-deferred.

Recent changes in the law have made tax-free rollovers more complicated than in the past. When you are eligible to receive a distribution from most retirement plans, you will receive a notice from the plan notifying you about your options. One of your options will be to authorize the plan to roll over your funds directly to an IRA of your choosing. This is the direct rollover discussed above. If you do not choose this option, the plan will keep 20% of your distribution and turn it over to the government as tax withholding. If you want your plan to pay your distribution to you for you to roll over into an IRA (an indirect rollover), the plan will still keep 20% of your distribution as tax withholding and you will only receive 80% of your distribution. This means that if you want to roll over 100% of your distribution, you must find other money to replace the 20% that was withheld. If you rollover only the 80% that you receive, you will be taxed on the 20% that is withheld and that is not rolled over!

Spousal Rollovers

In some cases when a person with an IRA or other retirement plan dies and the money goes to the surviving spouse, the surviving spouse does not want the money. What should you do if the money is coming to you and you have to pay taxes on it, but you don't want it yet? Here's the solution: Take the money and "roll it over" into a spousal IRA. Now you're being treated very much as your spouse was. The money, which you would otherwise have to pay income tax on, can be put into a spousal rollover IRA with no current income tax due. It is a good idea not to mix these funds with your own IRA because of certain excise taxes which apply. Also, you can't take your spouse's IRA and roll it into your retirement plan. Only the spouse of a deceased plan participant or IRA owner is eligible to make such a rollover and defer the income tax until the surviving spouse attains the age of 70 years and six months, at which point the spouse must start taking distributions. If anyone other than a spouse is named as a beneficiary of retirement benefits, the longest that income tax can be deferred is five years. That is why it is often a good idea to name your spouse as the beneficiary of retirement benefits.

Five-Year Averaging

The Internal Revenue Code does give certain recipients who select a lump sum distribution a break when it comes to taxation of the distribution. Recognizing the hardship that may result when income earned over many years is received and taxed in a single year, the Internal Revenue Code provides that certain recipients can take the retirement lump sum distribution and divide it by five. The tax is figured on this one-fifth of the amount of the distribution and then that tax is multiplied by five. While dividing by five and then multiplying by five sounds like it would produce the same result; it doesn't because the rates are progressive. It is better to have one-fifth of the property taxed at a low rate and then have that multiplied by five rather than have all the property taxed at the top rate. Before you take a lump sum distribution you should determine whether you are eligible to use this five-year averaging method. For example, if you are not age 59 1/2 at the time of the distribution or, in the case of death, at the time of death, generally you or your beneficiary may not use the five-year averaging method and must pay tax on the entire distribution as ordinary income.

Excess Distributions

Occasionally, a person may manage to accumulate a large enough amount in a retirement plan to trigger a special federal excise tax. This excise or penalty tax is a flat 15%, and it is imposed by the IRS in addition to any federal income tax or estate tax otherwise due. The federal excise tax can be triggered in two ways: one is by an "excess distribution" during your lifetime; the other is by an "excess accumulation" at your death.

Generally, an excess distribution is any distribution received over $150,000 (although the threshold applicable to you may be more or less). If a lump sum distribution is used instead of annual distributions, the excess is generally the amount over $750,000.

Excess Accumulations

IRS also imposes a 15% excise tax in the case of excess accumulations in a retirement plan at the time of a person's death. If an estate will have this much money accumulated in *all* IRA and other retirement plans, certain steps need to be taken. This 15% federal excise tax may *not* be reduced either by the $600,000 equivalent exemption or by the marital deduction. The result is that it is possible to have funds passing to a surviving spouse that are free of federal estate tax by reason of the marital deduction, but nevertheless are subject to the 15% federal excise tax. When the surviving spouse dies, the federal government is going to take an estate tax bite. There is an exception to this heavy taxation. Under a recent change in the tax law, the 15% federal excise tax on property passing to a surviving spouse may be deferred until the death of the surviving spouse. Whether this is desirable or not can be determined only after sitting down and doing some calculations, since it is necessary to consider any retirement plan benefits the surviving spouse may have on his or her own account.

Death Taxes

Since the retirement plan account or IRA is an asset the owner earned, it will be included in the owner's estate for state inheritance and federal estate (or "death") tax purposes. The beneficiary will usually be the spouse, since in most cases federal law now requires that the spouse be the beneficiary unless the spouse waives that right. Since all assets which pass outright to a surviving spouse are fully deductible for death tax purposes, if retirement plan benefits are paid directly to the surviving spouse, the benefits should not cause any death taxes to arise. In instances where there is no surviving spouse, the usual death tax rules apply and the IRA or qualified plan may cause substantial death taxes to arise.

IRAs and Retirement Plans

As we have seen, the rules concerning retirement plans and IRAs are complex. They require careful study because there are so many exceptions to the general statements. The correct answer depends in many instances on when the IRA or retirement plan was started, whether the contributions to the IRA were deductible or nondeductible, whether they are the result of a spouse's efforts or your own efforts, whether you are an owner or a "highly compensated employee," whether you have sufficient sums in your retirement plan or IRA to be considered by the government as excessive and thereby subject to the 15% federal excise tax, and many other variables. Nevertheless, it is essential to deal with retirement plans and IRAs because of the large sums of money held in these types of plans. The 15% federal excise tax for excessive accumulations can cause considerable problems and will require special planning.

With proper planning, however, the substantial amounts contained in IRAs and retirement plans can be directed to the surviving spouse or dealt with in such a fashion that the goals of planning for retirement and of passing assets on to loved ones can be accomplished with a minimum of tax. This can be done only with careful planning and an awareness of the complexities inherent in such plans.

In this chapter, you will learn:

- what the benefits of life insurance are
- what types of policies are available
- insurance terms
- interpolated terminal reserve
- assignment of insurance policies
- cash value
- what income tax advantages life insurance has
- dividends
- borrowing
- death tax aspects
- whether to transfer policy ownership
- irrevocable life insurance trust
- who should be the beneficiary of the policy
- what death tax treatment to expect
- how to determine the right amount of insurance

16

LIFE INSURANCE

Life insurance is no longer the simple life insurance of past years. New types of policies serve a variety of purposes. Let's review life insurance over the years.

In 1941, the Supreme Court described life insurance as "a device to shift and distribute the risk of loss from premature death." Even today, "risk shifting" remains the basic test of whether an arrangement will be considered life insurance and, therefore, entitled to favorable tax treatment. There are statistics ("mortality tables") concerning the life expectancy of an individual of any specific age, the percentage of individuals of the same age who can be expected to die during the year, and any other classification that may be of interest. Insurance companies use these mortality tables to predict the amount of benefits they will

181

have to pay to policy holders. The premiums for traditional life insurance policies are based on the amount of such benefits together with insurance company's charges which cover the insurance company's other anticipated costs and expenses, and investment results. The new types of policies may contain a separate investment component in addition to insurance protection that accrues to the insured. These investments are funded through higher premiums, the amount of which may fluctuate, often at the policy owner's discretion. Some policies do not even guarantee a minimum death benefit and, therefore, have a substantial built-in element of risk. Because of the proliferation of products intended to serve as tax shelters or short-term investments, Congress enacted new definitions and new rules to identify and govern life insurance for tax purposes.

Traditionally, life insurance was purchased to provide funds for the family after the breadwinner's (then ordinarily the husband's) death. Rarely was there any thought of insuring the wife who worked in the home. Insurance was not intended to be an investment. It was not purchased as a tax-advantaged savings plan. All that has changed in recent years. We'll discuss some of the common types of life insurance policies currently available, and their advantages and disadvantages. We'll talk about the economics of purchasing life insurance. Today, many people are more interested in the investment possibilities than in the death benefits.

For estate planning, life insurance is still used to replace the earning power of the family breadwinner or, as is more frequent today, breadwinners. Couples should not overlook the economic value of the services performed by a spouse, and life insurance may be a welcome source of funds after a spouse's death.

Life insurance is also purchased to provide readily available cash in an estate. Death taxes become due nine months after the date of death. If cash is not otherwise available, the personal representative of a taxable estate may be forced to sell estate assets at bargain prices to pay taxes. When death taxes are extremely high, insurance is often the best source of funds to pay these death taxes.

There is a third reason for life insurance, a very real reason that is rarely discussed, either by the life insurance industry or by estate planners. After the death of a spouse, there is a feeling of considerable loss. If the survivor is a wife who does not work outside the home or was not included in the management of the family finances, there may be distressing feelings of economic vulnerability. A grieving survivor who has limited experience in managing money and is unfamiliar with the family's financial situation naturally feels a little frightened and very ill at ease when faced with numerous financial decisions and responsibilities after the death of a spouse. Life insurance provides a substantial amount of cash on short notice with few questions or choices. There is a high degree of comfort on seeing a large check come from the insurance company and knowing "At least I have this." Even when the insurance proceeds are not a financial necessity, they often fill a very real, personal need. The vulnerability and lack of financial acumen of a grieving spouse may be strong arguments for establishing a trust to receive the insurance proceeds.

Finally, life insurance can be helpful when a large asset of the estate is ownership in a closely held business (a business owned by a small number of individuals, a family, or other close group). An immediate infusion of cash may be necessary for a variety of reasons: to offset the economic loss the business faces on the death of a person who is important to its operation, to provide to the business or the remaining owners sufficient funds to purchase the decedent's share, or to enable the decedent to leave the business to the children who are active in its operation and give the other children a comparable cash inheritance. This is a complex area that we will cover later in this chapter.

We have seen that life insurance is one way to meet certain real needs of the estate. The cash proceeds, which may be substantial, are available to provide for the emotional well-being and comfort of the survivors, to replace the earning power of the breadwinner, to provide liquidity for death taxes, and to serve possible business purposes. Though not everyone needs or wants life insurance, it should be considered in the estate planning process.

With that brief introduction, let's talk about some of the types of life insurance policies and some of the terms used in the life insurance industry. There are numerous variations of these products as well as a multitude of available options.

Life Insurance and Death Taxes

Life insurance in the eyes of the Internal Revenue Service is inherently testamentary. This means that the Internal Revenue Service will seek diligently to apply death tax to life insurance. All the usual rules about including in an estate the property at its fair market value as of the date of death apply. But in the case of life insurance, the estate also includes any life insurance owned by the decedent or life insurance given away three years from the date of his or her death. Therefore, life insurance is even more taxable than ordinary property. If Ted gives away $50,000 worth of stocks and bonds, and dies within three years, the fair market value of those stocks and bonds at the time of his death is not brought back into his estate. However, let's say that Ted owns a life insurance policy which will pay $500,000 upon his death. If Ted gives away the policy at a time when the fair market value of the policy is $50,000, and if Ted dies within three years of making his gift of the policy, then the amount which is included in Ted's estate for death tax purposes is the full amount of the death proceeds, or $500,000. Life insurance in the estate plan area needs special attention.

Whole Life Insurance

One of the traditional forms of life insurance is called whole life or straight life. Whole life insurance has three components. One is the pure underwriting risk portion of the premium — the mortality risk. This portion is used by the insurance company (the "insurer") solely to offset the expense of paying out the face value of the policy.

The second component is the administrative cost of the policy. After all, the insurance company has to pay for its building. It may have to pay its shareholders, officers, employees, and, of course, commissions to the life insurance salesmen.

The third component of whole life insurance is the investment factor. Whole life premiums remain level during the life of the policy even though the underwriting risk increases as the insured grows older. During the early years of the policy when the insured is younger, the amount of the premium is higher than the pure actuarial risk of the insured's death. As the policy and the insured become older, the premiums are less than the cost of protection. The excess advance premiums paid in the beginning years are invested by the insurance company. These advance payments result in a cash value within the policy. Most insurance companies allow whole life policy owners to borrow back the paid-in dollars, at a reduced rate. While the lower rate may justify borrowing from your policy rather than another source, this feature should be kept in perspective when making the decision to purchase insurance. After all, the company is lending you money you paid to it in advance, which it is holding for you. Whole life may be preferred by young families getting started because of the savings aspect and because premiums can be paid in installments over the life of the policy.

Endowment Insurance

Endowment insurance functions like whole life, but with a set value or face value to be paid out at the end of a particular term. Endowment insurance is not as frequently used in today's insurance marketplace and in fact may gradually be disappearing except in specialized applications.

Universal Life Insurance

Universal life insurance is a relatively new product. Instead of the traditional savings-type plan of whole life insurance, the universal life policy has a special investment component and, in some instances, risk built in. The universal life policy does not have the level premium that the whole life policy does. Instead, the policy holder may put as much money into the insurance plan as he or she wishes each year. The important thing to remember about universal life insurance is that the owner of the policy has the investment control of the life insurance policy, not the insurance company. With regular whole life, the insurance company manages the investment factor. With universal, the individual can select from a broad spectrum of investment vehicles ranging from Treasury bills to much more aggressive investments. If the owner is wise and lucky in investments, then the value will grow much faster than if regular whole life had been purchased and the insurance company were managing the investments. Conversely, if you do not do as well as the insurance company could, then the value of your policy will be less.

The interest earned by the universal life policy is tax-advantaged. No current tax is paid on the increasing value which results from the investments. Tax is not paid (it is "deferred") until money is actually taken out of the universal life policy. This tax-deferment feature gives the life insurance policy a significant advantage over other types of investments. The money that would have gone to pay income taxes remains with the policy and is available to earn interest. Over a long period of time, the additional value generated by money that would have been paid for taxes can be substantial. For this reason, universal life policies became very popular during periods of high inflation, when interest rates and taxes were very high.

Responding to perceived abuses, in 1984 Congress passed strong rules prohibiting certain highly investment-oriented life insurance contracts from being called life insurance and being treated as life insurance for tax purposes. These rules require that life insurance policies act more like insurance and less like investment vehicles.

Term Life Insurance

A term life insurance policy is issued by the insurance company for a specific limited period of time, generally one, five, or ten years. The term policy has a lower premium than other types of life insurance because it has no cash value. Premium dollars pay only for the administrative cost and insurance risk that the insured will die before the term of the policy is up. Usually, the premium is established on a yearly basis and increases each year as the insured grows older. If the insured dies during the period of the policy, the designated beneficiary will receive the face amount of the policy. If the policy term ends before the insured's death, the beneficiary receives nothing. There is no value to the policy after the term has passed.

A term policy is also a popular form of insurance for young adults because it provides maximum insurance for the least cash. Some term policies are automatically renewable for a number of years, though premiums usually increase as the insured ages.

Another option allows the term policy to be converted into other types of insurance when the higher insurance premiums will not strain the family budget. But term insurance isn't just for young people with limited resources. Sometimes insurance protection is only needed for a specific period of time.

Parents or grandparents may purchase term insurance on the life of one or both parents, renewable for 20 years, at the birth of each child. If a parent dies before the child is 20, this relatively inexpensive policy insures that money will be available to replace the economic support which would have been provided by the parent. The insurance can be a decreasing term policy in which the amount of coverage is reduced as the child grows older, offsetting the increased cost of the insurance. Those concerned about inflation or the cost of college may prefer to keep a level amount of coverage and pay the higher premium each year.

Term policies are frequently used in business transactions when it is desirable to have a party insured for a limited number of years and not for an entire lifetime. An example might be a particularly important employee (a "key man") who is expected to be with the company for 10 years. If he dies during that period, the company will suffer significant economic loss. For this reason, the company with limited cash to spend on life insurance takes out a term life insurance policy ("key man insurance") on its employee. The insurance proceeds that will be paid to the company if the insured dies will cover at least a portion of the economic loss the company sustains as the result of the death.

Both term and whole life insurance are frequently used in closely held corporations when the corporation and the shareholders agree in advance about the purchase and sale of corporate stock from a decedent stockholder's estate. These contracts (referred to as "buy-sell agreements" or "cross-purchase agreements") may require the transfer of shares, allow the corporation a right of first refusal if the shares are to be sold, give the corporation and remaining shareholders the right to purchase the shares, permit the estate to require that the shares be purchased, or whatever else everyone agrees to. Buy-sell agreements and cross-purchase agreements are widely used, with good reason. Rick and Rob may have worked together over the years to build a successful business. When Rick dies, his wife

Pat may not want the stock. She needs cash and doesn't care about the business now that Rick is no longer a part of it. Pat typically will have a hard time finding a buyer for Rick's part interest in the corporation. Rob has a valid concern, but no control, over who buys the shares. With the insurance proceeds, Rob can buy Rick's shares of stock and Pat will get the value of her husband's shares.

When there is a buy-sell agreement requiring the purchase of stock, and it is funded with life insurance, each shareholder can be assured of a cash purchaser for his or her closely held corporate stock. With the insurance in place, the surviving shareholders know the necessary cash will be available to pay for the deceased shareholder's stock. All this can be accomplished for a relatively low premium.

Single Premium Life Insurance

Sometimes it makes good economic sense to pay all the life insurance premiums of a policy at one time, so there is a single premium life insurance. This type of policy has aspects of whole life, but instead of relatively small premiums being paid out over a long period of time, the premiums are all grouped together, a credit is given for early payment, and the single premium is paid. The life insurance is then in force for the lifetime of the individual. The single premium policies are frequently used by people who are in high-income tax brackets and have enough cash to make a substantial payment. By making this early payment, they receive the income-tax benefit of tax deferral. Having the insurance company invest the advance payment portion of their premium is like having a savings account which earns interest tax-deferred until withdrawal. There are policies that allow the insured to decide whether the funds are invested in stocks, bonds, real estate, or other forms of investment. Of course, the more control the individual has over the investment, the less the policy looks like insurance.

In estate planning, single premium policies are also used as gifts. A wealthy individual can purchase a substantial single premium life insurance policy on her or his own life and transfer it to a trust, to individuals, or to a charity. The single premium which has been paid in a lump sum will be considerably less than the face value of the policy. When the policy is transferred by gift, the value for gift tax purposes is very close to the cash value of the policy. Assuming that a relatively young person could purchase a $100,000 face value policy for a lump sum premium cost of $30,000 or less, the policy could be given to three individuals without any transfer tax. (Remember the insured can transfer $10,000 per year per beneficiary free of gift tax.) With three individuals owning the policy, that's the $30,000 actual cash value of the policy, even though it has a face value on the insured's death of $100,000. If the insured dies, $100,000 of value has been transferred out of his or her estate at no actual transfer tax cost. However, as we will see later in this chapter, there are some significant problems in transferring life insurance that is owned by the insured. It is much better for the insured to transfer the cash to the individuals who will ultimately own the policy and have the premiums paid by them than to purchase the policy and transfer it.

Second-to-Die Life Insurance

One of the hot new items being offered by the life insurance industry is known as joint life insurance, survivorship coverage, or "second-to-die" coverage. The thrust of this type of life insurance is that the coverage insures more than one life. The death benefit is payable *only* upon the death of the *second* insured. Typically, these policies are on the lives of a husband and wife.

As we saw earlier, in most situations involving a husband and wife of a long-term marriage, there will be no tax upon the death of the first spouse because of the · complete marital deduction for assets passing to the surviving spouse. The life insurance industry created the second-to-die coverage to provide liquidity to estates at the time of the death of the second spouse, when substantial amounts of cash would be needed to pay the death taxes.

Premiums are remarkably low for second-to-die coverage. The reason for this is that insuring two people extends the life expectancy actuarially and the cost of the mortality risk is less than insuring just the younger person alone. After all, there is always the outside chance, which actuaries and other persons who study mortality tables must consider, that the younger person would be killed in an accident or unexpectedly develop a fatal illness. In fact, sometimes, it can be very useful to use second-to-die coverage when one of the parties is essentially uninsurable because of health problems or advanced age. The insurance company will accept the mortality risk of insuring the older person, or the person who is unhealthy, when coupled with the younger person or the healthy person, and the premiums are not excessive. Second-to-die life insurance is also used in estate planning when made part of a gifting program with a view of providing funds to pay death taxes. Frequently, with this type of insurance, the funds to purchase are transferred by the parents to the children. The children then use these funds to purchase the policy. The children name themselves as the owners of the policy and as the beneficiaries of the policy proceeds. The insureds are the parents of the children.

The policy does not pay off when one parent dies — only when the surviving parent dies. Since the children are the beneficiaries of the insurance policy, they now have substantial amounts of money with which to pay the death taxes or to use as an inheritance.

Terminology

After this short overview of the types of policies, let's look at a few of the more commonly used terms in life insurance. Many people may be unaware that the designations of owner, insured and beneficiary in their life insurance policies have very significant consequences. The owner of the policy is the individual shown as having the right to change the policy, to cash it in, to modify it, or to give it to some other person. The insured is the person whose life is being covered by the insurance policy. The beneficiaries are those who would receive the money from the insurance company upon the insured's death. The insurance company, by contract with the owner, has agreed to pay the value to the beneficiary of the policy if the insured dies.

These concepts are pretty simple. The problem arises in failing to think through who the owner should be, who the beneficiaries should be, and who the insured should be. All too frequently, the insured is the owner. If the insured is the owner at the time of death, the full face value of the insurance policy will be included in his or her estate. For this reason, it is often better for estate planning purposes to have someone other than the insured own the policy.

Interpolated Terminal Reserve Value

The interpolated terminal reserve value is the value that the IRS and the Tennessee Department of Revenue will use when calculating the value of most life insurance policies for gift tax purposes. Generally, the cash value and the interpolated terminal reserve value are similar except in the first few years when the interpolated terminal reserve is generally significantly lower.

It is important to establish the value of a life insurance policy before making a gift of the policy. Most insurance companies will provide you with interpolated terminal reserve value. If your insurance agent is not familiar with this term, you need to be firm and insist that the agent ask the company for the amount. Gift splitting between spouses in connection with the $10,000 annual exclusion from gift tax can be used to make gifts of insurance. If the owner of the policy is married and the spouse joins in the gift, the couple can give away a life insurance policy with a current value of less than $20,000 without incurring any gift tax, provided this is the only gift they make to that individual during the calendar year. They must, of course, file an informational joint gift tax return, but no tax is due. Also, the marital deduction for gift tax applies to the transfer of a life insurance policy to a spouse. An unlimited amount of life insurance may be given to a spouse as a gift without any gift tax.

Cash Value

The cash value on a policy is the amount of money you can get if you turn your policy back to the company and "cash it in." Whole life policies frequently have a substantial cash value because of the savings component in the premiums. On the other hand, term insurance has no cash value because the premiums are solely the actuarial risk that the insured may die before the actuarial tables say they will. Usually, term payments are on a year-to-year basis. In any event, the cash value is almost always significantly less than the face value that is due when the insured dies. For example, Herb owns a $100,000 term policy issued on a year-to-year basis on the life of his wife, Meg. If Meg dies during the term of the policy, their children, the beneficiaries, receive the $100,000 face value of the policy. On the other hand, if Herb dies during the term of the policy and Meg is still alive, the value of this term insurance, which is an asset of Herb's estate, might be less than $500.

Because of the difference between cash value and face value, people frequently make gifts of life insurance because they know that the transfer tax cost is based on the cash value or interpolated terminal reserve, whichever is higher, but the value for death tax purposes if the policy is still owned by the insured is the death proceeds, which is almost always much higher.

Assignment of Insurance Policies

Assignment of insurance policies is quite common. Banks frequently ask to have any insurance policies assigned to them insuring the life of the debtor. This way, they are more certain that they are going to be paid if the debtor dies. The beneficiary is the person who receives the death benefit proceeds. If there is a loan outstanding on these death benefit proceeds, the amount that the individual beneficiary actually gets is reduced by this loan value.

Dividends

Some insurance companies pay dividends on their insurance. This sounds like a dividend on stock, but it is different. The dividend on a life insurance policy is a return of excess premium. Sometimes an insurance company will find that it has excess dividends because of unforeseen (but favorable) circumstances. It will do one of three things: send back some of these excess premiums in the form of a cash dividend, provide an additional period of a year's coverage "free," or treat the dividend as being for the payment of additional amounts of insurance.

Borrowing

Borrowing against insurance policies frequently makes good sense. Under the older types of policies, the rate of interest charged for borrowing against the policy is very low compared to contemporary interest rates. Because of this, people sometimes will borrow against their life insurance policies to receive the loan proceeds and turn around and buy more life insurance with them. That borrowed money is "cheaper" than if they had taken the money from somewhere else because the "cost" of the money is less when borrowing against the policy than from other sources.

These loans, usually at favorable interest rates, cause interest to be assessed. These interest expenses on life insurance policies are treated like any other form of consumer interest. They are not deductible under the tax law. The old advice about borrowing against your life insurance policy and investing the proceeds for sound financial management no longer applies as often because of the change in the tax law. The loss of the interest deduction, the decline in interest rates, and the fact that the interest is fully taxable causes the financial planner to calculate carefully before making the recommendation to borrow against the life insurance policy.

Life Insurance and Income Taxes

Since we're looking at life insurance as an investment vehicle as well as a way of providing easily accessible cash, let's look at how life insurance is treated for income tax purposes. Life insurance does have some tax advantages. While it is probably not correct to say that life insurance is income tax-free, it certainly is income tax-advantaged. If you invest $100 in stock, you must pay capital gains on that stock if it goes up when you sell it. In the meantime, you must pay ordinary income tax on the dividends produced by that stock. Similarly, if you take that same $100 and invest it in a treasury obligation, a CD, or some other interest-yielding investment, you must pay income tax each year on that interest. However, when you give that same money to an insurance company and purchase whole life insurance, you do not have to pay income tax on the investment part of your premium. The "invested" money is free to grow. By being reinvested, it earns more interest, which is reinvested and earns even more interest.

However, like all things, there comes a time when the piper must be paid, particularly if the owner is seeking lifetime benefits. If you take out of the life insurance investment plan more than you put in, you must pay income taxes on the excess over the amount that was paid in. These are considered to be ordinary income payments and are taxed at the ordinary income rate. The government considers that you first get back the money that you put in, and what you get back above this is treated like interest or dividends.

Upon the insured's death, when the beneficiary receives the death benefits, the lump sum paid to the beneficiary is free from income tax. Sometimes, the death benefit proceeds are left with the insurance company under one of the settlement options the insurance companies offer. Under some of the settlement options, the interest earned by those death benefits is free of income tax until distributed.

For these reasons, life insurance does receive some significant benefits under the income tax law. The next question then becomes, what type of treatment does the insurance policy receive under the death tax law?

Withdrawing Funds

The 1986 tax law significantly changed the picture concerning the income tax consequences of withdrawing funds from certain types of life insurance policies. Generally, withdrawals may be made from a life insurance policy's cash values without incurring an income tax. However, these withdrawals are usually treated as income in the case of withdrawals within 15 years after a universal life insurance policy is set up. Owners of universal life insurance policies should be extremely cautious about withdrawals. In fact, if any life insurance policy does not meet certain requirements, withdrawing funds from the policy can cause income taxes to arise unexpectedly. Never take withdrawals from a policy until you check the income tax consequences.

Death Tax Aspects

The death tax aspects of life insurance are perhaps some of the most interesting areas in the whole field of death tax. First of all, we're dealing with what are typically large amounts of very liquid assets, which may be subject to very high tax levels. Further, special rules apply to life insurance to make it more taxable than any other type of asset. It is easier to make a mistake on the ownership and the naming of beneficiaries with life insurance than with other assets.

Frequently, life insurance is included in the estate because the person who died was the owner of the policy. If the decedent had any aspects of ownership at all, then it is likely that the insurance policy will be included in the insured-owner's estate. For this reason, in a taxable estate, it is almost always desirable to have someone other than the insured own the policy. Having the insured and the owner be the same person is a sure way to increase the death tax and reduce the ultimate amount that will go to the beneficiaries.

If the insurance proceeds are to be paid to the trustee of the owner's living trust or paid to the personal representative of the owner's estate, these proceeds or death benefits will also be included in the owner's estate. The full cash proceeds paid will be taxed upon death. The death tax starts at 37% and goes to 55%, so the death tax on this insurance money can be very high. It is better to have the owner and the beneficiary be a surviving spouse or perhaps another beneficiary if there is no surviving spouse. In this way, the proceeds will not be payable to the owner's personal representative or trustee, and will not be included in his estate for this reason.

Transfer of Ownership

For reasons noted above, people frequently give away the ownership of an existing policy. To keep the insurance proceeds out of the insured's estate, the insured must transfer *all* rights of any type of ownership in the policy. There must be a complete and full transfer with no strings attached. The owner must give up the right to change the beneficiary, to surrender the policy, to pledge it for a loan, or to cash in its cash surrender value. The transfer of the ownership must take place at least three years before the insured dies, and the likelihood of the owner ever getting the policy back must be less than one chance in 20.

If there is a greater chance than one in 20 that the insured will get the policy back, or if the owner dies within three years after transferring the policy, or if there are any "strings" on the transfer, the IRS and the Tennessee Department of Revenue will add the value of the policy back in the estate. What this means is that it is very important to transfer all incidents of ownership. Because of these special rules, life insurance, far from being one of the least taxable items in an estate, is one of the most taxable items.

Irrevocable Life Insurance Trust

The irrevocable life insurance trust has been with us for some time, and yet these trusts are by no means clear and well settled in the law.

What are these? What do they do? What good do they do? The irrevocable life insurance trust first of all is a trust. A trust is created that names an individual or corporation to serve as trustee. The beneficiaries are always someone other than the person creating the trust, and the trust is irrevocable. Irrevocable in this case means just that. It is irrevocable. It is cast in stone. You may be wondering, why would you ever want to create a trust which is cast in stone and which you never, ever could change, amend, alter, revoke, or have anything to do with ever again? The answer lies in the nature of life insurance and the death tax law.

Life insurance, when you purchase it, always costs significantly less than the death benefit. Some clever person might say, "I have an idea! I will purchase some life insurance and put it in an irrevocable trust so it is completely out of my estate. When I die, the face value of that policy will be paid to my beneficiaries, but it will never be taxed. I didn't own it at the time of my death and therefore, there could be no death tax on it." In fact, this clever approach has been used. However, the government felt it was losing too much death tax revenue. It then passed a law which said you could not have life insurance transferred to a trust and die within three years without having the entire face amount of the policy taxed to your estate.

Buying life insurance and then gifting it is a disaster on two counts. First, the full face value is included in your estate if you die within three years, and this will generate a great deal of death tax. Second, there's no extra money to pay the death taxes. While the insurance is included in the estate for tax purposes, the actual money on that policy went to the beneficiaries. They are not obligated to provide money to pay for the death tax unless certain and not very common provisions are inserted in the will.

Life Insurance Trusts and the Prearrangement Problem

Therefore, people very soon stopped transferring life insurance into these irrevocable life insurance trusts. They said to themselves, "If we don't transfer the life insurance, then maybe what we ought to do is transfer money into the trust. We'll let the trustee buy the life insurance." This works in many, but not all, instances. After all, the government does know what is going on. And most people won't transfer substantial amounts of money to the trust unless they know what the trustee is going to do with that money.

Frequently, people will decide on an amount of life insurance and find out what the premiums would be. Then they set up the trust and transfer that amount of cash or assets into the trust. Not too surprisingly, the trustee decides to purchase life insurance at just the right amount of money to pay the premiums. The IRS does not like this practice. There have been a number of cases dealing with this and similar types of problems involving irrevocable life insurance trusts. The government has tried many tactics to cause the face value of the policy to be included in the estate, even though the person who died did not own the policy and never did own it.

The IRS has a long history of attacking prearranged insurance trusts. In a 1990 Tennessee case, the IRS asserted that the trustee of the irrevocable life insurance trust was acting as the "mere agent" of the insured. The insured drafted the trust, designated the beneficiaries, selected an insurance policy for the trustee to purchase, and provided the money to purchase the policy and to pay the premiums. In fact, the insured had the power to remove the trustee at will and held the position as chairman of the bank's trust committee! In spite of these facts, the court rejected all of the IRS's arguments and decided that, because the insured had never held any incidents of ownership in the policy of insurance, the life insurance proceeds were not included in the estate of the insured. It is less likely these days that the IRS will try to attack an irrevocable life insurance trust (assuming it was set up correctly!), because in a 1991 case, the government was forced to pay attorney's fees to the estate of the insured after the government lost its challenge of the insurance trust. The court held that the IRS could not justify its decision to take the taxpayer to court yet again, after losing so many cases in so many jurisdictions.

When the irrevocable life insurance trust is set up correctly, it works very, very well. Maybe you're thinking about buying some term insurance. This is the type of insurance that insures you on a year-to-year basis. It has a relatively low premium for a relatively high payoff on death. Rather than just buying it in your own name and having it included in your estate, you set up an irrevocable life insurance trust. The bank down the street agrees to serve as trustee for a reasonable fee. You transfer $4,500 to the trust every year. Each year, the trustee buys term insurance. You create this trust at age 55 as a nonsmoker. Five years later, you die. A reasonable face amount for this term insurance to pay would be $600,000 upon death.

Look what's happened. You have shifted $22,500 out of your estate and yet the beneficiaries of that trust, who may well be your children or grandchildren, get $600,000 tax-free. The money can be used by the trustee for their health, maintenance, support, and education. Funds in the trust could be used to make sure that the grandchildren go to college or that the children have additional funds for retirement — all free of death taxes. There has been a tremendous savings. This is the reason people keep coming back to irrevocable life insurance trusts. They provide a tremendous opportunity for transferring assets free of death tax.

Who Should the Beneficiary of the Policy Be?

Naming the estate is usually not a good choice. This is not an absolute rule. However, naming the estate as the beneficiary is going to cause the policy proceeds to be subject to federal and state death tax if the total estate exceeds $600,000.

Suppose the estate is not subject to death tax because it is not going to meet the minimum figure of $600,000. Someone may say it doesn't make any difference then, and it is just as easy to have the policy payable to the estate. Many would not argue with this point. However, they should also mention that, by making the policy proceeds payable to the estate, you increase the size of the probate estate and will probably increase the costs in administrating the estate (probate expense). Sometimes, this is the only logical way to handle the proceeds because they are to be divided among a number of people. However, if you do not have a number of beneficiaries, it might be better to have the policy proceeds paid directly to the beneficiary. The beneficiary will get the money faster and the money he or she receives will not be subject to personal representative's and attorney's fees.

How Much Insurance?

How much insurance you should carry is one of the most important questions and sometimes the most difficult. To know the correct answer requires a well-operating crystal ball. However, even without supernatural guidance, it is possible to make some educated guesses as to how much insurance you need. Various rules of thumb exist: eight times earnings or ten times earnings or, maybe, five times earnings. Not surprisingly, many life insurance agents push for the higher multiple in hopes of selling a larger insurance policy. The use of such rules of thumb may work in some areas, but they can be worse than useless for life insurance and may give the insured an unwarranted sense of security. If the decision based on an earnings multiple is in fact the right amount, it is solely the result of luck.

Step-by-Step Plan

Let's consider a step-by-step plan for deciding how much life insurance you need for estate purposes. First, figure your current assets and liabilities, being very honest about them. If you are careful in listing your assets, you will probably be surprised at their total value. Since you are looking at life insurance from a death tax standpoint, put down the full value of joint property held with a surviving spouse. The full value of these properties will be subject to tax upon the death of the surviving spouse, so the full value is important.

Second, project the values of the assets and liabilities out to a reasonable period, say five to 10 years from now. If you figure further out than this, you're merely speculating, and a shorter period of time may not be very helpful.

Third, see if your estate plan provides for the payment of death taxes on your death or if these death taxes will be deferred until the death of the surviving spouse through use of the marital deduction. Be sure you are satisfied with your estate plan and that you have all the necessary documents to successfully carry out that plan.

Fourth, compute the death taxes that would be due on your estate using the values and liabilities five or 10 years out. Be sure to add in any administration costs and other expenses to which your estate may be subjected. If you have a corporate executor, anticipate that the charge will probably be between 1% and 2% of the estate. If your assets are passing through probate, anticipate that the cost of carrying these assets through probate will be approximately 1% to 2% for attorney's fees. If your assets are passing through an *inter vivos* trust, anticipate that your corporate trustee will charge you 1% to 2% for handling these assets and approximately 1% for attorney's fees, and that there will be additional charges for preparing death tax returns which should be figured in at approximately one-half of 1%.

A word of caution about these numbers: it is impossible to make accurate estimates for every possible situation that could occur in the state of Tennessee. Some personal representatives will charge more; others less. Family members may charge nothing at all to act as personal representative. Attorney's fees vary considerably depending on the time, the responsibilities, and the difficulties, among other factors. It is not considered bad form to ask your attorney what he or she estimates the legal fees would be on the estate if the estate were administered today and there were no unusual complications. Your attorney should be able to give you a reasonable range of figures.

After you look at what the anticipated death taxes will be, see if there is a way to decrease this cost. Would it be better to go to a type of estate plan that defers the death taxes, or would it be better to pay some taxes initially? Deferring taxes always is appealing. In some instances, however, it is better to pay the death taxes at the first death. Property that is taxed at the time the first spouse dies can appreciate without having the increased value subject to tax at the death of the surviving spouse. Because the rate of death tax increases as the value of the estate increases, you can usually get some benefit from the lower rates when both spouses pay some taxes.

These decisions generally require a considerable amount of working with the numbers and assumptions of growth rates, present value of dollars, and other factors. Most people, however, opt to defer the death tax in its entirety, using the unified credit (see Chapter 9) to shelter the first $600,000 from tax and passing the balance to a surviving spouse. If there are substantial assets, the $600,000 may be given outright to individuals other than the spouse. More often a trust (a "credit shelter trust") is used so that the income from the $600,000 will be available for the surviving spouse during his or her life before being distributed to the other individuals.

It is now time for a word of comfort. If you have been doing some of these computations, you realize that there are a tremendous number of assumptions being made in each step. You don't know how the death tax law is going to change or even what the death tax rates will be. You don't know whether you will still have the full marital deduction or a $600,000 unified credit. You don't know what the growth rate of money is going to be or how your assets will change in value. You don't know what your expenses and debts are likely to be. In short, there are many assumptions which necessarily cause this exercise to produce only a best guess. However, it is the best guess that you can make. Having considered these matters, you may want to purchase additional life insurance. If, at the time the taxes are due, it looks as though the estate will have substantial liquidity because of cash, publicly traded securities, a buy-sell agreement for closely held stock, or from any other source, then the money to pay these taxes may not have to be raised through life insurance. It may be possible simply to sell the securities. They will have a date-of-death basis even if they were bought for much less years ago, so there should be little or no capital gains tax.

On the other hand, your assets may be highly illiquid, or held in forms not readily converted to cash, such as stock in closely held companies and real estate. In this case, it may be desirable to have more life insurance to provide cash to pay the taxes due within nine months of your death. Some people purchase enough life insurance to pay all of the death taxes, because they want to preserve their real estate, stocks, bonds, and other investments and leave their entire estate to their children "intact."

Another factor to consider is the financial needs of your spouse following your death. If your spouse has substantial assets or a job that provides a sufficient income for your family, the need for insurance on your life decreases.

All in all, the question of how much life insurance to have cannot be readily reduced to rules of thumb. The questions in this chapter and their answers will lead you to a general sense of how much life insurance you need. At that point, you are better equipped to make a decision on the amount of life insurance than you would have been in trying to apply an arbitrary rule of thumb. Even after making the review and considering all the factors in determining how much life insurance seems appropriate, don't forget that just as your life changes so does your need for the life insurance. Check back on your assumptions every three or five years. Are there changes in family situations or personal financial situations? What about inflation? Is there more discretionary money so that the cost of buying some additional life insurance wouldn't cut into the family budget in such a large way?

Summary

We have discussed most of the different types of life insurance — whole life, term life, universal life, single premium, and second-to-die. You have seen how life insurance is treated for income tax purposes and death tax purposes. You also have seen a step-by-step plan for how to determine how much life insurance you need. Life insurance can be confusing for the layman, but it offers liquidity and security at a time when these two items can be very important to those left behind.

In this chapter, you will learn:

- what probate is
- what is necessary to get probate started
- why it takes so long
- who can be a personal representative
- what the duties of personal representatives (executors) are
- how creditors' claims and distributions are handled

17

PROBATE

So much has been said about probate, it seems appropriate to include a short chapter on it in this book on estate planning. Estate planning looks to the probate process and what happens during administration of a person's estate. You should have a passing familiarity with what happens in probate if you are to have full understanding of estate planning for the Tennessean.

Probate in Tennessee differs from probate in many states in that the procedure and even the philosophy in Tennessee reflects a feeling that the process should be free of judicial activism. This feeling is much stronger here than in other states. The greater weight of the responsibility for the administration of a person's estate falls on the personal representative and, if the personal representative chooses to hire an attorney, on the attorney for the estate. These are the persons responsible for seeing that the deceased person's assets are handled as he or she wished. The "personal representative" is appointed by the court to "represent" the "person" who has died. The personal representative is also called an "executor" if there is a will, and an "administrator" if the person died without a will.

Probate includes gathering together the assets of the person who has died, paying his or her bills, filing tax returns, and other things that must be done. Actually, the word probate comes from a Latin word meaning "to prove." Its most narrow definition is the

203

action of proving the will is the final will of the deceased person or, alternatively, proving that he or she died without a will. In general terms, however, probate is the entire process, that is, the handling of the estate with the lawyers and courts from the beginning of the court proceeding through the final distribution of the assets to the beneficiaries and the closing of the estate.

We will talk about what actually happens on a day-to-day basis in a typical estate. What do the personal representatives do? What do the attorneys do? What do the judges do? What is the point of all this?

Initial Conference with Attorney

Let us take what might be called a typical estate of a man we will call Adam Nemo. We begin with a call to the attorney's office telling us that Mr. Nemo has passed away. One of the children is calling. She has come down to be with her mother, the widow. She wants to know what to do. In many instances, the response will be to take care of family matters and notify friends and relatives who should receive word of Mr. Nemo's death. When it is convenient for the family, Mrs. Nemo and the children should meet with the attorney to discuss the estate. The attorney will probably tell them also that when they come in, they should bring with them a general idea of the assets and Mr. Nemo's will.

The family comes to the attorney's office, bringing the will, a number of papers reflecting financial information, and a host of questions. While it is high drama and beloved by movie producers and television series, more often than not the attorney does not formally gather the family together and in solemn tones "read the will." Usually, the family has already read the will. They know exactly what it says. The will is written in reasonably good English and they have no difficulty understanding what Mr. Nemo had to say and what he wanted to have done with his assets. Their concerns now are, "What do we do next? How long will this take and how much will it cost?"

Petition for Administration and Order Admitting Will to Probate and Appointing Personal Representative

Commencement of the estate is usually done with the filing of the Petition for Administration. This probate court form and other typical probate court forms discussed in the following paragraphs are in Appendix L. The petition says that Mr. Nemo has died, states his residence, and names his next of kin. It requests that Mrs. Nemo, the person named in his will, be appointed as the personal representative and gives the court an idea of the general nature of the assets and whether the estate is worth more than $600,000 or less (to let the court know whether death tax returns will be due the state and federal governments, or if the simpler Tennessee "short form" return will be required).

Oath of Personal Representative

The court will require an oath of the personal representative. The oath is a solemn assurance that the person seeking to be personal representative will be diligent in administering the estate. If the personal representative lives outside the state of Tennessee, he or she will usually be permitted to serve alone, without the requirement that an in-state person be appointed as well; however, the court will require that the out-of-state personal representative sign a designation of the secretary of state of Tennessee as a resident agent. The designation of resident agent is the person who will be served with any legal papers when the personal representative is not located in Tennessee.

Letters of Administration

When the petition and oath are filed, together with the original will and the court filing fee of approximately $125, the court will review the petition, the oath, and the will, and if satisfied that everything seems to be correct, will enter an order directing that the will be admitted as the Last Will and Testament of Mr. Nemo. The court will further direct that Letters of Administration be issued to Mrs. Nemo as the personal representative after she posts a bond. A bonding company agrees to post a bond that Mrs. Nemo will carry out her duties as personal representative; if she does not and steals the money, the bonding company will make up the loss. In most cases, courts will waive the filing of a fiduciary bond if the will directs that no bond be posted. If a person dies without a will, the courts will require a bond, which significantly increases the cost of administering the estate; however, if all the beneficiaries of the estate are adults and they agree to waive a bond, the courts will usually excuse the bond requirement even in a case in which there is no will. Since Mr. Nemo's will waives bond, the court will not require a bond and Letters of Administration are issued to Mrs. Nemo.

Letters of Administration are formal authorizations from the court addressed to any person who has assets or financial information concerning Mr. Nemo, directing them to give this information to the person appointed as his personal representative — in this case, Mrs. Nemo. This gives the personal representative full authority to find all assets, and to request bank accounts or other information necessary to gather together (marshal) the assets. In many instances, the attorney will ask the personal representative to sign a form directed to any person having information concerning Mr. Nemo's assets asking that they release this information to a law firm or attorney. This will save the personal representative a great deal of time. If general inquiries are made, the personal representative by signing this form can have the attorney write the various financial institutions and request that they respond in writing, providing information concerning bank accounts, savings accounts, certificates of deposit, loans outstanding, or any other information that is necessary. Once the court issues the Letters of Administration, the estate is formally opened and the personal representative is in business.

Proof of Service and Notice of Administration

After the personal representative is appointed, a Notice to Creditors will appear in the paper or be otherwise published. The purpose of the Notice to Creditors is to tell creditors that if they have any claims against the estate, they should file a claim form with the court within six months advising the personal representative of their claim. If the creditors are notified that they should file such a claim and fail to do so, they may be barred for failure to file a claim within six months, as provided in the notice.

These notices are typically published in the newspaper so that creditors get as much notice as possible. The United States Supreme Court has ruled that the personal representative has a duty to creditors, or people who may be creditors, to tell these creditors that the person has died, that the creditor should file a claim in court, and that failure to file a claim may cause it to be barred. Before the estate can be closed, the personal representative must file an affidavit with the court stating that he or she has personally notified all potential creditors of this information.

The personal representative must also file an affidavit with the court stating that a copy of the will has been provided to all people who are named in the will as beneficiaries, and that the will has been admitted by the court as the Last Will and Testament and that the estate is being administered. If anyone objects to the will or objects to the person serving as personal representative, the objecting person has two years following the date the Order of Probate was entered in which to object formally to the validity of the will or to the appointment of the personal representative. If he or she fails to do so within two years, it will be nearly impossible later to start a will contest or similar action.

Inventory and Proof of Service of Inventory

While the Notice to Creditors' six-month period is running, the diligent personal representative will compile a list of Mr. Nemo's assets and liabilities, at least to the best extent possible. The list of assets will come from Mr. Nemo's financial papers. They will also come from responses from financial institutions with whom he had dealt as well as other sources such as business associates. Once the information concerning financial assets is available, an Inventory will be filed with the court. The Inventory will list all property other than real estate, which would include items such as furniture, furnishings, automobiles, bank accounts, stocks, bonds, and other types of assets. It is worth noting again here that this Inventory is filed with the court, and it is available to people who might want to read it just to find out "what he was worth." Like the bond requirement, however, if the will waives the requirement of the filing of the Inventory, or if all the beneficiaries of the estate are adults and they agree to waive this requirement after death, then no Inventory will normally be required by the courts.

Personal Representative's Proof of Claim

After the six-month Notice to Creditors' period has ended, the Inventory will have been filed and the personal representative and the attorney will know the approximate value of the assets in the estate and will also know the claims outstanding in the estate. If the estate is worth less than $600,000, a "short form" Tennessee inheritance tax return will be due (although there will almost never be any inheritance tax owed). Once the short form is filed with the state, a Non-Taxable Certificate is issued to the personal representative, who must file the certificate with the court before the estate can be closed. The next steps are to pay off creditors and to distribute the estate to the beneficiaries. In many instances, this takes seven or eight months. But it frequently takes longer than this because of factors beyond the control of the attorney or personal representative. If Mr. Nemo's assets exceed $600,000, a long-form Tennessee inheritance tax return and a federal estate tax return must both be filed, death taxes may be due, and either or both governments may audit their respective returns.

The initial petition requires the personal representative to tell the court whether or not he or she believes that the estate is greater than $600,000. The reason for this is so that the court will check and ask the personal representative to close the estate if 15 months have passed since the probate estate was started. If there is an estate tax return to be filed, the court knows that it may be well over 18 months from the date of death before the personal representative can close the estate because the state and the federal governments must both review and accept the returns and clear the estate of liability for any further death taxes.

Frequently, if there are dollar gifts in the will, these will be taken care of at the end of the six-month period, leaving a substantial reserve to cover contingencies that might arise for the payment of the death taxes. The personal representative may be personally liable for unpaid federal taxes on the federal estate tax return and will want to be sure there are plenty of assets in the estate to cover any tax liabilities. These tax liabilities might also include past unpaid income taxes, withholding taxes, or inheritance or estate taxes. The personal representative may also sell assets. Sometimes, if the person who has died does not have a surviving spouse, the children will want to sell the real estate in Tennessee to raise cash and reduce the expense of maintaining the property. They frequently will discuss this with the attorney and contact a real estate broker in order to get the property on the market early during the administration of the estate.

Accountings

Since the personal representative is handling other people's money, he or she has to prepare accountings. Accountings can be handled in one of two ways: formal, court accountings listing all assets, receipts and disbursements, and simplified accountings. Many attorneys prefer simplified accountings which show beneficiaries the inventory values, income coming in, payments going out and the remaining balance available for distribution to the beneficiaries. These informal accountings cover all the information which most of the beneficiaries would like to have in order to be assured that the estate has in fact been properly handled. Once they receive this information, if they are entirely satisfied with the way the estate has been managed, they may file a consent saying that they have received an accounting, that they are satisfied with the accounting which they received, and that they waive any formal court accounting. Alternatively, the will can excuse the requirement of formal accountings as well. Such simple accountings are used whenever possible in the majority of estates because it is a straightforward way to handle accountings and it speeds up the settlement of the estate. (The courts vary throughout the state of Tennessee in their willingness to allow estates to be closed without accountings, so you should check with your attorney to find out how the court in your county handles the requirement to produce a formal accounting in order to close the estate.)

If the beneficiaries are not satisfied for any reason, the personal representative must file a formal accounting in court and the beneficiaries will be given copies of the accounting and told to review it and to file any objections. The court reviews the objections and can require the personal representative to respond to concerns that the beneficiaries have as to the administration of the estate, and particularly regarding the accounting of the personal representative. In our case, Mrs. Nemo was the sole beneficiary. As such, she did not have to file any accounting at all if she did not wish to.

Final Distribution; Petition to Close; Order Closing the Estate

Once the beneficiaries are satisfied with the proceedings in the estate, the personal representative will make a distribution of the remaining assets to the beneficiaries. The beneficiaries will file their receipts and waivers as to further proceedings. The beneficiaries sign a Receipt and Release stating that they are satisfied with the way the estate has been handled, that they have received their share of the estate, and that they are content that the estate may now be closed. The personal representative, upon receiving these Receipts from beneficiaries, files the Petition to Close. This shows that the interested parties have all consented to the way the estate has been handled and asks that the personal representative be discharged from further responsibility in connection with the estate. The judge typically enters these orders after reviewing the file. The judge wants to be satisfied with everything that has taken place.

Summary

As we have described it, the probate process makes sense and sounds fairly simple. Why then does it take so long and cost so much? Actually, the probate part of handling an estate shouldn't cost so much. What takes a lot of time and causes some of the expense are all the related matters that come up in handling a person's estate. There are hundreds of questions that come up regarding income taxes, estate taxes, cash needs, how to handle particular assets, what to do about Social Security, joint property, Medicare, Blue Cross/Blue Shield, problems with beneficiaries, and all the other complexities with which human life is so richly woven.

CONCLUSION

We've come a long way. We started in the beginning to talk about estate planning for the Tennessean. That estate planning process began with thinking about estate planning, not only in the context of dollars and cents, but also in terms of individuals and what would be best for them. We have covered a great deal of ground and all of it, hopefully, rather less painfully than is suggested by the complexities involved in estate planning. This is one of the more complex areas of the law. It deals with the highly technical aspects of the Internal Revenue Code and yet at the same time with the very vague and generalized questions of what is best for all concerned.

We worked through the usual documents of wills, powers of attorney, living wills, and living trusts. Then we gradually took on more complicated areas of estate, inheritance and gift taxes, and charitable giving. We moved even further through life insurance, probate, joint property and estate planning, and on to charitable remainder trusts, irrevocable life insurance trusts, and some of the less common estate planning documents. To be sure, there are still more exotic aspects of estate planning, which is a very fluid and, at times, rapidly changing discipline.

New concepts and new documents appear on the scene and yet these are rarely the magic bullet everyone is looking for. It is unlikely that such a magic bullet will ever be invented. Occasionally, a new concept will be discovered and many wonderful qualities will be attributed to it. It pays to stop and carefully analyze these new concepts. Almost always, they turn out to be not quite as good as originally described, and yet there may be strong reasons for using them. Living trusts are a good example — neither a quack remedy nor a miracle cure.

When considering estate planning, it is always a good idea to consult a qualified, professional person. Too much money is riding on the outcome to try to do things inexpensively or on your own. Qualified estate planning help is one of the best bargains going. Almost always, a qualified estate planning professional can show you ways that will save you money, save your beneficiaries money and, at the same time, set the stage so that your assets can be managed and transferred to your ultimate beneficiaries in a way that meets your wishes and reflects your personal goals and philosophy.

It is our hope that, with the tools described in this book, Tennesseans will be well-equipped to go forward with a clear understanding of the basic concepts of estate planning and to apply these concepts to their own lives. There will be less mystery and more satisfaction with the entire process of transmitting wealth from one generation to another — responsibly, quickly, and with a minimum of expense and red tape.

CONFIDENTIAL ESTATE PLANNING QUESTIONNAIRE

Date: _____

I.　FAMILY DATA

YOURSELF:

Full Name: _____ Social Security No.: _____
Home Address: _____ Phone: _____
Business Address: _____ Phone: _____
Details on all prior marriages: _____
Occupation: _____

YOUR SPOUSE:

Full Name: _____ Social Security No.: _____
Home Address: _____ Phone: _____
Business Address: _____ Phone: _____
County of Residence: _____ Date, Place of Birth, Citizenship: _____
Details on all prior marriages: _____
Occupation: _____

CHILDREN:　Names, Dates of Birth, City and State of Residence: _____
_____
_____

CHILDREN OF PRIOR MARRIAGES:　Names & Dates of Birth, Custodial Parent:_____
_____

PARENTS (FOR EACH SPOUSE):　Names, Dates of Birth and Death:_____
_____
_____

II.　ESTATE PLANNING DECISIONS:　Remember, you may name more than one person to serve in any position (e.g., Co-Executors).

A.　EXECUTOR:

	For Your Estate (name, city, state)	For Spouse's Estate (name, city, state)
Executor:	_____	_____
1st Successor:	_____	_____
2nd Successor:	_____	_____

B.　TRUSTEE(S): (To manage assets of minor children/spouse/other relatives)

	For Your Estate (name, city, state)	For Spouse's Estate (name, city, state)
Trustee:	_____	_____
1st Successor:	_____	_____
2nd Successor:	_____	_____

C.　GUARDIAN(S):

	For Your Estate (name, city, state)	For Spouse's Estate (name, city, state)
Guardian:	_____	_____
1st Successor:	_____	_____
2nd Successor:	_____	_____

III.　ESTATE PLANNING GOALS:　Please describe your overall estate planning goals.
_____
_____

IV. **ITEMS TO BRING WITH YOU WHEN YOU COME IN FOR OUR CONFERENCE:**
1. A copy of your most recent Will and any Codicil(s)
2. Copies of all Divorce Decrees/Settlement Agreements
3. Copies of all prior Gift Tax Returns
4. A copy of your Federal Tax Return for the last year
5. Copies of any Buy-Sell Agreements you have signed
6. A copy of any Pre-Nuptial Agreement you have signed
7. Copies of any trusts that have been created by or for you
8. Copies of deeds <u>and</u> tax receipts to any real property you own.

V. **FINANCIAL DATA**

A. REAL ESTATE*

	Identification (map & parcel #)	Market Value	Mortgage/Lien	Owner Joint? Wife? Husband?
Principal residence				
Other residences				
Realty Partnerships				
Rental Realty				
Farms				

*Please locate the deeds and tax receipts.

B. STOCKS & BONDS

Publicly Traded				
Closely held				

(If closely held, what percentage owned? _____)

C. PERSONAL PROPERTY

Bank Accounts				
CDs				
Annuities				
Notes Receivable				
Autos, Boats				
Furn/Jewelry/Silver				
Partnerships				
Business Property				
Interests in Trusts				
Other				

D. INSURANCE

YOU: LIFE INSURANCE ON YOUR LIFE (Please list all policies on your life, whether owned by you, your spouse, others or your business.)

Policy Type	Owner	Face Value	Mortgage/Lien	Beneficiary

OTHER INSURANCE (Include disability, accident and health): _____

SPOUSE: LIFE INSURANCE ON YOUR SPOUSE'S LIFE (Please list all policies on your life, whether owned by you, your spouse, others or your business.)

Policy Type	Owner	Face Value	Mortgage/Lien	Beneficiary

OTHER INSURANCE (Include disability, accident and health): _____

E. RETIREMENT PLAN ASSETS

Identification   Current Value   Owner   Beneficiary
_____   _____   _____   _____
_____   _____   _____   _____

F. TOTAL LIABILITIES - Current Balances Due

Mortgages: _____
Notes Payable: _____
Divorce Obligations: _____

G. ESTIMATED WORTH OF SPOUSES' COMBINED ESTATES AFTER DEATH

Add market
values from A - E above and subtract liabilities: _____

_____   _____
SIGNATURE   SIGNATURE

© Anne M. McKinney, P.C. 1995

GENEALOGICAL CHART

Paternal   Maternal

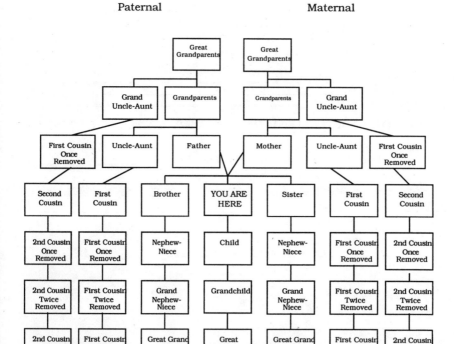

ADMINISTRATIVE POWERS OF FIDUCIARIES

35-50-110. Specifically enumerated fiduciary powers which may be incorporated by reference. — Without diminution or restriction of the powers vested in the fiduciary by law, or elsewhere in this instrument, and subject to all other provisions of this instrument, the fiduciary, without the necessity of procuring any judicial authorization therefor, or approval thereof, shall be vested with, and in the application of such fiduciary's best judgment and discretion in behalf of the beneficiaries of this instrument shall be authorized to exercise, the powers hereunder specifically enumerated:

(1) In behalf of my estate, to join my spouse (if living), or the personal representative of the estate of my spouse (if deceased), in the execution and filing of a joint income tax return to the United States, or to the state of Tennessee, or any other governmental taxing authority (or a joint gift tax return, if and when such a joint return is authorized by law), if the fiduciary, in the exercise of the fiduciary's best judgment, believes such action to be for the best interests of my estate, or will result in a benefit to my spouse (or the estate of my spouse) exceeding in amount any monetary loss to my estate which may be caused thereby;

(2) To continue, to the extent and so long as in the exercise of the fiduciary's best judgment it is advisable and for the best interests of my estate so to do, the operation or participation in the operation of any farming, manufacturing, mercantile and/or other business activity or enterprise in which at the time of my death I am engaged, either alone or in unincorporated association with others;

(3) In behalf of my estate, to perform any and all valid executory contracts to which at the time of my death I am a party, and which at the time of my death have not been fully performed by me, and to discharge all obligations of my estate arising under or by reason of such contracts;

(4) Pending the administration of my estate, to permit any beneficiary or beneficiaries of this will to have the use, possession and enjoyment, without charge made therefor (and without the fiduciary thereby relinquishing control thereof), of any real property or tangible personal property of my estate which, upon completion of the administration of my estate, will be distributable to such beneficiary or beneficiaries when, if, and to the extent that, such action will not adversely affect the rights and interests of any creditor of my estate, and in the judgment of the fiduciary it is appropriate that such beneficiary or beneficiaries have the use and enjoyment of such property, notwithstanding that it may be subjected to depreciation in value by reason of such use. The exercise of this power will not constitute a distribution of the property with respect to which it is exercised; and, whether or not exercised, neither the power nor the exercise thereof shall be deemed a constructive or actual distribution of the property to which it relates;

(5) During the fiduciary's administration of the estate, and subject to all the other provisions of this instrument, to receive and receipt for all of the assets of the estate, and to have exclusive possession and control thereof;

(6) By public or private sale or sales, and for such consideration, on such terms and subject to such conditions (if any) as in the judgment of the fiduciary are for the best interests of the estate and the beneficiaries thereof, to sell, assign, transfer, convey, or exchange any real or personal property of the estate, or the estate's undivided interest in such property, or any specific part of or interest therein (including, but not limited to, standing timber, rock, gravel, sand, growing crops, oil, gas and other minerals or mineral rights or interests), and to grant easements on real property of the estate, and to participate in the partition of real or personal property in which the estate has an undivided interest; and to accomplish any such transactions by contracts, endorsements, assignments, bills of sale, deeds or other appropriate written instruments executed and delivered by the fiduciary in behalf of the estate, and to acknowledge the execution of such instruments in the manner provided by law for the acknowledgment of the execution of deeds when such acknowledgments are required or appropriate;

(7) For such consideration, on such terms and subject to such conditions (if any) as in the judgment of the fiduciary are for the best interests of the estate and the beneficiaries thereof, to lease, for terms which may exceed the duration of the

estate, any real or tangible personal property of the estate, or any specific parts thereof or interests therein (including, but not limited to, oil, gas and other mineral leases); and to accomplish such leases by appropriate written instruments executed and delivered by the fiduciary in behalf of the estate, and acknowledge the execution of such instruments in the manner provided by law for the acknowledgment of the execution of deeds when such acknowledgments are required or appropriate;

(8)   In behalf of the estate, borrow money; evidence such loans by promissory notes or other evidences of indebtedness signed by the fiduciary in the fiduciary's fiduciary capacity, to be binding upon the assets of the estate but not upon the fiduciary in the fiduciary's individual capacity; secure such loans by assigning or pledging personal property of the estate or by mortgages or deeds of trust or other appropriate instruments imposing liens upon real property or tangible personal property of the estate; and repay such loans, including principal and interest due thereon;

(9)   In behalf of the estate, borrow money from the fiduciary in the fiduciary's individual capacity and secure such loans in the same manner as though they were made by a third person;

(10)   Enter into contracts binding upon the estate (but not upon the fiduciary in the fiduciary's individual capacity) which are reasonably incident to the administration of the estate, and which the fiduciary in the exercise of the fiduciary's best judgment believes to be for the best interests of the estate;

(11)   Settle, by compromise or otherwise, claims or demands against the estate, or held in behalf of the estate;

(12)   Release and satisfy of record, in whole or in part, and enter of record credits upon, any mortgage or other lien constituting an asset of the estate;

(13)   Abandon and charge off as worthless, in whole or in part, claims or demands held by or in behalf of the estate which, in the judgment of the fiduciary, are in whole or in part uncollectible;

(14)   Pay taxes and excises lawfully chargeable against the assets of the estate which are in the possession or under the control of the fiduciary, including, but not limited to, *ad valorem* taxes upon real and personal property of the estate which became due and payable prior to such property coming into the hands of the fiduciary, or which become due and payable while such property remains in the fiduciary's possession or under the fiduciary's control; excluding, however, income taxes payable by distributees, assessed with respect to income which has been distributed by the fiduciary pursuant to the provisions of this instrument;

(15)   Repair and maintain in good condition real and tangible personal property of the estate so long as such property remains in the possession or under the control of the fiduciary;

(16)   Invest liquid assets of the estate, and from time to time exchange or liquidate and reinvest such assets, pending distribution thereof, if and when such investments in the judgment of the fiduciary will not impede or delay distribution thereof pursuant to the provisions of this instrument or as otherwise by law required, and in the judgment of the fiduciary are advisable and for the best interests of the estate and the beneficiaries thereof. In making such investments the fiduciary shall be guided by the "Prudent Man Rule" as authorized and defined in § 35-3-117; and the investments thus authorized shall be understood to include, but not to be limited to, loans secured by mortgages, or liens otherwise imposed, upon real or personal property;

(17)   Subject to the making and keeping of appropriate records with respect thereto, which will at all times clearly identify the equitable rights and interests of the estate therein, invest funds of the estate in undivided interests in negotiable or nonnegotiable securities, or other assets, the remaining undivided interests in which are held by the fiduciary in a fiduciary capacity for the use and benefit of other beneficiaries;

(18)   Retain investments which initially come into the hands of the fiduciary among the assets of the estate, without liability for loss or depreciation or diminution in value resulting from such retention, so long as in the judgment of the fiduciary it is not clearly for the best interests of the estate, and the distributees thereof, that such investments be liquidated, although such investments may not be productive of income or otherwise may not be such as the fiduciary would be authorized to make;

(19)   At any time and from time to time, keep all or any portion of the estate in liquid form, uninvested, for such time as the fiduciary may deem advisable, without liability for any loss of income occasioned by so doing;

(20) Deposit funds of the trust in one (1) or more accounts carried by the fiduciary, in a clearly specified fiduciary capacity, in any one (1) or more banks and/or trust companies whose deposits are insured under the provisions of the Federal Deposit Insurance Act as now constituted or as the same may be hereafter amended; and if the fiduciary be itself a bank or a trust company, and is otherwise qualified, the fiduciary may serve as such depository;

(21) Deposit for safekeeping with any bank or trust company (including the fiduciary itself if the fiduciary be such a bank or trust company) any negotiable or nonnegotiable securities or other documents constituting assets or records of the estate;

(22) Bring and prosecute or defend actions at law or in equity for the protection of the assets or interests of the estate or for the protection or enforcement of the provisions of this instrument;

(23) Employ attorneys, accountants or other persons whose services may be necessary or advisable, in the judgment of the fiduciary, to advise or assist the fiduciary in the discharge of the fiduciary's duties, or in the conduct of any business constituting an asset of the estate, or in the management, maintenance, improvement, preservation or protection of any property of the estate, or otherwise in the exercise of any powers vested in the fiduciary;

(24) Procure and pay premiums on policies of insurance to protect the estate, or any of the assets thereof, against liability for personal injuries or property damage, or against loss or damage by reason of fire, windstorm, collision, theft, embezzlement or other hazards against which such insurance is normally carried in connection with activities or on properties such as those with respect to which the fiduciary procures such insurance;

(25) Allocate items of receipts or disbursements to either corpus or income of the estate, as the fiduciary in the exercise of the fiduciary's best judgment and discretion deems to be proper, without thereby doing violence to clearly established and generally recognized principles of accounting;

(26) In behalf of the estate, purchase or otherwise lawfully acquire real or personal property, or undivided interests therein, the ownership of which in the judgment of the fiduciary, will be advantageous to the estate, and the beneficiary or beneficiaries thereof;

(27) Construct improvements on real property of the estate, or remove or otherwise dispose of such improvements, when such action is in the judgment of the fiduciary advisable and for the best interests of the estate;

(28) Exercise in person or by proxy (with or without a power of substitution vested in the proxy) all voting rights incident to the ownership of corporate stock or the other securities constituting assets of the estate; and exercise all other rights and privileges incident to the ownership of such securities, including, but not limited to, the right to sell, exchange, endorse or otherwise transfer such securities, consent to (or oppose) reorganizations consolidations, mergers or other proposed corporate actions by the issuer of such securities, exercise or decline to exercise options to purchase additional shares or units of such securities or of related securities, and pay all assessments or other expenses necessary (in the judgment of the fiduciary) for the protection of such securities or of the value thereof;

(29) Employ any bank or trust company to serve as custodian of any securities constituting assets of the estate, and cause such securities (if they are nonassessable) to be registered in the name of such custodian or of its nominee, without disclosure that they are held in a fiduciary capacity; authorize such bank or trust company, as agent and in behalf of the fiduciary, to collect, receive and receipt for income derived from such securities, or the proceeds of sales, assignments or exchanges thereof made by authority and under the direction of the fiduciary, and to remit to the fiduciary such income or other proceeds derived from the securities; and pay to such custodian reasonable and customary charges made by it for the performance of such services; provided that any such action taken by the fiduciary shall not increase, decrease or otherwise affect the fiduciary's liability, responsibility or accountability with respect to such securities;

(30) Register nonassessable securities constituting assets of the estate in the name of the fiduciary or of the fiduciary's nominee, without disclosure that such securities are held in a fiduciary capacity, or hold such securities unregistered or otherwise in such form that the title thereto will pass by delivery, without, in any

such case, increasing, decreasing or otherwise affecting the fiduciary's liability, responsibility or accountability with respect to such securities;

(31) In making distribution of capital assets of the estate to distributees thereof under the provisions of this instrument, to make such distribution in kind or in cash, or partially in kind and partially in cash, as the fiduciary finds to be most practicable and for the best interests of the distributees; distribute real property to two (2) or more distributees thereof in division, or to partition such real property for the purpose of distribution thereof, as the fiduciary in the exercise of the fiduciary's best judgment finds to be most practicable and for the best interests of the distributees; and determine the value of capital assets for the purpose of making distribution thereof if and when there be more than one (1) distributee thereof, which determination shall be binding upon the distributees unless clearly capricious, erroneous and inequitable;

(32) (A) (i) Inspect and monitor property to which the fiduciary takes legal title (including interests in sole proprietorships, partnerships, or corporations and any assets owned by such business enterprises) for the purpose of determining compliance with environmental laws affecting such property, and respond or take any other action necessary to prevent, abate or clean up, on behalf of the trust or estate as shall be necessary, before or after the initiation of enforcement action by any governmental body, any actual or threatened violation of any environmental laws affecting property held by the fiduciary relating to hazardous substances or environmental laws;

(ii) Refuse to accept property in trust if the fiduciary determines that any property to be donated to a trust estate is contaminated by any hazardous substances, or such property is being used or has been used for any activities, directly or indirectly involving hazardous substances, which could result in liability to the trust or estate or otherwise impair the value of the assets held therein;

(iii) Settle or compromise, at any time, any and all claims against the estate or trust which may be asserted by any governmental body or private party involving the alleged violation of any environmental laws affecting property held in the estate or trust;

(iv) Disclaim any power granted by any document or any statute or rule of law which, in the sole discretion of the fiduciary, may cause the fiduciary to incur personal liability under any environmental laws; and

(v) Decline to serve as fiduciary if the fiduciary reasonably believes that there is or may be a conflict of interest between it in its fiduciary capacity and in its individual capacity because of potential claims or liabilities which may be asserted against it on behalf of the estate or trust resulting from the type or condition of assets held therein;

(B) (i) The fiduciary shall be entitled to charge the cost for any inspection, insurance, review, abatement, response or cleanup, or any other remedial action, as authorized in this subdivision (32), against the income or principal of the estate or trust and shall not be personally responsible therefor. The fiduciary shall not be personally liable to any beneficiary or any other party for any decrease in value or exhaustion of assets in the estate or trust by reason of the fiduciary's compliance with any environmental laws, specifically including any reporting requirements under such laws;

(ii) While acting in good faith and according to traditional fiduciary standards, the fiduciary shall not be considered an "owner," "operator" or other party otherwise liable for violation of environmental laws unless the fiduciary has actually caused or contributed to such violation;

(C) For the purposes of this subdivision (32), "hazardous substances" means any substance defined as hazardous or toxic or otherwise regulated by any federal, state or local law, rule or regulation relating to the protection of the environment or human health. Such laws are referred to in this subdivision as "environmental laws"; and

(33) Do any and all other things, not in violation of any other terms of this instrument, which, in the judgment of the fiduciary, are necessary or appropriate for the proper management, investment and distribution of the assets of the estate in accordance with the provisions of this instrument, and in such fiduciary's judgment are for the best interests of the estate and its beneficiaries. [Acts 1963, ch. 110, § 3; T.C.A. § 35-618; Acts 1991, ch. 182, § 2.]

Durable Financial Power of Attorney
of
John Doe

KNOW ALL MEN BY THESE PRESENTS:

    1.   **Power of Attorney.** That I, John Doe, of Knox County, Tennessee, do hereby make, constitute and appoint Jane Doe, of Knox County, Tennessee, as my true and lawful attorney-in-fact, but if Jane Doe should be or become unable or unwilling to serve as my attorney-in-fact, then I do hereby make, constitute and appoint Daughter Doe, of Knox County, Tennessee, to act as my successor attorney-in-fact for me and in my name, place and stead and on behalf of me for my use and benefit to do each of the following things:

    (a)   **General Powers.** Generally to do, sign, or perform in my name, place and stead any act, deed, matter, or thing whatsoever, that ought to be done, signed, or performed, or that, in the opinion of the attorney-in-fact ought to be done, signed, or performed in and about the premises, of every nature and kind whatsoever, to all intents and purposes whatsoever, as fully and effectually as I could do if I were personally present and acting. The enumeration of specific powers hereunder shall not in any way limit the general powers conferred herein;

    (b)   **Monies.** To receive from or disburse to any source whatever monies through checking or savings or other accounts or otherwise, to endorse, sign and issue checks, withdrawal receipts, or any other instrument, and to open or close any accounts in my name alone or jointly with any other person;

    (c)   **Real and Personal Property.** To buy, sell, lease, alter, maintain, pledge, or in any way deal with real and personal property and to sign each instrument necessary or advisable to complete any real or personal property transaction, including, but not limited to, deeds, deeds of trust, closing statements, options, notes, and bills of sale;

    (d)   **Tax Returns.** To perform any and all acts that I might perform with respect to any and all federal, state, local and foreign taxes, for prior tax years as well as for tax years ending subsequent to the date of this Power of Attorney, including, but not limited to, the power (i) to make, execute and file returns, amended returns, powers of attorney, and declarations of estimated tax, joint or otherwise, (ii) to represent me before any office of the Internal Revenue Service or other taxing authority with respect to any audit or other tax matter involving any tax year or period, (iii) to receive confidential information, (iv) to receive, endorse, and collect checks refunding taxes, penalties or interest, (v) to execute waivers of restrictions on assessment or collection of deficiencies in tax, (vi) to execute consents extending the statutory period for assessment or collection of taxes, (vii) to execute and prosecute protests or claims for refund or applications for correction of assessed value, (viii) to execute closing agreements, (ix) to prosecute, defend, compromise or settle any tax matter, and (x) to delegate authority to or substitute another agent or attorney respecting any such taxes or tax matters;

    (e)   **Insurance.** To acquire, maintain, cancel, or in any manner deal with any policy of life, accident, disability, hospitalization, medical, or casualty insurance, and to prosecute each claim for benefits due under any policy; however, no such power shall be construed or used to give any incident of ownership to my attorney-in-fact in any life insurance policy on my life or on the life of my attorney-in-fact;

    (f)   **Support.** To provide for my support and protection and for the support and protection of my spouse, including, without limitation, provision for food, lodging, housing, medical services, recreation, and travel;

    (g)   **Safe Deposit Box.** To have free and private access to any safe deposit box in my name, alone or with others, in any bank, including authority to have it drilled, with full right to deposit and withdraw therefrom or to give full discharge therefor;

This Instrument Prepared by
Anne M. McKinney, Attorney at Law
Anne M. McKinney, P.C.
Suite 700, Arnstein Building
505 Market Street
Knoxville, Tennessee 37902

(h) **Money from U.S. or Other Government.** To receive and give receipt for any money or other obligation due or to become due to me from the United States, or any agency or subdivision thereof, and to act as representative payee for any payment to which I may be entitled, and to effect redemption of any bond or other security wherein the United States, or any agency or subdivision thereof, is the obligor or payor, and to give full discharge therefor;

(i) **Agents.** To contract for or employ agents, accountants, advisors, attorneys, and others for services in connection with the performance by said attorney-in-fact of any powers herein;

(j) **Bonds.** To buy United States government bonds redeemable at par in payment of any United States estate taxes imposed at my death;

(k) **Borrowing.** To borrow money for any of the purposes described herein, and to secure such borrowings in such manner as my attorney-in-fact shall deem appropriate, and use any credit card held in my name for any of the purposes described herein;

(l) **Bank Accounts.** To establish, utilize and terminate checking and savings accounts, money market accounts and agency accounts with financial institutions of all kinds, including securities brokers and corporate fiduciaries;

(m) **Investments.** To invest or reinvest each item of money or other property and to lend money or property upon such terms and conditions and with such security as my attorney-in-fact may deem appropriate, or to renew, extend, or modify loans, all in accordance with fiduciary standards of Tennessee Code Annotated § 35-3-117;

(n) **Continue Business.** To engage in and transact any and all lawful business of whatever nature or kind for me and in my name, whether as partner, joint adventurer, stockholder, or in any other manner or form, and to vote any stock or enter voting trusts;

(o) **Dues and Contributions.** To pay dues to any club or organization to which I belong, and to make charitable contributions in fulfillment of any charitable pledge made by me;

(p) **Additions to Revocable Trust.** To transfer any property owned by me to any revocable trust created by me with provisions for my care and support;

(q) **Litigation.** To sue, defend, or compromise suits and legal actions, and to employ counsel in connection with the same, including the power to seek a declaratory judgment interpreting this power of attorney, or a mandatory injunction requiring compliance with the instructions of my attorney-in-fact, or actual and punitive damages against any person failing or refusing to follow the instructions of my attorney-in-fact;

(r) **Reimbursement.** To reimburse the attorney-in-fact or others for all reasonable costs and expenses actually incurred and paid by such person on my behalf;

(s) **Employee Benefit Plan.** To create, contribute to, borrow from and otherwise deal with an employee benefit plan or individual retirement account for my benefit, to select any payment option under any employee benefit plan or individual retirement account in which I am a participant or to change options I have selected, to make "roll-overs" of plan benefits into other retirement plans, and to apply for and receive payments and benefits;

(t) **Execution of Forms.** To execute other power of attorney forms on my behalf which may be required by the Internal Revenue Service, financial or brokerage institutions, or others, naming the attorney-in-fact hereunder as attorney-in-fact for me on such additional forms;

(u) **Release of Information.** To request, receive and review any information, verbal or written, regarding my personal affairs or my physical or mental health, including legal, medical and hospital records, to execute any releases or other documents that may be required in order to obtain such information, and to disclose such information to such persons, organizations, firms or corporations as my attorney-in-fact shall deem appropriate;

(v) **Funeral Arrangements.** To make advance arrangements for my cremation and/or funeral if I have not already done so; and

(w) **Substitutes.** To appoint a substitute or substitutes to perform any of the acts that my attorney-in-fact is by this instrument authorized to perform, with the right to revoke such appointment of a substitute or substitutes at the pleasure of my attorney-in-fact, and any such authorization to a substitute shall not terminate with the death or disability of my attorney-in-fact.

2.   Ratification. I hereby ratify and confirm each act done or caused to be done by my attorney-in-fact in and about the premises by virtue of this power of attorney.

3.   Inducement. For the purpose of inducing any party to act in accordance with the powers granted in this power of attorney, I hereby warrant that if this power of attorney is terminated for any reason whatsoever, I and my successors will save such party harmless from any loss suffered or liability incurred by such party in acting in accordance with this power of attorney prior to the time on which any person has actual notice of such revocation or termination. **Any party may rely upon a photocopy of this Power without production of the original.**

4.   Durability. This power of attorney shall not be affected by any disability, incompetence, or incapacity which I may suffer at any future time or times, whether or not the same shall be adjudicated by any court, it being my intent that the authorizations and powers granted herein shall remain exercisable notwithstanding any such subsequent occurrence.

5.   Exculpation. Under no circumstances shall my attorney-in-fact incur any liability to me for acting or refraining from acting hereunder, except for such attorney's own willful misconduct or gross negligence.

6.   Revocation. This power of attorney shall remain in full force and effect until it is revoked by written notice duly recorded in the Register's Office of Knox County, Tennessee.

7.   Nomination of Conservator. If, after execution of this durable power of attorney, incompetency proceedings are initiated either for my estate or my person, I hereby nominate as my conservator for financial matters for consideration by the Court, Jane Doe, of Knox County, Tennessee, but if Jane Doe should be or become unable or unwilling to act as my conservator, then I hereby nominate Daughter Doe, of Knox County, Tennessee, to serve as my successor conservator.

IN WITNESS WHEREOF, I have signed this power of attorney this ___ day of January, 1996.

_____
John Doe

_____   _____
Witness   Witness

STATE OF TENNESSEE   )
                                                    : ss
COUNTY OF _____   )

On this ___ day of January, 1996, before me, _____ (Notary Public), personally appeared John Doe, _____ and _____, personally known to me (or proved to me on the basis of satisfactory evidence) to be the persons whose names are subscribed to this instrument, and acknowledged that they executed it as their free act and deed.

_____
Notary Public

My Commission Expires:

_____

LIST OF FINANCIAL POWERS

T.C.A. § 34-6-109. Attorney in fact — Powers. — Without diminution or restriction of the powers vested in the attorney at law, by law or elsewhere in the instrument and subject to all other provisions of the instrument, the attorney in fact, without the necessity of procuring any judicial authorization therefor, or approval thereof, shall be vested with and in the application of such attorney in fact's best judgment and discretion on behalf of the principal shall be authorized to exercise the powers specifically enumerated in this section:

(1)   Generally to do, sign or perform in the principal's name, place and stead any act, deed, matter or thing whatsoever, that ought to be done, signed or performed, or that, in the opinion of the attorney in fact, ought to be done, signed or performed in and about the premises, of every nature and kind whatsoever, to all intents and purposes whatsoever, as fully and effectually as the principal could do if personally present and acting. The enumeration of specific powers hereunder shall not in any way limit the general powers conferred herein;

(2)   Receive from or disburse to any source whatever moneys through checking or savings or other accounts or otherwise, endorse, sign and issue checks, withdrawal receipts or any other instrument, and open or close any accounts in the principal's name alone or jointly with any other person;

(3)   Buy, sell, lease, alter, maintain, pledge or in any way deal with real and personal property and sign each instrument necessary or advisable to complete any real or personal property transaction, including, but not limited to, deeds, deeds of trust, closing statements, options, notes and bills of sale;

(4)   Make, sign and file each income, gift, property or any other tax return or declaration required by the United States or any state, county, municipality or other legally constituted authority;

(5)   Acquire, maintain, cancel or in any manner deal with any policy of life, accident, disability, hospitalization, medical or casualty insurance, and prosecute each claim for benefits due under any policy;

(6)   Provide for the support and protection of the principal, or of such principal's spouse, or of any minor child of the principal or of such principal's spouse dependent upon the principal, including, without limitation, provision for food, lodging, housing, medical services, recreation and travel;

(7)   Have free and private access to any safe deposit box in the principal's individual name, alone or with others, in any bank, including authority to have it drilled, with full right to deposit and withdraw therefrom or to give full discharge therefor;

(8)   Receive and give receipt for any money or other obligation due or to become due to the principal from the United States, or any agency or subdivision thereof, and to act as representative payee for any payment to which the principal may be entitled, and effect redemption of any bond or other security wherein the United States, or any agency or subdivision thereof, is the obligor or payor, and give full discharge therefor;

(9)   Contract for or employ agents, accountants, advisors, attorneys and others for services in connection with the performance by the principal's attorney in fact of any powers herein;

(10) Buy United States government bonds redeemable at par in payment of any United States estate taxes imposed at principal's death;

(11) Borrow money for any of the purposes described herein, and secure such borrowings in such manner as the principal's attorney in fact shall deem appropriate, and use any credit card held in the principal's name for any of the purposes described herein;

(12) Establish, utilize, and terminate checking and savings accounts, money market accounts and agency accounts with financial institutions of all kinds, including securities brokers and corporate fiduciaries;

(13) Invest or reinvest each item of money or other property and lend money or property upon such terms and conditions and with such security as the principal's attorney in fact may deem appropriate, or renew, extend, or modify loans, all in accordance with the fiduciary standards of § 35-3-117;

(14) Engage in and transact any and all lawful business of whatever nature or kind for the principal and in the principal's name, whether as partner, joint adventurer, stockholder, or in any other manner or form, and vote any stock or enter voting trusts;

(15) Pay dues to any club or organization to which the principal belongs, and make charitable contributions in fulfillment of any charitable pledge made by the principal;

(16) Transfer any property owned by the principal to any revocable trust created by the principal with provisions for the principal's care and support;

(17) Sue, defend or compromise suits and legal actions, and employ counsel in connection with the same, including the power to seek a declaratory judgment interpreting this power of attorney, or a mandatory injunction requiring compliance with the instructions of the principal's attorney in fact, or actual and punitive damages against any person failing or refusing to follow the instructions of the principal's attorney in fact;

(18) Reimburse the attorney in fact or others for all reasonable costs and expenses actually incurred and paid by such person on behalf of the principal;

(19) Create, contribute to, borrow from and otherwise deal with an employee benefit plan or individual retirement account for the principal's benefit, select any payment option under any employee benefit plan or individual retirement account in which the principal is a participant or change options the principal has selected, make "roll-overs" of plan benefits into other retirement plans, and apply for and receive payments and benefits;

(20) Execute other power of attorney forms on behalf of the principal which may be required by the Internal Revenue Service, financial or brokerage institutions, or others, naming the attorney in fact hereunder as attorney in fact for the principal on such additional forms;

(21) Request, receive and review any information, verbal or written, regarding the principal's personal affairs or the principal's physical or mental health, including legal, medical and hospital records, execute any releases or other documents that may be required in order to obtain such information, and disclose such information to such persons, organizations, firms or corporations as the principal's attorney in fact shall deem appropriate; and

(22) Make advance arrangements for the principal's funeral and burial, including the purchase of a burial plot and marker, if the principal has not already done so. [Acts 1991, ch. 197 § 3.]

Durable General Power of Attorney for Health Care of John Doe

KNOW ALL MEN BY THESE PRESENTS:

1.   **Durable Power of Attorney for Health Care.** That I, John Doe, of Knox County, Tennessee, do hereby make, constitute and appoint Jane Doe of Knox County, Tennessee, as my attorney-in-fact for my health care, but if Jane Doe is unwilling or unable to serve as my attorney-in-fact, then I do hereby nominate Daughter Doe of Knox County, Tennessee, to serve as my successor attorney-in-fact for health care, for me and in my name, place, and stead and on behalf of me for my use and benefit to act for me as follows: My attorney-in-fact is authorized in the sole and absolute discretion of my attorney-in-fact to exercise the powers granted herein relating to matters involving my health and medical care. I desire that my wishes as expressed herein be carried out through the authority given to my attorney-in-fact by this document despite any contrary feelings, beliefs or opinions of members of my family, relatives, friends, conservator, or guardian. In exercising such powers, my attorney-in-fact should first try to discuss with me the specifics of any proposed deci - sion regarding my medical care and treatment if I am able to communicate in any manner, however rudimentary. My attorney-in-fact is further instructed that if I am unable to give an informed consent to a proposed medical treatment, my attorney-in - fact shall give, withhold or withdraw such consent for me based upon any treatment choices that I have expressed while competent, whether under this document or otherwise. If my attorney-in-fact cannot determine the treatment choice I would want made under the circumstances, then my attorney-in-fact should make such choice for me based upon what my attorney-in-fact believes to be in my best interests. Accordingly, without limiting the foregoing general authority my attorney-in-fact is authorized as follows:

(a)   **Gain Access to Medical Records and Other Personal Information.** To request, receive and review any information, verbal or written, regarding my personal affairs or my physical or mental health, including medical and hospital records, and to execute any releases or other documents that may be required in order to obtain such information, and to disclose such information to such persons, organizations, firms or corporations as my attorney-in-fact shall deem appropriate.

(b)   **Employ and Discharge Health Care Personnel.** To employ and dis - charge medical personnel including physicians, psychiatrists, dentists, nurses, and therapists as my attorney-in-fact shall deem necessary for my physical, mental or emotional well-being, and to pay them (or cause to be paid to them) reasonable com - pensation.

(c)   **Give, Withhold or Withdraw Consent to Medical Treatment.** To give or withhold consent to any medical procedure, test or treatment, expressly including surgery and artificial life support, such as respiration, forced feeding, and artificially provided nourishment, fluids, and hydration; to arrange for my hospitalization, conva - lescent care, hospice or home care; to summon paramedics or other emergency medical personnel and seek emergency treatment for me, as my attorney-in-fact shall deem appropriate; and under circumstances in which my attorney-in-fact determines that certain medical procedures, tests or treatments are no longer of any

This Instrument Prepared by
Anne M. McKinney , Attorney at Law
Anne M. McKinney, P.C.
Suite 700, Arnstein Building
505 Market Street
Knoxville, Tennessee 37902

benefit to me or, where the benefits are outweighed by the burdens imposed, to revoke, withdraw, modify or change consent to such procedures, feedings, tests and treatments, as well as hospitalization, convalescent care, hospice or home care which I or my attorney-in-fact may have previously allowed or consented to or which may have been implied due to emergency conditions. My attorney-in-fact's decisions should be guided by taking into account (a) the provisions of this document, (b) any reliable evidence of preferences that I may have expressed on the subject, whether before or after the execution of this document, (c) what my attorney-in-fact believes I would want done in the circumstances if I were able to express myself, and (d) any information given to my attorney-in-fact by the physicians treating me as to my medical diagnosis, and the intrusiveness, pain, risks and side effects associated with the treatment.

(d) **Exercise and Protect My Rights.** To exercise my right of privacy and my right to make decisions regarding my medical treatment even though the exercise of my rights might hasten my death or be against conventional medical advice.

(e) **Authorize Relief From Pain.** To consent to and arrange for the administration of pain-relieving drugs of any kind or other surgical or medical procedures calculated to relieve my pain, including unconventional pain-relief therapies which my attorney-in-fact believes may be helpful, even though such drugs or procedures may lead to permanent physical damage, addiction or hasten the moment of (but not intentionally cause) my death.

(f) **Grant Releases.** To grant, in conjunction with any instructions given under this Article, releases to hospital staff, physicians, nurses and other medical and hospital administrative personnel who act in reliance on instructions given by my attorney-in-fact or who render written opinions to my attorney-in-fact in connection with any matter described in this article from all liability for damages suffered or to be suffered by me; to sign documents titled or purporting to be a "Refusal to Treatment" and "Leaving Hospital Against Medical Advice" as well as any necessary waivers of or releases from liability required by a hospital or physician to implement my wishes regarding medical treatment or non-treatment.

(g) **Provide For My Residence.** To make all necessary arrangements for me at any hospital, hospice, nursing home, convalescent home or similar establishment and to assure that all my essential needs are provided for at such a facility.

(h) **Provide For Companionship.** To provide for such companionship for me as will meet my needs and preferences at a time when I am disabled or otherwise unable to arrange for such companionship myself.

(i) **Consider Medical Directive.** To consider the contents of a Medical Directive, if I have prepared such a Medical Directive and attached it hereto; however, my attorney-in-fact shall not be bound to follow the Medical Directive unless it is in my best interests to do so.

(j) **Make Advance Funeral Arrangements.** To make advance arrangements for my funeral and burial, including the purchase of a burial plot and marker, and such other related arrangements as my attorney-in-fact shall deem appropriate, if I have not already done so myself.

(k) **Make Anatomical Gifts.** To make anatomical gifts which will take effect at my death to such persons and organizations as my attorney-in-fact shall deem appropriate and to execute such papers and do such acts as shall be necessary, appropriate, incidental or convenient in connection with such gifts.

(l) **Authorize An Autopsy.** To authorize an autopsy if my attorney-in-fact deems it appropriate for any reason.

2. Ratification. I hereby ratify and confirm each act done or caused to be done by my attorney-in-fact in and about the premises by virtue of this power of attorney.

3. Inducement. For the purpose of inducing any party to act in accordance with the powers granted in this power of attorney, I hereby warrant that if this power of attorney is terminated for any reason whatsoever, I and my successors will save such party harmless from any loss suffered or liability incurred by such party in acting in accordance with this power of attorney prior to the time on which any person has actual notice of such revocation or termination. **Any party may rely upon a photocopy of this Power without production of the original.**

4. Durability. This power of attorney shall not be affected by any disability, incompetence, or incapacity which I may suffer at any future time or times, whether or not the same shall be adjudicated by any court, it being my intent that the authorizations and powers granted herein shall remain exercisable notwithstanding any such subsequent occurrence.

5. Exculpation. Under no circumstances shall my attorney-in-fact incur any liability to me for acting or refraining from acting hereunder, except for such attorney's own willful misconduct or gross negligence.

6. Revocation. This power of attorney shall remain in full force and effect until it is revoked by written notice duly recorded in the Register's Office of Knox County, Tennessee.

7. Nomination of Conservator For My Person. If, after execution of this durable power of attorney for health care, incompetency proceedings are initiated for my person, I hereby nominate as the conservator of my person for consideration by the Court, Jane Doe, of Knox County, Tennessee. If Jane Doe should be or become unable or unwilling to serve in this capacity, then I nominate as the successor conservator of my person, Daughter Doe of Anderson County, Tennessee.

IN WITNESS WHEREOF, I have signed this power of attorney this _____ day of January, 1996.

_____
John Doe

I declare under penalty of perjury under the laws of Tennessee that the person who signed this document is personally known to me to be the principal; that the principal signed this durable power of attorney in my presence; that the principal appears to be of sound mind and under no duress, fraud, or undue influence; that I am not the person appointed as attorney-in-fact by this document; that I am not a health care provider, an employee of a health care provider, the operator of a health care institution nor an employee of an operator of a health care institution; that I am not related to the principal by blood, marriage, or adoption; that, to the best of my knowledge, I do not, at the present time, have a claim against any portion of the estate of the principal upon the principal's death; and that, to the best of my knowledge, I am not entitled to any part of the estate of the principal upon the death of the principal under a will or codicil thereto now existing, or by operation of law.

_____   _____
Witness   Witness

STATE OF TENNESSEE   )
                          : ss
COUNTY OF _____   )

On this _____ day of January, 1996, before me, _____ (Notary Public), personally appeared John Doe, _____ and _____ (witnesses), personally known to me (or proved to me on the basis of satisfactory evidence) to be the persons whose names are subscribed to this instrument, and acknowledged that they executed it as their free act and deed.

                                                    _____
                                                    Notary Public

My Commission Expires: _____

WARNING TO PERSON EXECUTING THIS DOCUMENT

This is an important legal document. Before executing this document you should know these important facts.

This document gives the person you designate as your agent (the attorney-in-fact) the power to make health care decisions for you. Your agent must act consistently with your desires as stated in this document.

Except as you otherwise specify in this document, this document gives your agent the power to consent to your doctor not giving treatment or stopping treatment necessary to keep you alive.

Notwithstanding this document, you have the right to make medical and other health care decisions for yourself so long as you can give informed consent with respect to the particular decision. In addition, no treatment may be given to you over your objection, and health care necessary to keep you alive may not be stopped or withheld if you object at the time.

This document gives your agent authority to consent, to refuse to consent, or to withdraw consent to any care, treatment, service, or procedure to maintain, diagnose or treat a physical or mental condition. This power is subject to any limitations that you include in this document. You may state in this document any types of treatment that you do not desire. In addition, a court can take away the power of your agent to make health care decisions for you if your agent (1) authorizes anything that is illegal or (2) acts contrary to your desires as stated in this document.

You have the right to revoke the authority of your agent by notifying your agent or your treating physician, hospital or other health care provider orally or in writing of the revocation.

Your agent has the right to examine your medical records and to consent to their disclosure unless you limit this right in this document.

Unless you otherwise specify in this document, this document gives your agent the power after you die to (1) authorize an autopsy, (2) donate your body or parts thereof for transplant or therapeutic or educational or scientific purposes, and (3) direct the disposition of your remains.

If there is anything in this document that you do not understand, you should ask a lawyer to explain it to you.

WARNING PROVIDED BY: **WARNING RECEIVED BY:**

_____   _____
Anne M. McKinney   John Doe
Anne M. McKinney, P.C.

Living Will
of
John Doe

I, John Doe, willfully and voluntarily make known my desire that my dying shall not be artificially prolonged under the circumstance set forth below, and do hereby declare:

If at any time I should have a terminal condition and my attending physician **and one other licensed physician** have determined there is no reasonable medical expectation of recovery and which as a medical probability, will result in my death, regardless of the use or discontinuance of medical treatment implemented for the purpose of sustaining life, or the life process, I direct that medical care be withheld or withdrawn, and that I be permitted to die naturally with only the administration of medications or the performance of any medical procedure deemed necessary to provide me with comfortable care or to alleviate pain.

ARTIFICIALLY PROVIDED NOURISHMENT AND FLUIDS: By checking the appropriate line below I specifically:

_____ authorize the withholding or withdrawal of artificially provided food, water, or other nourishment or fluids.

_____ **DO NOT** authorize the withholding or withdrawal of artificially provided food, water, or other nourishment or fluids.

ORGAN DONOR CERTIFICATION: Notwithstanding my previous declaration relative to the withholding or withdrawal of life-prolonging procedures, if as indicated below I have expressed my desire to donate my organs and/or tissues for transplantation, or any of them as specifically designated herein, I do direct my attending physician, if I have been determined dead according to Tennessee Code Annotated § 68-3-501(b), to maintain me on artificial support systems only for the period of time required to maintain the viability of and to remove such organs and/or tissues, **provided that such means as are used for removing and/or preserving parts of my body shall be at no additional expense to my estate.** By checking the appropriate line below I specifically:

_____ desire to donate my organs and/or tissues for transplantation.

_____ desire to donate my: _____.

_____ **DO NOT** desire to donate my organs or tissues for transplantation.

In the absence of my ability to give directions regarding my medical care, it is my intention that this declaration shall be honored by my family and physician as the final expression of my legal right to refuse medical care and accept the consequences of such refusal.

The definitions of terms used herein shall be as set forth in the Tennessee Right to Natural Death Act, Tennessee Code Annotated § 32-11-103. I understand the full import of this declaration, and I am emotionally and mentally competent to make this declaration. **Any party may rely upon a photocopy of this Living Will without production of the original.**

IN ACKNOWLEDGMENT WHEREOF, I do hereinafter affix my signature on this the _____ day of January, 1996.

_____

John Doe

We, the subscribing witnesses hereto, are personally acquainted with and subscribe our names hereto at the request of John Doe, an adult, whom we believe to be of sound mind, fully aware of the action taken herein and its possible consequence.

We the undersigned witnesses further declare that we are not related to John Doe by blood or marriage; that we are not entitled to any portion of the estate of John Doe upon his decease under any will or codicil thereto presently existing or by operation of law then existing; that we are not the attending physician, an employee of the attending physician or a health facility in which John Doe is a patient; and that we are not a person who, at the present time, has a claim against any portion of the estate of John Doe upon his death.

We the undersigned witnesses further declare that this instrument was signed by John Doe in our presence and we, at his request and in his presence, and in the presence of each other, have hereunto subscribed our names as witnesses the date and year above set out.

_____
Witness

_____
Witness

Subscribed, sworn to and acknowledged before me by John Doe, and subscribed and sworn to

before me by _____ and _____, witnesses, this ___ day of January, 1996.

_____
Notary Public

My Commission Expires: _____

NOTE: **The portions of the text appearing in bold have been added by the authors; the Tennessee statutory form for the living will does not contain these provisions.**

FUNDING AND ADMINISTERING YOUR TRUST AGREEMENT
Transferring Assets to Your Trust

It is most important that assets be transferred to your trust. If assets are not transferred to the trust, then they will not be subject to the terms of the trust agreement until after your death. The number of assets and the type of assets placed in the trust will vary from person to person. Below are some suggestions on transferring the various types of assets.

1. **Stocks and bonds**. Securities may be transferred through your stockbroker with re-registration so that they are no longer in your individual name, but are registered in your name as the trustee as follows:

"JOHN DOE tte u/a dtd June 1, 199X, f/b/o JOHN DOE et al."

This means JOHN DOE as Trustee under agreement dated June 1, 199X, for the benefit of JOHN DOE, and others.

Generally, your stockbroker or others in his or her office will request to see a copy of your Trust Agreement. They need to know that the Trust Agreement does exist, and they may want to check several of its provisions. The Declaration of Trust you signed can be used for this purpose.

Street Accounts. Frequently, stockbrokers will hold securities for you as trustee in what is known as a "street account" or "street name account" or "nominee account." This means that the stockbrokers' company will hold the securities in its name and then follow your instructions as trustee for the trading of securities. You do not receive physical delivery of the securities; they are simply held by the stockbroker for you.

Bank Custody Accounts. When a corporate fiduciary such as a bank is named as successor trustee, securities and similar assets can often be delivered to the bank trust department to hold in custody following your instructions as the current trustee. Sometimes the securities are placed in the bank nominee's account, which is an account very similar to the broker's street account. The bank, however, will charge a fee for holding the securities and transmitting any dividends or interest to you. This arrangement can be useful to establish a working relationship with the bank's trust department in order to see how they perform with a custody account, before they become your successor trustee.

The bank's trust investment department can be called upon to upgrade the service which the bank is rendering from a custody account to an investment management account. With an investment management account, the trust department gives advice concerning the buying and selling of your securities. Occasionally, the client who is serving as trustee will decide to turn the entire management of the trust over to the trust department and resign as trustee.

Unregistered Securities. Many people have what are known as bearer bonds. Typically, these are municipal bonds and have no individual owner's name on them; they belong to whoever holds them. This type of ownership is fraught with potential problems, since anyone who holds the security is considered to be the owner. This means that the bearer bond has to be treated just as cash.

We recommend that bearer bonds be kept in a Tennessee safe-deposit box, with a note in the following form attached to the bearer bonds:

> "For value received, I hereby sell, assign and transfer to JOHN DOE as trustee u/a dated June 1, 199X, the following described bearer bonds (here describe the bonds by name, denomination, due date and interest rate on the bonds).
>
> Dated this _____ day of _____, 199__.
>
> Signature _____."

We also recommend that the original broker's confirmation slip be either retained with the bond or kept in your separate records. This confirmation slip will also establish who originally purchased the bearer bond. Do not place bearer bonds in a joint box unless the bearer bonds are intended to be made joint, and you discuss this with the attorney who assisted you in the trust. The appropriate notations should then be made with a memorandum attached to the securities stating that they are held as joint tenants with right of survivorship with the named individual.

2. **Tennessee Real Estate.** Real estate requires some care to correctly transfer the title of the real estate to your trust. Real estate held in Tennessee or a note and mortgage to be transferred to the trust should be transferred by a deed or an assignment of mortgage by special instruments drafted by an attorney who practices real estate or trust law. Generally, this transfer will be accomplished by a special type of deed. The same is also true of an assignment of the note and mortgage.

It is a good idea to record your Declaration of Trust in the Register of Deeds Office before the deed transferring the real property into your trust is recorded. Again, the attorney who is assisting you with the transfer of your realty to the trust can also help guide you with these details.

3. **Out of State Real Estate.** The conveyance of real estate located outside the State of Tennessee can present special problems. Each state's laws are different, and the real estate is governed by the law of the state in which the real estate is located. It is important that an attorney who is experienced in both real estate law and trust law in the state where the real estate is located be retained to transfer the real estate to the trust. That attorney should review the Trust Agreement and the Declaration of Trust to make sure that the terms of the trust agreement and declaration will not be in conflict with that state's law.

4. **Bank Accounts.** Checking accounts, savings accounts, certificates of deposit, and similar types of accounts including money markets may be treated very much as securities. The registration may be as follows:

"JOHN DOE as Trustee u/a dated June 1, 199X, f/b/o
JOHN DOE et al."

This title should appear on all of the documents creating the account. Frequently, the financial institution will shorten the title in informal correspondence to just JOHN DOE, Trustee. This is perfectly permissible, but the title in the bank's registry of accounts should be in the longer form.

5. **Life Insurance.** Generally, if you are the owner of the life insurance and you are the insured, it is not necessary to transfer the life insurance policy to the trust. The primary purpose of many trusts is to avoid having the assets subject to probate, and life insurance on your life will avoid probate if the proceeds have been made payable to the trust or to an individual, depending upon your overall estate plan. To direct the life insurance proceeds into your trust, you should use the language suggested in the company's change of beneficiary form. If no language is suggested, the primary beneficiary should be "The Trustees of The John Doe Trust dated June 1, 199X." The secondary or contingent beneficiary should be "The Estate of John Doe." Life insurance which you own which insures the life of another, such as a spouse or child, should be transferred to the trust in most instances. Insurance companies also provide forms for transferring the ownership of life insurance policies. You may contact your life insurance company for their form to transfer the ownership of life insurance you hold on the life of another to your trust.

6. **Tax Identification Number.** When registering securities, bank accounts or other assets, you may be asked for a tax identification number for the trust. As long as you or your spouse serves as a trustee of your trust, the tax identification number for your trust is your Social Security number.

Several years ago, trusts such as yours were required to apply for a separate taxpayer identification number. The law has now changed, and it is no longer necessary to use a special tax identification number in most cases.

Administering Your Trust

As trustee, you are the person responsible for administering the trust and the trust assets. As the grantor, you have the right to alter or amend the trust any time you choose. You can revoke it, or take the income or take principal if you choose. However, even though the interests which you have as the grantor, beneficiary and as trustee are all-inclusive, it is important that certain formalities be observed.

You should keep good records. While you may know what has transpired, the successor trustee may find it very difficult to follow your record-keeping system. Assets transferred in the trust, transferred out of the trust, assets which are purchased, sold, and all other transactions involving trust assets should be clearly documented. Your tax basis for the assets transferred to the trust should be determined and recorded. If the assets which are in the trust are substantial and you find the record keeping burdensome, then a professional bookkeeper or an accountant or a bank with a trust department may be utilized to provide the record-keeping services.

The same degree of care which you exercised over your assets before they were shifted to your trust should be continued after the assets are transferred to the trust. Stocks, bonds and particularly bearer bonds should be kept in a safe-deposit box and clearly identified as noted above. Insurance should be carried on property in the appropriate amounts.

Trust assets which you hold as trustee may be kept in the joint box or in a box which is in your name alone. However, these assets should be clearly shown and registered to the trustee so that there is no confusion as to the ownership of these assets.

Reporting the Trust for Tax Purposes

Your trust is considered, while you are alive, to be in many respects your alter ego. This is true for federal income tax purposes. In reporting trust income for federal income tax purposes it is only necessary that you report the trust income in the appropriate schedules on your own personal 1040. It is not necessary to file a separate trust income tax return, so long as either you or your spouse is serving as a trustee or co-trustee. However, if neither of you is able to serve as a trustee or co-trustee, then a separate income tax return must be filed and a new tax identification number must be acquired for your trust.

Making Gifts From Your Trust

If you decide to make a gift of money or property from your trust to another person, and you want to avoid gift tax by using the $10,000 annual exclusion, it is _very_ important that you follow this procedure:

1. First, the trustee should transfer the money or property to your individual name, by placing it in your bank account or re-registering the asset in your name.

2. Then, make the gift from yourself, as an individual, to the person you choose.

3. If you are disabled, the trustee should transfer the money or property to your attorney-in-fact, so that he or she can make whatever gifts are authorized in your power of attorney for financial matters.

FEDERAL UNIFORM GIFT AND ESTATE TAX RATE SCHEDULE

If the amount with respect to which the tentative tax to be computed is:	The tentative tax is:
Not over $10,000	18% of such amount
Over $10,000 but not over $20,000	$1,800 + 20% of the excess of such amount over $20,000
Over $20,000 but not over $40,000	$3,800 + 22% of the excess of such amount over $20,000
Over $40,000 but not over $60,000	$8,200 + 24% of the excess of such amount over $40,000
Over $60,000 but not over $80,000	$13,000 + 26% of the excess of such amount over $60,000
Over $80,000 but not over $100,000	$18,200 + 28% of the excess of such amount over $80,000
Over $100,000 but not over $150,000	$23,800 + 30% of the excess of such amount over $100,000
Over $150,000 but not over $250,000	$38,800 + 32% of the excess of such amount over $150,000
Over $250,000 but not over $500,000	$70,800 + 34% of the excess of such amount over $250,000
Over $500,000 but not over $750,000	$155,800 + 37% of the excess of such amount over $500,000
Over $750,000 but not over $1,000,000	$248,300 + 39% of the excess of such amount over $750,000
Over $1,000,000 but not over $1,250,000	$345,800 + 41% of the excess of such amount over $1,000,000
Over $1,250,000 but not over $1,500,000	$448,300 + 43% of the excess of such amount over $1,250,000
Over $1,500,000 but not over $2,000,000	$555,800 + 45% of the excess of such amount over $1,500,000
Over $2,000,000 but not over $2,500,000	$780,800 + 49% of the excess of such amount over $2,000,000
Over $2,500,000 but not over $3,000,000	$1,025,800 + 53% of the excess of such amount over $2,500,000
$3,000,000 and larger	$1,290,800 + 55% of the excess of such amount over $3,000,000

NOTE: The unified credit and rates below 55% are phased out on estates over $10,000,000 so the rate is a flat 55% on taxable estates in excess of $21,040,000.

NOTE: From the tentative tax should then be subtracted the tax credit of $192,800 (same as the equivalent exemption of $600,000) to figure the actual tax.

STATE AND FEDERAL DEATH TAXES

Taxable Estate:	Actual State and Federal Tax Due and Payable

(The actual tax has the equivalent exemption already figured in.)

$ 225,000 through $600,000	0
$ 650,000	$ 18,500
$ 700,000	37,000
$ 750,000	55,500
$ 800,000	75,000
$ 900,000	114,000
$ 950,000	133,500
$ 1,000,000	153,000
$ 1,250,000	257,250
$ 1,500,000	372,500
$ 1,750,000	491,550
$ 2,000,000	609,800
$ 2,500,000	863,100
$ 3,000,000	1,132,400
$ 3,500,000	1,407,700
$ 4,000,000	1,679,000
$ 4,500,000	1,946,300
$ 5,000,000	2,212,800
$ 5,500,000	2,476,100
$ 6,000,000	2,583,000
$ 6,500,000	2,833,000
$ 7,000,000	3,083,000
$ 7,500,000	3,333,000
$ 8,000,000	3,583,000
$ 8,500,000	3,833,000
$ 9,000,000	4,083,000
$ 9,500,000	4,333,000
$10,000,000	4,583,000

TENNESSEE GIFT TAX RATE SCHEDULE

CLASS A GIFTS If the taxable gifts amount is:	The gift tax is:
Not over $40,000	5.5% of such amount
Over $40,000 but not over $240,000	$2,200 + 6.5% of the excess of such amount over $40,000
Over $240,000 but not over $440,000	$15,200 + 7.5% of the excess of such amount over $240,000
Over $440,000	$30,200 + 9.5% of the excess of such amount over $440,000

CLASS B GIFTS If the taxable gifts amount is:	The gift tax is:
Not over $50,000	6.5% of such amount
Over $50,000 but not over $100,000	$3,250 plus 9.5% of the excess of such amount over $50,000
Over $100,000 but not over $150,000	$8,000 plus 12% of the excess of such amount over $100,000
Over $150,000 but not over $200,000	$14,000 plus 13.5% of the excess of such amount over $150,000
Over $200,000	$20,750 plus 16% of the excess of such amount over $200,000

TENNESSEE INHERITANCE TAX RATE SCHEDULE

If the taxable gifts amount is:	The gift tax is:
Not over $600,000	$0
Over $600,000 but not over $640,000	5.5% of the excess of such amount over $600,000
Over $640,000 but not over $840,000	$2,200 + 6.5% of the excess of such amount over $640,000
Over $840,000 but not over $1,040,000	$15,200 + 7.5% of the excess of such amount over $840,000
Over $1,040,000	$30,200 + 9.5% of the excess of such amount over $1,040,000

NOTE: If the Tennessee inheritance tax figured using the table above is less then the federal credit allowed for state death taxes, Tennessee has a separate estate tax to soak up the difference. This is usually called a "pick-up" tax.

GIFTS TO MINORS

	Outright Gift	Custodianship	Guardianship	Regular Trust	Sec. 2503(b) Trust	Sec. 2503(c) Trust
May Income be used for Minor?	No	Yes	Yes	Trust controls	Mandatory Distribution	Discretionary Distribution
Use of Principal for Minor?	No	Yes	Yes	Trust controls	Trust controls	Trust controls
Fiduciary Qualifications	None	Any adult or trust company	Court-approved	Donor choice	Donor choice	Donor choice
Judicial Supervision	No	No	Yes	No	No	No
Tax Risk to Donor if Fiduciary	No	Yes	No	Possible	Possible	Possible
Accounting	No	Records kept; possible accounting	Yes, court required	Records kept; possible accounting	Records kept; possible accounting	Records kept; possible accounting
Investments	Unlimited	Limited	Limited	Generally, as donor authorized in trust	Generally, as donor authorized in trust	Generally, as donor authorized in trust
When Minor Gets Title	Immediately	Immediately	Immediately	On termination income or earlier distribution of trust	On termination income or earlier distribution of trust	On termination income or earlier distribution of trust
When Minor Gets Possession	Immediately	Age 21	Age 18	Trust controls	Trust controls	Generally, at age 21
When Minor Can Dispose of Gift Property	Generally, at age 18	Age 21	Age 18	Trust controls	Trust controls	Generally, at age 21

MARITAL DEDUCTION

Residuary Trust Share Plan

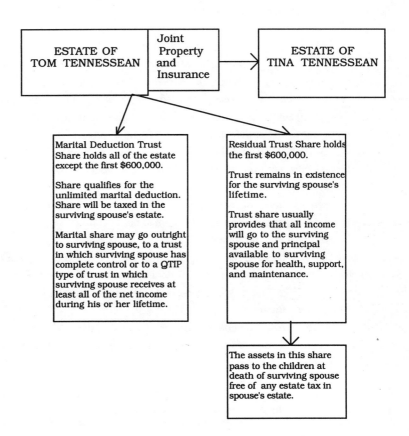

ANTENUPTIAL AGREEMENT
OF
JOHN DOE AND JANE SOON-TO-BE-DOE

THIS ANTENUPTIAL AGREEMENT is made this _____ day of January, 1996, by and between John Doe (herein called John), a resident of Knox County, Tennessee, and Jane Soon-To-Be-Doe (herein called Jane), a resident of Knox County, Tennessee.

WITNESSETH:

John and Jane plan to marry. In anticipation of their marriage, they desire to fix and determine by this Antenuptial Agreement the rights and claims that will accrue to each of them in the estate and property of the other by reason of the marriage, and to accept the provisions of this Agreement in lieu of and in full discharge, settlement, and satisfaction of all such rights and claims; and

WHEREAS, both John and Jane have made a full disclosure to the other of all relevant financial information concerning his or her financial worth and income; and

WHEREAS, John and Jane have each been afforded the opportunity to retain independent legal counsel in order to be fully advised of his or her rights and liabilities under this Agreement and under applicable law; and

WHEREAS, John and Jane have fully considered the effect and consequences of all of the provisions of this Agreement upon their respective pecuniary condition and situation, and upon their mutual rights and obligations, and they have each concluded and hereby acknowledge that this Agreement is fair and equitable, and each seeks to be bound by this Agreement.

NOW, THEREFORE, in consideration of their forthcoming marriage to each other, and in further consideration of the mutual promises and undertakings set forth in this Agreement, John and Jane agree as follows:

1.   **Responsibilities for Debts.** Both parties agree that each will be responsible for debts which he or she contracted before marriage. Each party will be responsible for his or her own debts which are incurred during their marriage.

2.   **Mutual Release of Rights in Separate Property of the Other.** All property, real and personal, of whatsoever nature and wheresoever situated, including but not limited to any and all retirement, pension, deferred compensation or similar plans or accounts (hereinafter collectively referred to as "retirement benefits") and any insurance policies or the proceeds thereof, (a) owned by either party as of the effective date of this Agreement or (b) acquired on or after the effective date of this Agreement by either party in such party's separate name or jointly with another, shall be the sole and separate property of such party (such assets are hereafter sometimes collectively referred to as the "Separate Property" of John or Jane, or of both) and shall be enjoyed by such party and subject to such party's disposition as if the parties had never married, even though the earnings of either party may have been applied so as to enhance the value of such property and even though any appreciation in such property may have been attributable to the personal services, skill, effort and work of either of the parties. John and Jane each hereby waives, releases, and relinquishes any and all right, title, estate and interest, statutory or

otherwise, which either may have or acquire under present or future law, in any and all Separate Property of the other.

3. **Mutual Release of Rights in Assets Upon the Death of the Other.** John and Jane each hereby waives, releases and relinquishes all right, title, estate and interest, statutory or otherwise, including but not limited to homestead, year's support allowance, exempt property, spousal elective right to take against the Will, intestate share, and the right or preference to act as personal representative of the estate of the other, which either may acquire under present or future law as the spouse, widow or widower, heir, heir-at-law, or next-of-kin in the Separate Property or estate of the other at the other's death. John and Jane each consent and agree that the estate of the other shall descend to his or her heirs-at-law, legatees or devisees, as may be prescribed by his or her last will and testament or by the law of the state in force, as though no marriage had taken place between them.

4. **Ownership of Assets.** With respect to the ownership of their Separate Property, John and Jane hereby acknowledge and agree that after their marriage John and Jane shall each be entitled to keep and retain sole ownership and control of all of their Separate Property, whenever acquired. Should the parties agree to own an asset jointly (either as tenants by the entirety or as joint tenants with right of survivorship), such as a joint checking account, savings account, residence, or any other joint asset or interest, such joint ownership shall not be considered as a waiver of any provision of or a relinquishment of any right under this Agreement.

5. **Execution of Additional Documents.** John and Jane shall at any time upon request by the other, execute, acknowledge and deliver any and all instruments reasonably necessary or appropriate to carry into effect the intention of the parties as expressed in this Agreement, and to make this Agreement effective in any jurisdiction in which either of them has property. The parties further specifically agree to execute any documents necessary or required in order to effect their waiver, release and relinquishment of all right, title, estate and interest in and to any retirement benefits of the other.

6. **Voluntary Transfers Permitted.** The purpose of this Agreement is to limit the rights of each party in the assets of the other in the event of the death of either of the parties or in the event of their separation or divorce. However, this Agreement shall not be construed as placing any limitation on the rights of either party to make voluntary gifts to the other during his or her lifetime, and to make transfers of his or her assets to the other by Will or otherwise at death, and to name the other as the personal representative of his or her estate. However, John and Jane acknowledge that neither has made any representations or promises of any kind whatsoever to the other with respect to any such transfers, conveyances, or fiduciary relationships. John and Jane each understands that the other may write, revise, or revoke a Will prior to, in contemplation of, or after their prospective marriage, and each agrees that any Will, and any codicil of such Will, shall not be deemed to be revoked by their marriage and/or by the subsequent birth or adoption of children to such marriage. It is further agreed that, if John or Jane should decide to designate the other as a legatee, devisee, or beneficiary either under the terms of his or her Will or otherwise, such designation shall not be construed as an amendment of this Agreement, or a waiver or relinquishment of any rights under this Agreement, or as the creation of any obligation from one to the other aside from the obligations that are contained in this Agreement (and aside from the specific obligations, if any, that are contained in any Will or other document designating the other as a legatee, devisee, or beneficiary after such document becomes irrevocable).

7. **Right to Property Settlement in the Event of Separation or Divorce.** John and Jane each agrees with the other that this Agreement and the mutual releases given by each to the other in their respective Separate Property as defined herein shall apply and shall constitute the division of property and the settlement of all of their rights to such Separate Property in the event that either party institutes against the other a divorce proceeding, a proceeding for permanent or temporary separation, or a proceeding for separate maintenance and support. Each party agrees with the other that in such event, he or she will not seek, in any such proceeding, to

enforce or claim any rights in the Separate Property of the other, or seek to divide or settle rights in said property in any manner other than that provided in this Agreement. Both parties further agree with each other that each will not assert or claim any other rights in or to the Separate Property of the other, whether owned prior to the marriage or acquired during the marriage, whether now or hereafter given by applicable law, which are inconsistent with the terms of this Agreement. The provisions of this Section 7 are not intended to limit or abridge in any way whatsoever the rights which either party might have against the other for alimony, support, maintenance, and child support under applicable law in the event of a separation or divorce, but are only intended to settle rights in and to divide the assets subject to this Agreement.

8.   Alimony. Although the parties contemplate a long and lasting marriage, terminated only by the death of one of the parties, they also recognize the possibility of divorce. The parties understand that under existing Tennessee law, it may not be possible to waive alimony and support in an Antenuptial Agreement. Nevertheless, if their marriage is terminated, regardless of which party is at fault or initiates such action and regardless of jurisdiction, venue or location of such action, the parties hereby specifically agree that this Agreement, to the extent allowed by applicable law at the time of such divorce, shall serve as a bar or estoppel of either party to receive any alimony, whether *pendente lite*, or permanent, from the other party. This provision is agreed to by the parties with full knowledge of the alimony and support which might otherwise be available to either of them under applicable law.

John and Jane each acknowledges that this provision may not be enforceable under present Tennessee law. As provided in Section 16 for all provisions herein, this Section of the Agreement is severable, and any judicial determination that it is void or unenforceable shall not affect the validity or enforceability of any other terms, provision or Section of this Agreement. John and Jane each acknowledges that the terms and conditions set out in this Section are fair and equitable and are a true representation of what the parties believe to be the obligations owed to them by each other. Even if this Section is not effective, the parties desire that any future tribunal give great weight to the parties' statements and their agreement contained in this Section.

9.   Full Disclosure of Separate Property and Income. John and Jane each promises and represents to the other that he or she has disclosed to the other the nature, extent and value of his or her various assets, interests, sources of income and income for the past full calendar year. By execution of this Agreement, John and Jane each acknowledges receipt of the other's financial information, and confirms that he or she has reviewed such information, fully understands the nature and approximate value of the assets of the other, and each has conducted whatever investigation and made whatever inquiries he or she deemed necessary concerning such information.

10.   Informed Consent With Independent Legal Advice. John and Jane each declares that he or she fully understands the terms and provisions of this Agreement, that he or she has been fully informed of his or her legal rights and liabilities (or that he or she has been afforded the time and the opportunity to retain independent legal counsel and has chosen not to do so), that he or she believes that the provisions of this Agreement are fair, just and reasonable, that he or she signs this Agreement freely and voluntarily, and that he or she enters into this Agreement freely, knowledgeably, and in good faith, and not under duress or undue influence from the other or from any other persons not party to this Agreement.

11.   Governing Law. This Agreement shall be governed by and construed in accordance with the laws of the state of Tennessee, which laws, the parties understand, both by statute and common law, uphold the validity of such agreements.

12.   Community or Marital Property States. Should one or other, or both of the parties hereto, ever become domiciled in a community or marital property jurisdiction, or if their domiciliary jurisdiction should adopt such property rules, it is the intention of each party that neither community property, quasi-community property, marital nor quasi-marital property rules shall apply to either of them or to the assets of either of them.

13. Entire Understanding. This agreement contains the entire understanding of the parties, and there are no representations, warranties, promises, covenants, or undertakings, oral or otherwise, between them other than those expressly set forth in this Agreement. This Agreement is intended to cover all assets now owned by each party, and all assets which the parties may hereafter acquire, jointly and separately.

14. Binding Agreement and Termination. This Agreement shall become effective only upon the marriage of the parties, and shall inure to the benefit of, and shall be binding upon, the parties hereto, their heirs, personal representatives and assigns. The parties may, by written agreement executed personally by the parties (but not by an attorney-in-fact for either of them), modify or terminate this Agreement at any time.

15. Enforcement of Agreement. In the event that either party should seek to enforce the terms of this Agreement in a jurisdiction that fails or refuses to recognize its validity, such judicial determination shall not prevent the other party from seeking to enforce this Agreement in another jurisdiction.

16. Severability. In the event that any provisions of this Agreement shall be held invalid, unenforceable or void for any reason, the remaining provisions of this Agreement shall not be affected, said provisions being severable.

17. Assignment. This Agreement is personal to each of the parties hereto, and neither party may assign nor delegate any of his or her rights or obligations hereunder.

18. Headings. Headings to items herein are for convenience only and shall not be construed to have any effect or meaning with respect to the content of such terms.

IN WITNESS WHEREOF, the undersigned have executed this Antenuptial Agreement as of the date first above written.

_____   _____
John Doe   Jane Soon-To-Be-Doe

STATE OF TENNESSEE   )
                          :ss
COUNTY OF KNOX   )

On this _____day of_____ 1996, before me, _____ (Notary Public), personally appeared John Doe, personally known to me (or proved to me on the basis of satisfactory evidence) to be the person whose name is subscribed to this instrument, and acknowledged that he executed it. I declare under penalty of perjury that the person whose name is subscribed to this instrument appears to be of sound mind and under no duress, fraud, or undue influence.

_____
Notary Public

My Commission Expires: _____

ACKNOWLEDGMENT

STATE OF TENNESSEE   )
                           :ss
COUNTY OF KNOX   )

On this _____ day of _____ 1996, before me, _____ (Notary Public), personally appeared Jane Soon-To-Be-Doe, personally known to me (or proved to me on the basis of satisfactory evidence) to be the person whose name is subscribed to this instrument, and acknowledged that she executed it. I declare under penalty of perjury that the person whose name is subscribed to this instrument appears to be of sound mind and under no duress, fraud, or undue influence.

                                     _____
                                     Notary Public

My Commission Expires: _____

ATTORNEY'S CERTIFICATION

The undersigned, Anne M. McKinney, a member of the Tennessee Bar, hereby certifies, on behalf of Anne M. McKinney, P.C., that Anne M. McKinney, P.C., is counsel for and represents John Doe (John) in connection with the above Agreement and that as an attorney with Anne M. McKinney, P.C., she has explained fully to John his legal rights and liabilities under the Agreement; which include, but are not limited to, support and inheritance rights, and the effect that this Agreement has on such rights, including but not limited to, waiver of all rights of inheritance and waiver of other rights in the property of Jane Soon-To-Be-Doe.

Dated: _____, 1996

                               ANNE M. MCKINNEY, P.C.

By: _____
             Anne M. McKinney

ATTORNEY'S CERTIFICATION

The undersigned attorney, a member of the Tennessee Bar, hereby certifies that he is counsel for and represents Jane Soon-To-Be-Doe (Jane) in connection with the above Agreement and that he has explained fully to Jane her legal rights and liabilities under the Agreement; which include, but are not limited to, support and inheritance rights, and the effect that this Agreement has on such rights, including but not limited to, waiver of all rights of inheritance and waiver of other rights in the property of John Doe.

Dated: _____, 1996

                                     _____
                                Jane Soon-To-Be-Doe's Attorney

**IN THE CHANCERY COURT FOR ___ COUNTY, TENNESSEE
PROBATE DIVISION**

IN THE MATTER OF:)
)
THE ESTATE OF   )
JOHN DOE,   )
)
   Deceased,   )   No. _____
)
JANE DOE,   )
)
   Petitioner/Executor.   )

**PETITION FOR PROBATE OF WILL
AND GRANTING OF LETTER TESTAMENTARY**

TO: THE HONORABLE CHANCELLOR:

Your Petitioner shows the Court the following:

1.   **The Decedent.** The decedent, John Doe, died in ___ County, Tennessee, on (Date of Death), at the age of ___ years.

2.   **Decedent's Property.**

   (a)   <u>Real Estate</u>. The Decedent owned real estate in ___ County, Tennessee, at (address). Article V of Decedent's Will requires that the real estate be handled as property subject to Decedent's Will.

   (b)   <u>Personal Property</u>. The Decedent owned personal property subject to a court supervised administration valued at (more/less) than six hundred thousand dollars ($600,000).

   (c)   <u>Inventory, Bond and Accountings</u>. Article II, paragraph C of the Will excuses the requirements of the filing of an inventory, bond and accountings.

3.   **Decedent's Will.** Decedent left a Last Will and Testament dated ___ which was properly witnessed in the presence of a Notary Public by ____ and ____. A photocopy of the original Will is attached as <u>Exhibit A</u>, together with the Affidavit of Witnesses. The original document will be presented to the Court with this Petition.

4.   **Will Beneficiaries.** The names, birthdates, and addresses of the named beneficiaries under decedent's Will are as follows:

       <u>Name and Address</u>   <u>Birth Date</u>

5.   **Petitioner Identification.** The petitioner's name, relationship and mailing address are as follows:

       Jane Doe - Spouse
       (Jane's address)

Petitioner is appointed Executor of the decedent's estate in Article II, Paragraph A of the Will.

6.   **Inheritance Tax Information.** The estimated gross value of the decedent's estate for Tennessee Inheritance Tax purposes is (more/less) than six hundred thousand dollars ($600,000.00).

WHEREFORE, PETITIONER PRAYS:

1.   The original Will containing affidavits of the subscribing witnesses to the Will be accepted by the Court to the end that the Will may be proved and established and that probate of the Will may be granted and the same ordered for record;

2.   Petitioner be appointed to serve as Executor, that the Probate Clerk be directed to administer the oath and otherwise qualify the Executor and issue Letters Testamentary;

3.   Notice by publication be given to the creditors of the estate as required in Tenn. Code Ann. § 30-2-306; and notice be given the Department of Revenue as required in Tenn. Code Ann. § 67-8-406.

4.   All accountings, bond and inventory be excused; and

5.   The Petitioner be granted such additional relief as the Court may deem proper under the circumstances.

Submitted this _____ day of January, 1996.

Jane Doe, Petitioner

By   _____
      Anne M. McKinney
      Anne M. McKinney, P.C.
      Suite 700, Arnstein Building
      505 Market Street
      Knoxville, Tennessee   37902
      (423) 525-8700
      Attorney for Jane Doe

COST BOND

We acknowledge ourselves sureties for costs in this cause not to exceed the sum of Five Hundred Dollars ($500).

This the _____ day of January, 1996.

ANNE M. MCKINNEY, P.C.

By   _____
      Anne M. McKinney

STATE OF TENNESSEE   )
                        :ss
COUNTY OF _____   )

Personally appeared before me, ___, a Notary Public in and for the above named State and County, Jane Doe, the above named Petitioner who, being duly sworn by me, deposes and says that the statements in the foregoing Petition are true to Petitioner's knowledge, except as to matters therein stated to be upon information and belief, and these matters Petitioner believes to be true.

_____
Jane Doe, Petitioner

Sworn to and subscribed before me
this the _____ day of January, 1996.

_____
          Notary Public

My Commission Expires: _____

IN THE CHANCERY COURT FOR ___ COUNTY, TENNESSEE
PROBATE DIVISION

IN THE MATTER OF:)
)
THE ESTATE OF   )
JOHN DOE,   )
)
    Deceased,   )   No. _____
)
JANE DOE,   )
)
    Executor.   )

ORDER ADMITTING WILL TO PROBATE

Based on an examination of the Petition, the decedent's Last Will, the affidavits of the subscribing witnesses, the oath of the Petitioner, and the affidavit of Petitioner, the Court finds the following:

    A.   Decedent was a resident of ___ County, Tennessee;

    B.   Decedent died on ___, at the age of __ years;

    C.   Decedent left a Will dated (date of Will), which was properly signed and witnessed;

    D.   Petitioner was appointed Executor in Article II, Paragraph A of decedent's Will and was also excused from bond and the filing of an inventory or court accountings in Article II, Paragraph C, of decedent's Will; and

    E.   Decedent owned property at decedent's death which is subject to a Court supervised administration worth (more/less) than six hundred thousand dollars ($600,000.00).

Based on these findings, the Court orders the following:

    1.   That Decedent's Will dated ___ be admitted to probate;

    2.   That the Oath of Petitioner be accepted and letters testamentary be issued to Jane Doe;

    3.   That bond, accountings and an inventory are excused; and

    4.   That notice be issued to creditors and the Department of Revenue as required by Tenn. Code Ann. § 30-2-306 and § 67-8-408, respectively.

    ENTERED this _____ day of _____, 1996.

                                          _____
                                          Chancellor

APPROVED FOR ENTRY:

_____
Anne M. McKinney
Anne M. McKinney, P. C.
Suite 700, Arnstein Building
505 Market Street
Knoxville, TN 37902
(423) 525-8700
Attorneys for Petitioner, Jane Doe

IN THE CHANCERY COURT FOR ___ COUNTY, TENNESSEE
PROBATE DIVISION

IN RE:)
)
THE ESTATE OF   )
JOHN DOE,   )   No. _____
)
    Deceased,   )
)
JANE DOE,   )
)
    Executor.   )

AFFIDAVIT OF NOTICE TO CREDITORS

I, Jane Doe, Executor of the Estate of John Doe, do hereby state that, pursuant to Section 30-2-306 of the Tennessee Code Annotated, the required copies of the notice to creditors for this Estate have been sent to each creditor of the Decedent.

And further the affiant saith not.

_____
Jane Doe, Executor/Affiant

Sworn to and subscribed before me
this _____ day of_____, 1996.

_____
Notary Public

My Commission Expires:

_____

IN THE CHANCERY COURT FOR __ COUNTY, TENNESSEE
PROBATE DIVISION

IN RE:)
)
THE ESTATE OF   )   No. _____
JOHN DOE,   )
)
    Deceased,   )
)
JANE DOE,   )
)
    Executor.   )

AFFIDAVIT OF NOTICE TO BENEFICIARIES

I, Jane Doe, Executor of the Estate of John Doe, do hereby state that, pursuant to Section 30-2-301 of the Tennessee Code Annotated, the required copies of the Last Will of John Doe have been mailed or delivered to the residuary beneficiaries thereunder and copies of the dispositive paragraphs of said Will have been mailed or delivered to any of the beneficiaries thereunder receiving specific bequests.

And further affiant saith not.

_____
Jane Doe, Executor/Affiant

Sworn to and subscribed before me
this ____ day of _____, 1996.

_____

My Commission Expires:

_____

IN THE CHANCERY COURT FOR ___ COUNTY, TENNESSEE
PROBATE DIVISION

IN RE:	)
	)
THE ESTATE OF	) No. _____
JOHN DOE,	)
	)
Deceased,	)
	)
JANE DOE,	)
	)
Executor.	)

ORDER TO CLOSE ESTATE

Based on an examination of the record the Court finds the following:

1.   Petitioner is the qualified personal representative of this estate.

2.   The estate is solvent.

3.   The estate has been fully administered.

4.   Each claim filed against the estate has been paid. A Receipt and Release has been filed of record for each such creditor claim. All other debts have been paid.

5.   All inheritance and estate taxes due the state of Tennessee have been paid as evidence by certificate issued pursuant to T.C.A. § 67-8-420 which is attached as Exhibit A. All U.S. estate taxes have also been paid.

6.   This estate has been properly distributed.

7.   All the residuary distributees and legatees of this estate agree to close the estate without a detailed accounting.

8.   The attorneys fees and expenses of Anne M. McKinney, P.C. in the amount of $___ appear to be reasonable and proper.

Based on these findings, the fees and expenses of Anne M. McKinney, P.C. are approved, and the Court orders the estate closed without a detailed accounting, discharges the personal representative and surety, if any, and directs no copy of this final order must be sent to any of the distributees and legatees·of the Estate.

ENTERED this _____ day of _____, 1996.

_____
CHANCELLOR

APPROVED FOR ENTRY:

_____
Attyname, Attorney at Law
Anne M. McKinney, P.C.
Suite 700, Arnstein Building
505 Market Street
Knoxville, Tennessee 37902
(423) 525-8700

INDEX

253